Dynamic Leadership

GORDON FERGUSON

Dynamic Leadership

*Principles, Roles and Relationships
for a Life-Changing Church*

ILLUMINATION PUBLISHERS

Dynamic Leadership: *Principles, Roles and Relationships for a Life-Changing Church*
© 2012 by Gordon Ferguson and Illumination Publishers

All rights are reserved. No part of this book may be duplicated, copied, translated, reproduced or stored mechanically, digitally or electronically without specific, written permission of the author and publisher.

Printed in the United States of America.

ISBN: 978-0-9855749-3-2

Unless otherwise indicated, all Scripture references are from the Holy Bible, New International Version, copyright 1973, 1978, 1984 by the International Bible Society. Used by permission of Zondervan Bible Publishers.

Cover and interior book design: Toney Mulhollan.

About the author: Gordon Ferguson is a graduate of Northwestern State University and the Harding Graduate School of Religion. With more than 40 years of experience, he has served as an evangelist, elder and teacher. He trains ministers in the U.S., Eurasia and Asia. He emphasizes leadership training and teaching. Gordon has  also written eleven books and many audio/video teaching series. Gordon and his wife, Theresa, live in the Phoenix, Arizona area. For more articles and information see Gordon's web site at www.GFTM.org.

Illumination Publishers International
www.ipibooks.com
6010 Pinecreek Ridge Court
Spring, Texas 77379-2513

Acknowledgments

If any author attempted to acknowledge all who have helped make his work possible, it would be far too long to include in the book. In my case, it would likely dwarf the book. Thus, what we do is mention only those who have been most influential in the writing of the most recent book. Toney Mulhollan, a longtime friend, agreed to start handling all of my future work and even market my former books once I ended my work as a part of church staffs and started focusing on a teaching ministry. As a bona fide workaholic, he has published several second editions of earlier books, plus this present new book and many audio and video teaching sets. Paul Vasquez, his sales and marketing man, has shown great interest in my work and provided many suggestions for my future work.

Elizabeth Thompson, my copy editor, started off as basically an unknown person to me (although I have known and loved her parents, Sam and Geri Laing, for decades). Having been raised in such a strong family and having served in the ministry alongside her husband, Kevin, has uniquely prepared her for editing a book like this one. She is a novelist at heart, with a vocabulary and writing style to match, but is very much at home (painfully at times) with the mechanics of writing and also understands our movement of churches well. Through the editing process, she has edited both my writing and my heart in some unique ways—an unexpected but very appreciated blessing. With both of us sharing what she termed a "wackadoodle sense of humor," the editing process has been far more entertaining than any I have ever experienced!

Much thanks to all three of you in helping make this book become a reality!

TABLE OF CONTENTS

	Dedication	8
	Foreword by Wyndham Shaw	10
	Introduction	13

PART 1 – LEADERSHIP PRINCIPLES

Chapter One	Leaders Are Disciples and Servants	23
Chapter Two	The Gift of Leadership	37
Chapter Three	The Authority of Leadership	45
Chapter Four	Leadership Styles	58
Chapter Five	All Leaders Are Builders for God	70

PART 2 – LEADERSHIP ROLES

Chapter Six	The Role and Function of Elders	83
Chapter Seven	Qualifications, Selection and Appointment of Elders	99
Chapter Eight	Evangelists: Who They Are and What They Do	117
Chapter Nine	The Appointment of Evangelists and Others	133
Chapter Ten	Other Leadership Roles	147

TABLE OF CONTENTS

PART 3 – LEADERSHIP RELATIONSHIPS

Chapter Eleven — Relationships: 159
Historical Origins of Challenges

Chapter Twelve — Relationships: 178
Between Leaders and the Flock

Chapter Thirteen — Relationships: 189
Between Elders, Evangelists and Teachers

Chapter Fourteen — Relationships: 205
Team Leadership Principles

Chapter Fifteen — Relationships: 221
Team Leadership Practices

Epilogue: From Good to Great!   240

APPENDICES

Appendix One: Handle With Care!   243

Appendix Two: Matters of Conscience: A Deeper Look   249

Appendix Three: Shepherding Training Subjects   260

Appendix Four: Appreciating Our History   262

Appendix Five: Cooperation Proposals #1, #2, #3   270

Appendix Six: Church Discipline   291

Appendix Seven: Objective Negativity   298

Dedication

To be candid, every time I start writing a dedication page for a new book, I am strongly tempted to dedicate it to my wife Theresa, the love of my life. However, the full page dedication I wrote for *Romans: the Heart Set Free* pretty much encapsulates our love story. That allows me to dedicate other books to other people who have invaded my heart at the deeper levels.

I am excited to dedicate this book to the Greater Houston Church. My love affair with them started over three years ago through what I thought would be a one-time teaching visit. But something uniquely clicked between us that is still somewhat of a mystery to me. The leaders kept inviting us back for various types of teaching events and then began trying to persuade us to move there. For certain family reasons, this wasn't possible, but due to their perseverance, I offered to come for a year as much as we could when not traveling overseas. They jumped on that idea with a rapidity and intensity that added to the mystical nature of our relationship.

I had basically decided to devote my teaching efforts mainly to works in Asia and Eurasia, feeling that those churches were hungering and thirsting more for the teaching than were churches in the United States. Houston made me feel that they were an exception to my assumption. The end result was that in 2011 I spent one-third of my time in Phoenix and the rest in Asia, Eurasia and Houston, with the latter receiving most of our time and attention by a fair margin.

My role in Houston thus began as a leadership trainer and consultant, and unexpectedly morphed into the role of lead evangelist (at age sixty-nine, mind you!). When we began our labor of love, the leadership group said that they wanted Houston to become our home away from home. What actually happened is that it became like our home—period! I was the interim lead evangelist with the task of helping find a permanent replacement, which has just occurred, with the hiring of Doug and Angella Wens.

The morning after leaving Houston for the final (scheduled) time, I wrote a letter of appreciation, and near the end said this:

> In closing, let me say once again that we love you from the bottom of our hearts, and since you have given us enlargement of the hearts spiritually and emotionally, that expression of love carries more with it than it could possibly have two years ago. Thank you for everything. Whatever else the Lord has in mind for us, I can't imagine it will look much like what we have been through with you in the roles in which we served there. In that sense of roles, I think we have ridden in our last rodeo, and what more fitting place could that have occurred than in the place where the mother of all real rodeos is held each year. It was quite a ride and we thank all of you for it.

Houston church, we have opened wide our hearts to you and you have reciprocated in a marvelous way, opening wide your hearts to us. Words cannot express what you have come to mean to us, allowing us to become one in heart and soul with one of God's greatest congregations in one of the world's greatest cities. It was a ride to remember, a phrase that can be appreciated fully only by Texans! God bless you for loving us and serving him!

Foreword

Jesus healed many people with a single touch. The blind man in Mark 8 required a second touch to complete his healing. We as church leaders require multiple "touches" from Jesus to refine our vision, heal our wounds from past history and mature us in areas in which we have previously been blind.

In a "second touch" on the topic of leadership and team building, my dear friend and fellow builder, Gordon Ferguson, has offered another written treasure gleaned from God's wisdom over time. Gathered from his last ten years of travel, speaking in different churches and using his gifts as an elder, teacher and evangelist, Gordon builds on the initial concepts set forth in our joint effort of *Golden Rule Leadership*.

In his usual forthright manner, he commends the progress made by many individual church leaders and leadership teams. He also challenges us to consider what further clarity of concept and practice is needed in our personal evolution toward healthier and more effective church leadership.

I count Gordon as one of my best friends and thank God for his influence and partnership in my life! It is an honor to commend his latest thinking on a topic we both believe is vital for all churches and for their leaders to keep growing individually. His biblical depth and personal experience are combined in a compelling second touch on how to create spiritual and effective leadership teams at any stage and age of church growth.

I believe *Dynamic Leadership* is a must read for every evangelist, elder, teacher, deacon, board member and small group leader in our churches today! Building effective church leaderships is an evolving process that begins with the belief in team leadership as a concept. It then requires building your group as God raises up the men and women who are gifted, humble and spiritual enough to fulfill these functions. In addition to promoting the concept of team leadership, this book offers expanded biblical examples and practical insights in both the *why* and *how* to do it.

As the Boston church leadership continues to evolve in the understanding and practice of golden rule and team leadership, this latest collection of Gordon's best thoughts and biblical insight is sure to help us along the way.

Be prepared for the fact that Gordon brings up both painful and happy memories and experiences that many of us in the ICOC have shared in our journey toward heaven together. He does so not to relive the pain or to glory in past joys but to be sure we get the point of what God was teaching us about both good and bad! His assumption is that many of us have learned with deep conviction how to hold on to the good and leave the bad behind. But with positive aim, he drives home the lessons we all should have shared in together and looks to a future where the best is yet to come.

Since he is ten years older than I am (and I turn sixty this year), Gordon has lived and served long in God's kingdom on earth. This may be his best contribution of many great books written for our learning and maturity. I praise God to have been discipled, mentored and loved by Gordon Ferguson! I know of few men who have more humility, wisdom, courage, boldness and big-heartedness combined in one body! I treasure the years and special moments we have shared together (especially one day in June fishing on the Merrimack River just before he left Boston). God has blessed my life enormously by his friendship, fun and fellowship over the years we have worked together. I count them and him as some of my greatest blessings in life. I wholeheartedly commend this book to all who have known Gordon and our God and to those who will know both better by reading this book.

Introduction

Dynamic Leadership
Principles, Roles and Relationships for a Life-Changing Church

Dysfunction in leaders and leadership relationships will destroy the effectiveness of a church or a movement, but God has a plan for healthy kingdom-style leadership and relationships. It is that plan I hope to highlight in this book. You will likely quickly notice that this introduction is longer than most, and there is a good reason behind it. Keep reading and you will understand that reason and the importance of it. Your patience will be rewarded. I promise!

When people find out that I have written books, they often ask how I do it. Of course, they want to know what the process is, from beginning to end. One of the best answers is, "It varies from book to book." Another good answer would be, "It evolves." No matter what an author's idea is at the beginning of writing a book or even starting a chapter in a book, the final product often morphs into something different than the original idea. That is definitely true of this book on church leadership.

For example, my first conception of the title was: "Elders and Evangelists: Roles and Relationships." That subject has been on my mind and heart for years, having served in both roles and having experienced some of the challenges that often arise in the relationships between elders and evangelists. In my mainline Church of Christ days, a power struggle existed fairly consistently between men serving in these two roles, but philosophically it was usually agreed that the elders were "over" the preachers (they didn't typically use the term "evangelist"). After all, the elders were the ones who did the hiring and firing.

However, philosophical agreement doesn't mean that the struggle is over, as may be illustrated with the role of husband and wife. Most wives who claim to be Christians acquiesce to the statement in Ephesians 5:23–24 that the husband is the head of the wife and that she should submit to him in everything. And yet many of these same wives often become locked in a struggle with their husbands for emotional control of the relationship. Similarly, even those ministers who agree that the elders have the final say in decision-making may still struggle for the ultimate leadership control of the church.

In the days of the Campus Ministry Movement (which is what I call the earliest stage of what would become the International Churches of Christ), young evangelists generally made it clear that the evangelist should be "over" the elders. This position was taken primarily because of the challenges they had experienced with elders in campus ministry settings in mainline churches (challenges I understand fully!). In our present stage, most elders and evangelists have matured beyond such overt power struggles, but perhaps not entirely in their hearts. And there are some very sad examples of how such struggles have continued in certain places. Other relationship challenges between leaders in different roles have also surfaced, notably in some relationships between teachers and evangelists. Biblically, you would have to say that the three key leadership roles in the church are those of elder, evangelist and teacher. It is not surprising that Satan would try to raise and escalate relational challenges between those serving in these three key roles.

These issues are certainly pressing enough to write a book on the subject, not just to correct misunderstandings and abuses, but to clarify and give practical direction. In one sense, elders and evangelists are like the parents of the church. (Please, let's not worry about who is Mom and who is Dad—it's just an illustration of a principle.) Perhaps the teachers are like the big brothers, depending on their influence in a given church. When parents are not unified, the children are insecure; when they are unified, the children are secure. All leaders owe those whom they lead an atmosphere that produces the latter. Anything less is unloving leadership.

However, as I said, this book has evolved into something broader. The second title I had in mind when I first wrote this introduction was: "Church Leadership: Roles and Relationships." Biblically, church leadership is comprised of more roles than just those of elders and evangelists. Also, other leadership roles that are not mentioned in the Bible find their way into almost every church culture, because the needs of the flock are varied and numerous. For those reasons, the title of this book evolved into a broader approach. Now it addresses all types of leaders, those mentioned specifically in the Scripture as well as those not mentioned at all.

As I thought further about the title of the book, my thinking continued to evolve simply from considering the words within the title. Early on, I could see both roles and relationships needing due attention in a study of church leadership. But in the early planning stages, I viewed the term *role* as primarily academic and the term *relationship* as encompassing the really practical material. In other words, we first need to understand what the various leadership roles are, as defined by the Bible, and then we need to discuss how the people serving in those roles are to function in relationships—relationships between people in the specific leadership roles, then between individual leaders and also between leaders and the people under their leadership.

The intent of this book is to collect under one cover what can hopefully become a type of guide to the selection and appointment of all leaders, regardless of role—including roles not mentioned specifically in the Bible. Since some of these topics fall into the realm of uncharted territory, you can expect to find some surprises. For example, practices such as the appointment of evangelists have been commonplace, but the practices have been based primarily upon our traditions rather than upon a close examination of Scripture. We need to examine, or reexamine, our current practices and raise and answer questions regarding areas in which we have not yet established practices.

Further contemplation of the term "roles" also brings to mind other considerations that are eminently practical. A role is a function, and not who we are as a person. Thus, an elder or an evangelist is one serving within a specific function. What is he when he is not functioning in that capacity? That's a very relevant question, it seems to me. Asking the right questions can lead to some interesting and important contemplation. Together with what might be somewhat more academic in nature, these additional practical applications will serve to complete the foundation necessary for the mainly practical study of relationships involving leaders. Actually, from one perspective, nothing in the Bible is intended to be simply academic. All that God had written for us was designed to affect our lives, to make us more like him and his Son. To approach any part of the Bible as purely academic underlies a faulty hermeneutic in the first place. As I often say in reaching out to non-Christians, the Bible is a book of life, not a book of religion. In other words, it teaches us how to live in harmony with our Creator and with one another. It is not simply a book of history or a book of facts; it is a book that addresses our minds, our hearts and our lives as a whole.

As I developed the organization for the book and added materials from articles I had previously written, evolution occurred yet again, this time in the form of a sudden mutation. I thus found myself landing on a third and final title: *Dynamic Leadership: Principles, Roles and Relationships for a Life-Changing Church*.

Golden Rule Leadership: Perspectives, Ten Years Later

While this book evolved, it is itself an evolution of sorts from an earlier book on leadership that I wrote in a team effort with my dear friend and fellow elder at the time, Wyndham Shaw, entitled *Golden Rule Leadership*. I will have some things to say in this book about that book, including its initial reception. Some readers may be chagrined that I mention the past at all. But we as individuals are all products of our past environments, and others will never truly understand us, and we likely will not understand ourselves, without thinking about our backgrounds. The same may be said of congregations or of a movement as a whole. Therefore, I have chosen to refer to our past history as a movement at times, because without understanding our history, some will be confused or will miss some helpful lessons.

At worst, ignorance of history means that we are much more likely to repeat the mistakes of it. Being aware of past mistakes helps us deal with them personally in a healthy way, and enables us to understand others who may still need help in getting past them. Leaders who claim that our people are already past the past and don't need to hear any reminders of it are blissfully, but sadly, unaware of what is really present in the minds of a significant number of our grassroots membership. A part of this unwarranted assumption may be due to the fact that such leaders have learned lessons and made changes themselves, and now assume that all leaders have progressed to the same point. All have not.

Among the main themes of *Golden Rule Leadership* were appeals to leaders to examine themselves and their leadership style, and appeals to examine the whole practice of a one-man, top-down leadership approach that is based upon a single lead evangelist at the head of a church. At the time, such appeals were much harder for some leaders to even contemplate than the authors ever anticipated. Admittedly, we could have made some improvements in what we wrote, but some of the readers could have made some improvement in how they read.

After the book came out, I saw the need to add a chapter, which I actually wrote fairly quickly and we started including as a separate article, folded and placed in the front cover of the book. That article was entitled, "Golden Rule Followership." I also wrote another article that included the "Followership" material, and had it been a part of the original book, some negative reactions of leaders might have been avoided or at least lessened. Note that I mention negative reactions of leaders, because I do not recall anything but positive reactions by average members. That fact makes its own statement, and certainly raises some worthwhile questions. This second article is included as Appendix One in this book, and is entitled "Handle with Care."

Though we are aware that *GRL* had oversights, I still believe it is replete with very helpful material on leadership principles. If you have not read the book, or have not read it in a long time, I strongly recommend that you do so. While many of the people named have changed roles since we wrote the book, the principles are still very valuable. They will provide groundwork for this present book. The reactions of leaders at the time of writing *GRL* were as varied as they could possibly be. Many extremely positive reactions came from many directions, from leaders and non-leaders alike. Many very negative reactions came as well, mainly from leaders who were fairly high up on the leadership ladder at the time in our movement of churches.

Our present congregational evangelist in Phoenix, Gary Sciascia, was leading a church in New England at the time the book was published. He was a longtime friend of Wyndham's and a student of mine in our New England School of Ministry. His wife, Gail, read the book and asked Gary to read it. They very quickly asked the non-staff leaders in their congregation to read the book, after which they discussed it and made changes that they all supported. The result was that when the Henry Kriete letter came out in early 2003, their congregation remained on an even keel. Most other congregations did not weather that storm nearly so well.

A brother on the ministry staff in Boston at the time had an interesting observation along these lines: "*Golden Rule Leadership* was God's attempt to bring about repentance through his kindness (Romans 2:4), but when enough key leaders didn't pay attention, he sent the other letter." Sadly, I think that his statement was largely true. The "other" letter to which I refer contained a lot of truth, but was written in a general sense that implicated every leader and was so incendiary in tone that widespread damage occurred that could (and should) have been avoided. The unnecessary collateral damage left far more scars than it should have.

Quite a few leaders eventually expressed regrets at having negative initial reactions or at not having taken the time to really read our book with an open mind and heart, thus allowing changes to be made that could have averted more damage. What I have said here is in no way intended to say "I told you so." History is history in the sense that we cannot undo it. I made plenty of mistakes in leadership myself, for which I have apologized profusely and repeatedly, and thus I am not in any position to be casting stones. I just think we all need some historical perspective regarding past efforts to address leadership principles that may have been rejected at the time, but later have been accepted. That should help us read current material on the subject of leadership with more discernment. No one should read my book or any other without discernment. Paul described long ago what our attitudes in considering messages should be: "Now the Bereans were of more noble character than the Thessalonians, for they received the message with great eagerness and examined the Scriptures every day to see if what Paul said was true" (Acts 17:11). No writer should ask for more than that when others are considering what he has written.

With that background in mind, you might read or reread *Golden Rule Leadership*, and I strongly recommend that you read Appendix One. In it, both leaders and followers are addressed. Do keep in mind that most of us function in both roles in some settings in our lives, which should keep us from getting too polarized or critical. In God's kingdom, there is no "us" and "them"; there is only "us"—brothers and sisters standing on level ground at the foot of the cross, trying to help one another live the kingdom life.

Looking Back and Dreaming Forward

While we must learn from our past and deal with it appropriately, we cannot be crippled by it. On that note, I have been challenging all of us for years to deal with the past and move on. One of my favorite sermon titles of recent years was borrowed from the 20th anniversary theme of the church in the Philippines, "Looking Back and Dreaming Forward." Those two concepts are not mutually exclusive, and looking back means giving consideration to both the highs and lows of the past. We have all experienced some "conditioning" and thus have our "trigger points," which we should be fully aware of in order to avoid overreacting.

A related idea comes to mind as we talk about highs and lows, or positives and negatives. In Part 3 of this book, the material about relationships, I will use the word "challenges" fairly frequently. I do not see such terms as negative, but only wish to recognize that challenges are a part of leadership reality and life reality. As has often been preached, Abraham had to "face" the facts (Romans 4) before he could "faith" the facts. On the other hand, I don't intend to camp out only on the challenges, but will include some practical recommendations about relationship-building principles and practices.

This book will not be the last word on the subjects addressed, but I pray it will advance our understanding and practice of godly spiritual leadership. I heartily encourage other writers who have spent a lot of time contemplating leadership principles to put their thoughts into print. Although we as a movement have made much progress in the leadership realm, we all still have much to learn. Few subjects are more important to our continued progress as a movement of churches intent on restoring New Testament Christianity and reaching the world with the gospel in so doing.

With these introductory thoughts, I hope to have piqued your curiosity enough to engage your interest. I can promise that this book will take you to places you didn't anticipate, and the same will be true for me as my writing unfolds. Perhaps an apt challenge for all of us at this point is simply to say: *Let the evolution begin!*

Part One
Leadership Principles

Chapter One

Leaders Are Disciples and Servants

First and Foremost, Leaders Are Disciples

The basic definition of *disciple* is "learner" and "follower." The definition dictates that a disciple be a lifetime learner. The Great Commission in Matthew 28:19–20 makes this point abundantly clear, in that we must learn enough to be baptized and then be taught to obey all that Jesus commanded. It is regrettable that some devote themselves to study day and night in order to become Christians, but then appear to lose that desire to keep drinking deeply of the Word. The first part of the learning process leads to a spiritual birth, a rebirth. The second part of the process lasts for a lifetime and is a part of a continuing maturation process, a process that is to lead us toward becoming more and more like Jesus. Having a child born is the easier part of the process, compared to the task of raising them. The same is true of us as spiritual children.

To be a follower of Jesus means simply that our lives are devoted to walking in his steps. The apostle John stated it well in this passage:

> We know that we have come to know him if we obey his commands. The man who says, "I know him," but does not do what he commands is a liar, and the truth is not in him. But if anyone obeys his word, God's love is truly made complete in him. This is how we know we are in him: Whoever claims to live in him must walk as Jesus did (1 John 2:3–6).

The imitation of Jesus is our highest calling as a disciple, and it involves both learning of him and following him. The popular little catchphrase, "What would Jesus do?" deserves far more than being a mere catchphrase. It is the very essence of being a disciple of Jesus.

No wonder Jesus said, "If anyone would come after me, he must deny himself and take up his cross daily and follow me" (Luke 9:23). Some people, when doing a study on the concept of discipleship, assume that being a Christian is one level of being God's child, and being a disciple is a deeper level, but a level that is not for everyone. That concept is based on trying to harmonize the modern lifestyle that is commonly *called* Christianity with Christianity as the Bible describes it. There are not two acceptable levels of dedication and service to Jesus. He said clearly in the passage above, "if anyone." Here *anyone* means *everyone*—no exceptions. Later in Luke, Jesus puts it in a way that no one should be able to miss or to rationalize:

> Large crowds were traveling with Jesus, and turning to them he said: "If anyone comes to me and does not hate his father and mother, his wife and children, his brothers and sisters—yes, even his own life—he cannot be my disciple. And anyone who does not carry his cross and follow me cannot be my disciple.
>
> "Suppose one of you wants to build a tower. Will he not first sit down and estimate the cost to see if he has enough money to complete it? For if he lays the foundation and is not able to finish it, everyone who sees it will ridicule him, saying, 'This fellow began to build and was not able to finish.'
>
> "Or suppose a king is about to go to war against another king. Will he not first sit down and consider whether he is able with ten thousand men to oppose the one coming against him with twenty thousand? If he is not able, he will send a delegation while the other is still a long way off and will ask for terms of peace. In the same way, any of you who does not give up everything he has cannot be my disciple.
>
> "Salt is good, but if it loses its saltiness, how can it be made salty again? It is fit neither for the soil nor for the manure pile; it is thrown out.
>
> "He who has ears to hear, let him hear" (Luke 14:25–35).

Popular Christianity is often satisfied when it attracts large crowds. Jesus, on the other hand, was not interested in merely drawing a crowd. He was intent on making disciples, those willing to do anything, give up everything, and go anywhere for his cause. These intentions of his were not merely ideals—they were standards. When the crowds were not willing to follow him on his terms, he watched them walk away: "From this time many of his disciples turned back and no longer followed him" (John 6:66). In John 6, he was calling them to be disciples in the most graphic of terms. In verse 53, spiritual life is said to come from eating and drinking Jesus. In verse 56, such eating allows us to remain in Christ. Verse 57 says that we live by feeding on Jesus. Then verse 58 says that if we feed on the bread of Jesus, we will live forever. The emphasis on life through a relationship with Jesus is obvious.

Now look at other statements in the same chapter. Verse 35 says that if we come to Jesus, we will never go hungry, and if we believe in him, we will never go thirsty. In verse 40, Jesus says that all who look to the Son and believe in him will have eternal life. Verses 44–46 teach that this "coming to Jesus" is accomplished by listening to God and being taught by him. Then in verse 47, the result of listening to God is that "he who believes has everlasting life." Believing in Jesus is equated with eating him. Three times in the context, a reference is made to the "last day." In verses 39–40, if people look to Jesus and believe in him, they will receive eternal life and be raised up at the last day. In verse 44, those who come to Jesus by allowing the Father to draw them will be raised up at the last day. Then, in verse 54, eating Jesus' flesh and drinking his blood will cause a person to be raised up at the last day. The three passages are worded differently, but the meaning in context is the same in each. As Jesus said in verse 63, "The words I have spoken to you are spirit and they are life." He is discussing believing and obeying his words, not taking communion, as many mistakenly assume.

The crowds did not miss what Jesus was saying about being totally committed to him as disciples—learners and followers. Most of them walked away. Most people today still walk away once they understand what it really means to be a disciple of Jesus. Like the Rich Young Ruler (Luke 18:18–25), many want Christianity on their terms. They draw lines around areas of their lives; they are willing to dedicate some parts of life to Jesus but hold back other parts from him. However widely practiced this compartmentalized version of Christianity may be, it is totally unacceptable to Jesus. It is all or nothing with him, if we are truly to be his disciples.

So what does all of this have to do with a book on leadership? Everything. Unless our motivation is grounded solidly in the Bible, we will not make it long-term as disciples, and we have no right to be in leadership roles in God's family. Motivation means everything to God. We can perform the duties of a servant without having the heart of a servant, but if we have the heart of a servant, we will perform the duties of a servant. The issue of the heart is the issue, and the heart of the issue is the heart. *Why* we do what we do is always the ultimate question with God.

Primary Versus Secondary Motivations

Actually, the Bible teaches that there are primary motivations and secondary motivations, and all have a place at points in our Christian walk. But unless the primary motivation takes center stage in our hearts, we will not remain disciples of Jesus for a lifetime. The secondary motivations serve to attract us to Jesus initially, whereas the primary motivation keeps us "in Christ" as long as we live.

What are the secondary motivations? Seeing the love among disciples and being attracted by it is one of them (John 13:34–35). But eventually we will each be hurt by other disciples, and this motivation will lose its luster if something stronger isn't underneath it as a foundation. The fear of God and of Judgment Day is another secondary motivation (John 16:7–8; 2 Corinthians 5:10). The Proverbs remind us that the fear of God is the beginning of knowledge, but it is not the end (Proverbs 1:7; 9:10). In other words, fear gets our attention, but with maturity, "perfect love drives out fear" (1 John 4:18). Of course, fear in the sense of reverence and awe must remain in our heart toward the Creator of the universe.

A third type of secondary motivation comes from looking at the opposite side of the coin: desiring to enjoy the rewards of heaven. Haven't we all gone to a funeral or graveside and remembered these words:

> And I heard a loud voice from the throne saying, "Now the dwelling of God is with men, and he will live with them. They will be his people, and God himself will be with them and be their God. He will wipe every tear from their eyes. There will be no more death or mourning or crying or pain, for the old order of things has passed away" (Revelation 21:3–4).

The hope of heaven is a valid motivation that the Bible often speaks about, but it still cannot be our primary motivation.

Another secondary motivation has to do with finding a meaningful purpose in life. Jesus said, "For whoever wants to save his life will lose it, but whoever loses his life for me and for the gospel will save it. What good is it for a man to gain the whole world, yet forfeit his soul?" (Mark 8:35–36). Gaining the world means nothing on the scales of eternity. Having a life of purpose is what really counts. In the front of all my Bibles, I always inscribe a brief statement I once heard. It says, "Never give up your life for anything that death can take away." What can death take away? Everything except what you do *with* God and *for* God. Being right with God and helping others get right with God is all that ultimately matters.

However, the consideration of living a life of purpose is where leadership motivation can get derailed. It is logical to assume that being a leader is the best way to influence the most people—if we have the gift of leadership (Romans 12:8) and are given the opportunity to exercise it. But this is where some people get confused. Leadership becomes their main goal, rather than the goal of simply influencing people for God (which can be done in many ways). In other words, we can equate becoming a leader with our purpose to the point that leadership becomes *the* purpose of our lives instead of one means to fulfilling our purpose. In this case, leadership—which should never be more than a secondary motivation for coming into God's family— is not only misunderstood, but also becomes our primary motivation for being a disciple in the first place.

Our Primary Motivation

What is that primary motivation of which we speak? It is being motivated by the grace of God through the cross of Christ. Then being a disciple becomes only about learning from Christ in order to follow him; to represent him; to imitate him; to feed on him; to have an ever-growing relationship with him; to want to be with him for time and eternity. Was this not what Paul was saying in Philippians 3:7–11?

> But whatever was to my profit I now consider loss for the sake of Christ. What is more, I consider everything a loss compared to the surpassing greatness of knowing Christ Jesus my Lord, for whose sake I have lost all things. I consider them rubbish, that I may gain Christ and be found in him, not having a righteousness of my own that comes from the law, but that which is through faith in Christ—the righteousness that comes from God and is by faith. I want to know Christ and the power of his resurrection and the fellowship of sharing in his sufferings, becoming like him in his death, and so, somehow, to attain to the resurrection from the dead.

The Fruit of Mixed Motives

We have seen the consequences of muddled motivations in our own church leadership, particularly during the past tumultuous decade. When our churches went through times of upheaval, some leaders continued to follow God; others left him altogether. I've heard many disciples ask why some former leaders, even those who once led very powerfully, have lost their faith when they quit being leaders. Although the answers often contain varied and complicated elements that we need to explain further, the ultimate answer is to be found in the confusion of their motivations. For many of those people, being a leader became an end within itself, and thus it became their identity. Once they stopped leading, their question was "Who am I now?" rather than "*Whose* am I now?" A significant contributing factor was our churches' history of exalting one gift (leadership) above all other gifts, and to exalt one type of leader (evangelist) above all others. That huge mistake yielded serious consequences.

I am saddened that far too many leaders have fallen prey to this sort of misguided thinking, but the fact remains that I must be a disciple of Jesus, regardless of any role I have or don't have in his kingdom. I am his and he is mine, and all else is secondary—including whether I serve in a leadership role or not. If that is not my heart, then I am not a true disciple and I have no right to lead anyone for God. You may be thinking, "Wow—that's a hard teaching, Gordon!" True. But is it what Jesus teaches or not? That's the real issue, isn't it?

Years ago, I heard one very well-known leader say on several occasions that unless a certain brother remained on the staff of the church as a leader, that brother would fall away. Amazingly—staggeringly, shockingly—he was using that argument to convince people to stay on staff! It should have been used as an argument to take them *off* staff! If a person will only remain faithful to Jesus if he is a leader, then that person is not faithful in the first place. He is not a disciple as Jesus describes it. That is a hard teaching, but it is the only conclusion I believe to be in accord with the teaching of Jesus. I hope you can now understand why this chapter began with the statement that any leader must be first and foremost a disciple of Jesus. Disciple-leaders, and *only* disciple-leaders, are worthy of being followed and imitated. Leadership is only a role; being a disciple is who we *are*. Let's not get the two confused.

I do believe it is important to give some additional background explanation regarding why so many leaders from our churches have struggled once they have gotten out of leadership roles. I've already explained the bottom line truth—their primary motivation was off—but often there is more involved, which ushers in some of the complexity of the subject. For some of those leaders, their spirituality level was not equal to their leadership gift level. The reasons for that are varied. In our rush to appoint leaders in the past, we sometimes misjudged their spirituality and maturity, perhaps by equating their zeal to lead with godliness (and the two are definitely not the same). In some cases, had we allowed people more time to grow and helped them become more godly before appointing them, they might have done well. In other cases, some people just didn't have the spiritual capacity to become leaders. Only God knows which category such prematurely appointed leaders were in when they were given their roles. Finally, some of our experienced leaders worked on the premise that you could give leadership roles to people who had leadership gifts, and then help them to become spiritual later. That is called putting the cart before the horse, based on all that we have already studied about discipleship.

There were other contributing factors. During the biggest surge of our movement's upheaval, which began in early 2003, the criticisms of leaders reached ungodly heights. A saying that quickly developed among leaders during that time was, "We went from *hero* to *zero* overnight." We were all hurt deeply by the criticisms we received. I am in that same boat with the rest of the people who were in leadership roles during that time. If we are totally honest, most of us thought seriously about getting out of that leadership boat at some point along the way. I understand those feelings. Like all the people who stayed in leadership, I had to dig very deeply into my relationship with Christ to make it through the firestorm. But that is what we were called to do: deny self, take up our cross daily and follow Jesus. Sometimes that is so difficult to do that we beg God to take the cup of suffering away from us, just as Jesus did in Gethsemane. But like him, we must always return to the basics of discipleship and say, "Nevertheless, not my will, but yours be done." We confessed Jesus as Lord when we were baptized. There is never a valid excuse for going back on that confession—*never*! We must all remain disciples for a lifetime, whether serving in leadership roles or not. In my judgment, special kudos go to those who got off staff (for a variety of reasons) but remained faithful in spite of all the challenges they faced.

Second, Leaders Are Servants

The term "servant" is not a highly esteemed word in modern times, and it certainly wasn't in the society in which Jesus taught. By the world's definition, servants are the class of people under leaders, the people who serve leaders. Leaders direct servants, but they themselves aren't servants in the normal sense of that word. All of us were immersed in the world's concept of leadership prior to becoming disciples, and the depth of our immersion makes it difficult to extricate ourselves from worldly views. When we did come into the kingdom, some of us were led and trained by leaders who had figured out what "Golden Rule" leadership was, and others of us were led and trained by leaders who still functioned with worldly leadership concepts.

I recall a leader of a small group bringing a newer member of his group to see me and get some help resolving some feelings about his past. The group member was complaining about the way people had led him in the past, and if his story was accurate (and I don't assume it was, since I heard only his side), his point would have been valid. Interestingly, the small group leader observed that he felt very fortunate because he had always been discipled by people on the ministry staff and had therefore always received great training, help and encouragement. He'd never had a bad experience!

Why do I tell this story? Because some people with overly critical natures have assumed that everyone on our churches' ministry staff "in the old days" was worldly and unkind in their leadership. They assume that all leaders followed the worldly model of leadership and deliberately trained it into others. While that was the case far too often, it obviously was not universally true. The testimony of that small group leader gives strong evidence that many people on staff did in fact lead well! I have been under the leadership of some who exercised true spiritual leadership and others who exercised worldly leadership. Generalizing is not a healthy approach, for one size doesn't fit all. Besides that truth, the leaders who have remained in leadership during recent years have in the majority learned some valuable lessons and have made corresponding changes in how they now lead.

Servants or Masters?

But let's get back to the idea of leaders being servants. What does the Bible say about it? A key passage is Matthew 20:20–28:

> Then the mother of Zebedee's sons came to Jesus with her sons and, kneeling down, asked a favor of him.
>
> "What is it you want?" he asked.
>
> She said, "Grant that one of these two sons of mine may sit at your right and the other at your left in your kingdom."
>
> "You don't know what you are asking," Jesus said to them. "Can you drink the cup I am going to drink?"
>
> "We can," they answered.
>
> Jesus said to them, "You will indeed drink from my cup, but to sit at my right or left is not for me to grant. These places belong to those for whom they have been prepared by my Father."
>
> When the ten heard about this, they were indignant with the two brothers. Jesus called them together and said, "You know that the rulers of the Gentiles lord it over them, and their high officials exercise authority over them. Not so with you. Instead, whoever wants to become great among you must be your servant, and whoever wants to be first must be your slave—just as the Son of Man did not come to be served, but to serve, and to give his life as a ransom for many."

In this passage, a number of lessons just leap off the page. First, James and John were trained thoroughly in worldly leadership concepts—by their own mother! Second, three years of discipling by the Master had not yet eradicated their false concepts, so views of leadership must indeed be deeply ingrained. Third, the ten other apostles were indignant, not over their concern that their two brothers were sinfully ambitious, but over the fact that they were afraid that they had been beaten to the punch for the chief seats of honor! Fourth, worldly leadership is defined in two different ways here by Jesus: The first is that the Gentile rulers lord it over their people, and the second is that they exercise authority over them. Those are evidently two different things.

Lording over someone means basically to boss them around, perhaps threatening their job or position if they don't obey. It is a matter of how we treat people, our leadership manner. Exercising authority over them means to appeal to our authority as a basis for demanding obedience. In the first case, the one in authority would say, "You better do what I say or I'll fire you!" In the second case, he would say, "I'm the boss around here, and you are only a hireling, so you had better obey me!" Both approaches are closely related, but somewhat different. The first has more to do with the manner of treatment generally and the second has more to do with the basis of justifying that manner.

To give an example, a "Christian" husband might simply treat his wife harshly. Or he might quote Ephesians 5:22–24 to his wife and appeal to his authority as her head. Harsh treatment by a boss or by a husband is always wrong, and appealing to one's authority means that you have already lost your case, because the moment you pull "the authority card," you lose the respect of the other person. Good leaders *earn* respect; they don't demand it. The problem is that the world provides few examples of righteous leadership and many examples of unrighteous leadership. In a later chapter, I will examine the military model of leadership, a model that became all too common in the leadership style of our movement. There is a simple answer explaining how that unfortunate phenomenon occurred, but we will save that for later. Suffice it to say that when we come into the kingdom of God, most of us have much to unlearn and much to learn about leadership. The idea of becoming a slave for Jesus and a servant of all is not immediately attractive, to state it mildly.

The Greek Definition

We often overlook another underlying biblical principle regarding leaders and servanthood. It may be stated like this: "All leaders are deacons." What do I mean by that? I do not mean that all leadership roles are simply subsets of what we would call the deacon role, although some people have made that argument. (Although we'll save a thorough exploration of the deacon's role for later in the book, a deacon is generally understood to be a servant-leader in the church, with a particular role of service.) What I do mean is that the Greek term translated "deacon" in most of our English versions of the New Testament is often used in a broad sense of the term. When we see a version of the word *diakonos*, or "deacon," it is often used to refer to leadership in general, rather than to the specific role of a deacon. More important, every leadership role is covered under the umbrella of the term "deacon." Every leader, including Jesus himself, was also a servant (deacon).

It is not unusual for Greek terms to be used in a broader sense and in a narrower sense. For example, the word "disciple" is used of the Twelve apostles in a very specific sense and is thus used interchangeably with the word "apostle". Even the word "apostle" is used in a broader sense than just describing the Twelve (or Thirteen, after Paul became an apostle). In Acts 14:14, Barnabas is called an apostle; in Romans 16:7, it is possible that Andronicus and Junias, Paul's relatives, were also being called apostles (they were "outstanding among the apostles"); and in Galatians 1:19, the Lord's brother James is also called an apostle. The word "apostle," at its most basic definition, means "one sent on a mission." Thus, the terms "disciple" and "apostle" can be used in a special, restricted sense, or in a broader, more general sense. The context has to determine in which way the terms are being used.

Similarly, the word for servant describes all types of leaders in the New Testament, and is so used multiple times. The verb *diakoneō* denotes serving generally—to take care of others. The noun form, *diakonia*, denotes "service" or "ministry," and *diakonos* is used to describe "one who serves." Jesus used these words in Matthew 20 to describe the people who would lead in his kingdom. Note the word usage there: "Not so with you. Instead, whoever wants to become great among you must be your servant (*diakonos*), and whoever wants to be first must be your slave (*doulos*)—just as the Son of Man did not come to be served (*diakoneō*), but to serve (*diakoneō*), and to give his life as a ransom for many" (Matthew 20:26–28). All Christians are called to be servants (*diakonoi*), which shows that we must choose a very different path than is followed by the world. All roles of church leadership are servant roles, and anyone exercising a spiritual gift should recognize that he is but a servant who belongs to all the others in the church (Romans 12:5).

All leaders are first of all disciples, and then servants (deacons in the broad sense), as may be seen in the following examples:

1. Jesus (Romans 15:8)
2. The apostles (2 Corinthians 6:4)
3. Paul and Apollos (1 Corinthians 3:5)
4. Tychicus (Ephesians 6:21)
5. Epaphras (Colossians 1:7)
6. Timothy (1 Timothy 4:6)

Of the approximately thirty times that some form of the Greek term is used, it is almost always translated "minister" or "servant." When it is translated "deacon," the word refers to the more narrow usage, to the specific church leadership role. The word is used once to describe a female (Phoebe, in Romans 16:1), and more will be said about that in the chapter dealing with deacons. In my view, it would have been better not to translate the word as "deacon" in any passage. As with the terms "apostle" and "disciple," the context would provide sufficient evidence as to whether the word was being used in a general sense or in a more technical sense. This is the same mistake that translators made with the Greek term *baptizō* (literally "I immerse"). *Baptizō* was not translated, but rather transliterated and given English endings—"baptism" or "baptize"—for no good reason except tradition. At any rate, the point is clear: All leaders are first of all disciples and servants, and with that kept firmly in mind, they are then (and only then) ready to be spiritual leaders.

Titles, Positions, Roles and Functions

One final passage about leadership is worthy of our examination: Matthew 23:5–12. Here Jesus gives a righteous tirade against the Pharisees, one of the strongest denunciations of religious leaders to be found anywhere in the Bible. Read it carefully in the New American Standard Version (which is more faithful to the original language than the NIV):

> "But they do all their deeds to be noticed by men; for they broaden their phylacteries and lengthen the tassels *of their garments*. They love the place of honor at banquets and the chief seats in the synagogues, and respectful greetings in the market places, and being called Rabbi by men. But do not be called Rabbi; for One is your Teacher, and you are all brothers. Do not call *anyone* on earth your father; for One is your Father, He who is in heaven. Do not be called leaders; for One is your Leader, *that is*, Christ. But the greatest among you shall be your servant. Whoever exalts himself shall be humbled; and whoever humbles himself shall be exalted."

Jesus said here that we cannot be called "Rabbi," "Father" or "Leader." In the NIV, the third term is translated "Teacher" instead of "Leader." Since most of us use the NIV, let's take a closer look at its translation of verses 8–10:

> "But you are not to be called 'Rabbi,' for you have only one Master and you are all brothers. And do not call anyone on earth 'father,' for you have one Father, and he is in heaven. Nor are you to be called 'teacher,' for you have one Teacher, the Christ."

This translation of the passage is faulty on several counts. One,

"Master" in verse 8 is actually *didaskalos*, the common word for "teacher." "Master" is a poor translation. Teacher in verse 10 is actually *kathêgêtês*, which means "leader" and not "teacher." Teacher has already been used in verse 8, but this word in this verse is variously translated in other versions as "leader," "master" or "guide." Obviously the NIV does not translate the key words in this passage well, for whatever reason. Its translators would have done more justice to the original language by switching the words "Teacher" and "Master" in verses 8 and 10.

But just what is Jesus so strongly forbidding here? In short, he denounces the use of titles to describe what are actually only servant roles. For example, Paul said in Ephesians 4:11 that Jesus gave some to be teachers (with a small "t"). Paul called himself a teacher in 1 Timothy 2:7 and also said that he had been appointed as a teacher in 2 Timothy 1:11. He was not "Teacher Paul," but Paul who *served* as a teacher. He also said that he had dealt with the Thessalonian disciples as a *father* deals with his children (1 Thessalonians 2:11). More to the point is 1 Corinthians 4:15, which reads: "Even though you have ten thousand guardians in Christ, you do not have many fathers, for in Christ Jesus I became your father through the gospel." Thus, Paul was a spiritual father to those whom he had brought to Christ, but he wasn't "Father Paul." Finally, the term "leader" is used very positively in passages like Hebrews 13:7, 17 and 24—but with a lower case "l" and not a capital. With this in mind, I shudder to think back to a time when a certain leader in our churches was said to be *"The* Leader of *the* Movement." Was this not a title and therefore a flagrant violation of Jesus' teaching in Matthew 23?

As leaders, we have functions and designated roles, but we do not have titles. We should be respected and appreciated as leaders by those whom we lead (1 Thessalonians 5:12-13), but not exalted to a pedestal. Hero appreciation is one thing (and we do have heroes among us), but hero worship is quite another. The world's view of a great leader is one who is served by a great many; Jesus' view of a great leader is one who serves a great many. Near the end of the first section of this chapter, I made this statement: "Disciple-leaders, and *only* disciple-leaders, are worthy of being followed and imitated." I think we should expand it to read, "Disciple-servant-leaders, and only such leaders, are worthy of our following and imitating." May God help all of us who lead to not only state that truth, but to exemplify discipleship and servanthood as we lead. Let servant leadership describe who we *are*. Then we will have truly imitated our Master, the most humble servant of all!

Chapter Two

The Gift of Leadership

The Importance of All Gifts in the Body

> For by the grace given me I say to every one of you: Do not think of yourself more highly than you ought, but rather think of yourself with sober judgment, in accordance with the measure of faith God has given you. Just as each of us has one body with many members, and these members do not all have the same function, so in Christ we who are many form one body, and each member belongs to all the others. We have different gifts, according to the grace given us. If a man's gift is prophesying, let him use it in proportion to his faith. If it is serving, let him serve; if it is teaching, let him teach; if it is encouraging, let him encourage; if it is contributing to the needs of others, let him give generously; if it is leadership, let him govern diligently; if it is showing mercy, let him do it cheerfully (Romans 12:3–8).

The study of spiritual gifts is a topic that is certainly in vogue in many evangelical circles. In our movement, we have recently given much more attention to the understanding and application of gifts in the body of Christ. That emphasis is, of course, needed and commendable. Since leadership is one of the gifts listed in Romans 12, a book on the subject of leadership would be incomplete without discussing spiritual gifts. When we introduce this subject, we normally feel the need to mention that there is a clear difference in miraculous spiritual gifts (which were limited to the first-century church) and nonmiraculous spiritual gifts (of which Romans 12 speaks). I suppose that this comment is needed, but in one sense, all gifts from God are miraculous and extraordinary. I feel the need to state that as well.

Such lists as the list of gifts mentioned in Romans 12 are never intended to be all-inclusive. The Bible is written in a way that makes us dig deeper, and God intends that we should look at the Bible as a whole in order to get the big picture. For example, the New Testament contains many "sin lists," but none are exactly alike. We have to look at all of these lists, along with specific sins that are mentioned in isolation, to get the complete picture of sin. The same may be said of gifts, although in this chapter of the book we will concentrate only on the list of gifts in Romans 12, since it offers us sufficient information to cover the subject as it applies to leadership in general. Let's take a closer look at this key passage.

1. *Gifts Cannot Produce Pride*

First, notice that God warns us against pride before even speaking of the gifts (v. 3). Just prior to doing this, he said that we were to commit ourselves to him as living sacrifices and to avoid worldly thinking (Romans 12:1–2). Worldly thinking about our gifts is a very real challenge. These first three verses of the chapter are the foundation for understanding and using spiritual gifts in a righteous manner. Without a godly mindset, spiritual gifts minister to our pride. Thus, we must embrace the warning before proceeding to a further discussion of gifts.

2. *Gifts Exalt the Group*

Second, note that individual gifts are designed to help us become a more effective group, not to exalt us as individuals. We each belong to one another, and therefore our gifts belong to one another. Our gifts are for others and not just for us. Current teaching in the religious world generally includes a strong focus on the self. Statements like this one are commonplace: "Find your true self by discovering and exercising your gifts. Then your self-esteem can soar on wings of eagles!" As common as such statements may be, they are not simply uncommon in the pages of Scripture—they are nowhere to be found! The whole self-esteem movement is an invention of modern man, and (as is usually the case with unbiblical concepts) about 180 degrees off target. Jesus' call to discipleship begins with the words "deny yourself." Do we feel more fulfilled and better about ourselves by using our gifts for the good of others? Certainly. But the fulfillment and good feelings are a result of self-denial and serving others, not because we are seeking them as a goal. God always has rewards for righteous behavior, but the rewards come more as a by-product than anything else. The admonition to obey God and trust him in everything is always timely.

3. All Gifts Are Important

Third, we have different gifts, and none is said to be more important than any other. This introduces a subject that is often misunderstood. As I stated in an earlier chapter, we have tended strongly to exalt the gift of leadership above all others, and within the various leadership roles, we have exalted the role of evangelist above all other roles. But clearly this is man's doing and not God's. He never gives us any reason to make such distinctions. When we exalt one gift above another, we minister to the pride of those thus exalted and make the rest (even the clearly gifted) feel like second-class citizens. What a shame that is—and what a sin!

In *Golden Rule Leadership*, I addressed this issue in a way that I cannot improve on, so I will simply include a part of that segment:

> Truthfully, we are more humanistic than we may think. We value some gifts more than others, but I do not think God does. For example, my best gifts are more the up-front variety. I am a teacher and preacher with the gift of gab, and I write pretty well also. I often receive attention and praise for those gifts. I always remind myself that the Corinthian church members had perhaps more spiritual gifts than disciples in any other church, and yet they were the most unspiritual of the lot. Having gifts does not mean that we are spiritual; it only means that we have been blessed of God with gifts that are intended to bring him glory, not us. Properly understood, our gifts ought to humble us, not puff us up.
>
> My wife, Theresa, is a gifted person. In terms of Romans 12, she is much more gifted than I am in certain areas, especially these: serving, encouraging, giving and showing mercy. Her gifts are more the behind-the-scenes types of gifts, while my best gifts are not. What are often the results of these differences in our two sets of gifts? I receive most

of the notice, and she often feels less important than me to the church and even to God (I'm just being honest, and yes, we are working on viewing these things spiritually). Why? Because we tend to value the types of gifts that the world values—the more visible leadership gifts. Which types do you think God treasures most in us? Easy answer—the types that are most connected to character and heart. On Judgment Day, I would rather meet God with my beloved wife's gifts than with my own, without question. We need to develop God's viewpoint on these things.

4. Gifts Are Just That—Gifts!

Fourth, gifts are just that: *gifts* from God. How can we have pride in ourselves because we have received something we don't deserve? Paul addressed this point clearly in 1 Corinthians 4:7 with these words: "For who makes you different from anyone else? What do you have that you did not receive? And if you did receive it, why do you boast as though you did not?" Leadership is a gift from God, as are the other gifts mentioned in Romans 12. We are in no way superior because we have a particular gift or gifts. If we rely on them in a prideful manner, our gifts become obstacles to our own growth and to seeing our need for other people. For example, I have a reasonably good intellect (although my mind's *computer* is definitely slowing down with age!). Why do I have this? From a divine perspective, it is because of God's gifts. But from a human perspective, it is principally because of my gene pool. I could just as easily have been born with a low IQ or with significant learning disabilities. The fact that I have good learning capabilities has nothing to do with my value at all. As I often say when I preach, I'm the son of a redneck bricklayer from the wrong side of the tracks in the unimpressive state of Louisiana. For God to have used me in the ways he has demonstrates the point I am making here in an amazing way. Surely our Creator has quite a sense of humor!

5. Gifts Have Multiple Purposes

Fifth, gifts are designed to accomplish more than one purpose in the church. Obviously they are for the purpose of serving one another and thereby strengthening the body of Christ. But they have another important purpose that we sometimes miss. What if I don't have the "gift" of encouragement (and truthfully I don't)? Does that excuse me from encouraging people? Not at all. Even though I do not have the gift, I still have the *responsibility* to encourage. The New Testament is replete with passages that make this truth abundantly plain. The well-known verse in Hebrews 3:13 is sufficient testimony to that fact: "But encourage one another daily, as long as it is called Today, so that none of you may be hardened by sin's deceitfulness."

How do the gifts and responsibilities correlate? People with the gifts are role models for people without the same gifts, thus providing us with an example to help us better carry out our responsibilities. My wife has the gift of encouragement and has developed it to a high level of effectiveness. She has encouraged scores and scores of women to overcome their pasts and to do things I never thought they could do. She kept encouraging her own mother to become a disciple long past the point when I saw any hope for her at all. I was probably even unspiritual enough at times that I "encouraged" Theresa to give up and quit wasting her time. But she helped baptize her mother into Christ about two years before she died.

In my lack of faith, I wondered if my mother-in-law had become a true disciple—until I was able to spend time with her. We did not have a great relationship, and I knew that I would be the acid test of her repentance. By the way, I must admit here that I had my own faults in our strained relationship, even though I was already a disciple. The first time we got together after her baptism, it was obvious how much her heart had changed. Her growth helped me to change my part in that formerly difficult relationship, and we became close until her death. The last time I saw her alive was in a hospital on a Sunday, when we shared communion and a final parting. As I left her room, I simply said, "I love you and I will see you on the other side." And I will. Such are the stories produced by my wife's gift of encouragement, and her example has helped me to encourage others far better than I would have ever done on my own (although I still have much improvement to make in this area). I have only appreciation, not envy, for those who have gifts that I do not, because my spiritual family needs their gifts and I need their example.

6. Gifts Must Be Encouraged

Sixth, gifts have to be given an opportunity to be exercised. For every gift mentioned in Romans 12, we find the words "let him." *Let him* (or her) use the gift God has given, which implies several important points:

- Leaders must help people discover their gifts and empower them to use their gifts. Various tools are available to help us with this process.
- Once a person has a good idea of what their gifts are (and are *not*), they will need training, direction and opportunity.
- As they develop and use their gifts, we need to show much appreciation for all who serve in any capacity, and commend them often—*especially* those whose service is behind the scenes and can go unnoticed. Make a list of the people who serve in such areas and develop a plan to encourage them consistently.

All gifts are important to the healthy functioning of the body of Christ, and from what we have already seen, God may value the gifts in a very different way than we humans tend to do. As 1 Corinthians 12:12–13 teaches, we are unified by being baptized into Christ, where none is *inferior* to any other part of the body (vv. 14–20) and none is *superior* to any other part of the body (vv. 21–27). Keep in mind that this passage is also in the midst of a discussion about spiritual gifts. In our physical families, I hope we are very careful about making every child feel special and never inferior. In God's family, we cannot afford to do less. With genuine unity and appreciation for one another, let us rejoice in who God has made us in Christ and build each other up because we are all family!

The Importance of the Gift of Leadership

The final point in our list of lessons from Romans 12 is that leadership is indeed a gift of God for the church. A leaderless group is a confused and ineffective group. While all gifts are important to the health and growth of the church, little would ever be accomplished without effective leadership. I am grateful to have been given this gift and responsibility by God, and I have devoted my life to using it. I want to use it in the right way, but make no mistake about it: I enjoy using my gift (most of the time!). My leadership gift has found application in a number of ways, but the aspect I enjoy most is preaching and teaching. As Eric Liddell, the spiritually minded runner in the movie, *Chariots of Fire*, said: "When I run, I feel [God's] pleasure." Many times in preaching and teaching, I have exactly that same feeling—the feeling that I am doing what God created me to do.

I once heard an old preacher in his eighties quote Paul's comment in Galatians 1:15–16 about being set apart from birth to preach Christ, and he said that he felt the same way about his life. When I heard him, something stirred in my heart, a growing awareness that I felt much the same even at that early point in my career. After spending more than forty years in the preaching and teaching business, I have no doubt that these words also apply to me. If I had any say in the matter, I would choose to have my heart beat its last time when I was in the process of preaching the Word. I love God's word and count it a privilege beyond all comprehension and description to be able to share it with others.

I don't exercise this gift with any feeling of superiority—just gratitude. Of course, sometimes I wish I was anything but a leader, for leadership has some burdens known only to those who carry them. But generally I am one of those "lead, follow or get out of the way" people. Accomplishing little or nothing for God is nowhere to be found in my life's agenda. Years ago, I attended a time management type of seminar (although they described it as a "priority management program"). One of our exercises was to fill out a questionnaire about our priorities in the present and our dreams for the future. One question asked what our specific dreams were for the future. I gave the question some serious thought for quite a while before answering and wrote this simple statement: "My dreams for the future are to keep doing exactly what I'm doing now for as long as I can possibly do it." Someone asked, after seeing the movie *Bucket List*, what was on my bucket list (my list of things I want to do before I die). I replied, "I'm living it now." I have nothing else to add to my list, except going to heaven (which happens after we die anyway!). My gracious Father has given me a gift of leadership in his family, and I exercise it without apology. Although I haven't the faintest idea why he gave me this calling, I am a leader for him as long as I am still functional.

I don't view my gift as greater than other people's gifts, but I do view it as the greatest gift God could have given *me*. Similarly, I think God gave me the greatest wife in the world, which is to say, the greatest for *me*. I hope all husbands feel the same way about their wives.

I hope this example helps to illustrate how I can revel righteously in my gift of leadership without minimizing in any way another person's different gift. I hope that makes sense to you; it does to me. And I pray that you feel the same way about all the gifts God has blessed you with.

The reason I spend so much time talking about leadership, including the ways it can be misused and abused, is because it's my gift and I treasure it. I am protective of the gift in the sense that I want everyone to view it the right way and want all who have it to use it in a way that brings pleasure to the God who gave it to us. There's an old saying that goes something like this: "I can talk about my Mama, but I don't want to hear you do it." I am not saying that those without the leadership gift should not be able to talk about it, but I am saying that I have earned the right to discuss it candidly and in detail. It's my gift and I have been trying hard to use it to glorify God and bless his people for a long, long time. I love it and I want others to love it, and I will do all in my power to protect the way it is viewed and how it is used. In order to accomplish this lofty goal, taking the time to examine in depth the *authority* of leadership is absolutely essential, and to that subject we go next.

Chapter Three

The Authority of Leadership

Authority in God's Kingdom: A Very Serious Subject

As you can already tell, one of my major concerns about authority and leadership in the church is the temptation to have worldly perspectives that lead to harmful leadership styles. On the other hand, I am just as concerned that we will have another type of worldly view of authority—one that is equally damaging and totally inspired by Satan. I refer, of course, to a rebellious view toward authority. Years ago, I wrote a fairly comprehensive book on the subject of discipling, which is now out of print. To make the book more useful for newer disciples, a condensed version entitled *The Power of Discipling* took its place. The shorter version omitted several chapters, one of which addressed the topic of authority.

Since the original book is out of print and the chapter on authority contained some detailed material that is relevant to this present chapter, I am going to include segments of chapter 13 from the book *Discipling*. Read this material carefully, for it is biblically grounded and surprisingly sobering at points. Although its original intent was to examine the subject of authority generally and to examine specifically how it might apply to discipling relationships (or "one another relationships"), the material is applicable and helpful for our in-depth study of leadership. Following that material, I will offer some final practical observations on the subject, still aimed at helping us avoid an overreaction to authority. Our next chapter will address the other side of the coin, the improper application of authority—examined through some avenues not often traveled. Both extremes must be avoided like the plagues that they are. Here then is the material from the book *Discipling*:

Who Has Authority?

In this chapter, we want to examine the subject of authority in the church from a broad perspective, not just from the perspective of leadership in discipling relationships. It is hard to exaggerate the importance of authority in our world and in the church. Satan's hatred for authority tells us a great deal. He evidently became who he is through rebellion against the authority of God. Everything we are told about him makes it clear that he will do all within his power (which is considerable) to destroy authority and respect for it. As humans, we are never more satanic than when despising authority and encouraging others to do the same (2 Peter 2:10).

The Bible wastes no time in showing us Satan's hatred of authority and his devious way of undermining it. He approached Eve (Genesis 3) by saying that God had forbidden her and Adam to eat from *every* tree in the Garden. Eve responded by essentially saying, "No, it was really only *one* tree, but if we eat from it we will die." Satan pretty much replied, "Not true—God is lying to you because he doesn't want you to gain his knowledge." What was Satan doing here? Undermining trust in the authority of God. He has not changed his approach one iota in the millennia since Eve ate the forbidden fruit. He hates every form of authority (except his own; see Ephesians 6:12) and will continue his attempts to tear it down in every nation, society, and family, and certainly in the church of the Almighty God!

Search the pages of sacred history and you will find the same story repeated over and over. Moses, one of God's greatest leaders and the most humble one on earth (Numbers 12:3), had to deal incessantly with rebellion against his leadership. Even his own brother and sister rose up to question him. Just listen to their envious pettiness:

> "Has the Lord spoken only through Moses?" they asked. "Hasn't he also spoken through us?" And the Lord heard this (Numbers 12:2).

The root of rebellion against authority is pride and envy, pure and simple, whether by Satan, Aaron and Miriam—or by you and me!

But mark it down: God is listening, and he does not take rebellion lightly. Just read the rest of the account in Numbers 12 and see what happened to little sister. Since she was the one most directly punished, we can surmise that she was a true daughter of Eve and instigated the rebellion.

What do we find in the New Testament about this subject? As the only sinless man ever to live went about loving and serving perfectly, the supposedly spiritual folk were continually asking, "By what authority are you doing these things?" (See Matthew 21:23, Mark 11:28, Luke 20:2 and John 2:18.) Their little positions of worldly authority were being threatened by true spiritual leadership and they were listening very attentively as Satan whispered his lies and distortions in their ears. Paul, proclaimer of grace and model of humility, constantly had to defend his authority, much to his embarrassment. Reading 2 Corinthians 10–13 with this thought in mind shows us this point clearly. What we need to understand is that God always has leaders through whom he works, and Satan and his demons always incite rebellion against those leaders by filling men's hearts with pride, envy and distrust.

One additional note is needed before we move to specific biblical teaching about authority. Some leaders are themselves rebellious against any other authority besides their own. When leaders or "would-be" leaders rebel against true authority, they usually do so because of pride and envy. It is sometimes the case that others resist authority because of fear and mistrust, developed by having endured ungodly leadership. Such resistance is still viewed by God as rebellion, but the root cause is somewhat different. The seriousness of rebellion is obvious, but leaders who tempt followers to resist by leading in an unrighteous manner are just as guilty. On both sides of the coin we must be extremely careful. Godly leadership is absolutely essential, and godly followership is just as essential. God will not tolerate less.

The Provision for Authority

The need for authority exists in every group that has any purpose to accomplish. Without leadership and the authority inherent in it, no group can possibly achieve its purposes. In America (along with most of the rest of the world), society is bordering on chaos because of a breakdown of authority. The deterioration of homes and schools, former bastions for developing respect for authority, is nothing short of amazing. However, *no* organization can survive and flourish without authority. God's groups through the centuries required leadership and authority but did not always have the right kind of it. Without proper authority, God's nation suffered greatly (Judges 21:25). Moses could not lead the nation without the support of many other leaders exercising authority (Exodus 18:13–26). God placed leadership in the church in order to lead his people to maturity and productivity (Ephesians 4:11–16).

Essentially, two basic types of authority exist: authority based on position, and authority based on influence. In the case of authority wielded through influence, that influence may be based on one of two things: relationship or knowledge. Relationship authority is exercised when we trust someone enough to be influenced by their input. Knowledge authority is exercised mainly because we respect the knowledge or expertise of another person. For example, we go to the doctor and then do almost anything he says. Why? Not because he has any positional authority over us, and usually not because we have a close personal relationship with him. We simply trust his experience and training. The ideal authority would be a combination of relationship and knowledge.

Which kind of authority should we find in the church? Without a doubt, authority in the kingdom is to be viewed first of all as *relational* in nature. Even though everyone in a congregation cannot know all leaders on an intimate basis, we must *see* each other as family and work hard to build the *feeling* of family. Regarding the authority of *knowledge*, more experienced leadership will exert more influence than the less experienced. In a physical family, the older brothers and sisters teach the younger ones many valuable things. God never intended for the parents to be the sole trainers of the children. Older siblings and extended family members were all to have a part in the task. Surely this design is also a part of his plan for his spiritual family. Discipleship, as described in Matthew 28:19–20, is based upon these principles. God is the one with the greatest expertise, but we can and must learn much from others in the kingdom.

But what about positional authority in the church—do we have that? Because many religious people have seen church leaders wrongly exercise their authority in the past, they conclude that every vestige of positional authority is to be avoided. However, the Bible makes it clear that God has designated this type of authority in several realms, including in the church. The broad list would be:

1. Government: Romans 13:1–7; 1 Peter 2:13–17.
2. Masters (Employers): Colossians 3:22–24; 1 Peter 2:18–20.
3. Husbands: Ephesians 5:22–33; 1 Peter 3:1–7.
4. Parents: Ephesians 6:1–3.
5. Church leaders: 1 Thessalonians 5:12–13 (and the other passages to follow).

I remember spending hours with a young man in a foreign country discussing these issues. He admitted that positional authority was authorized by God in government, business, between husband and wife, and parents and children, but argued emphatically that it is *not* authorized in the church. Do you see the lack of logic in this line of reasoning? According to him, God instituted authority in every realm except the most important one! Of course, it is true that positional authority should not exist in isolation in the church, without being combined with the other types. However, positional authority definitely has a place in the kingdom.

Key New Testament Texts Regarding Spiritual Authority

To disciples who had a worldly view of authority, Jesus spoke these words:

> Jesus called them together and said, "You know that the rulers of the Gentiles lord it over them, and their high officials exercise authority over them. Not so with you. Instead, whoever wants to become great among you must be your servant, and whoever wants to be first must be your slave—just as the Son of Man did not come to be served, but to serve, and to give his life as a ransom for many" (Matthew 20:25–28).

The word for "authority" (v. 25) here is from the Greek *exousia*. Does Jesus' statement in this text thus rule out all authority in the church, as some claim? For starters, note that in verse 28, Jesus is using himself as an example of the right kind of leader, a servant leader. Yet, he has all authority (*exousia*) in heaven and on earth (Matthew 28:18). Does his having "all authority" indicate that only he has *exousia*? No, it cannot mean that, for in 2 Corinthians 10:8 and 13:10, Paul claims to have the authority (*exousia*) of an apostle. Since Jesus was given all authority by the Father, he then could imitate the Father by sharing his authority with the leaders he had chosen. Obviously Jesus is not ruling out all authority in the church, but he unquestionably is ruling out *positional only* authority in which people lord it over others and do not lead by example and relationship. (See 1 Peter 5:1–4 for a similar application.)

To a church where people were apparently becoming independent of leadership, the writer of Hebrews penned these words:

> Obey your leaders and submit to their authority. They keep watch over you as men who must give an account. Obey them so that their work will be a joy, not a burden, for that would be of no advantage to you (Hebrews 13:17).

The word "authority" in the NIV is not in the Greek, so the literal translation would be "obey and submit to them" (as leaders). The word "obey" is from the Greek *peithō*, and the literal meaning is "be persuaded." My young friend I mentioned earlier argued that the leader has no authority, but only the power of persuasion. While it is true that good leaders need to persuade their people from the Scriptures and with valid reasoning, this passage is not directed at leaders! Followers are commanded to *be persuaded*. Just as no leader can make us submit if we do not have a submissive heart, so no leader can persuade anyone who refuses to be persuaded. Even God pleads with us to be persuaded, for it is an issue of submission from the *heart* that he is after! The same word is found in James 3:3, which reads: "When we put bits into the mouths of horses to make them *obey* us, we can turn the whole animal" (emphasis added). People are not horses and leaders should not use bits, but the usage here shows us that the word is hardly a weak one.

Who are the leaders in Hebrews 13:17? They are recognized congregational leaders with a designated work in the church, for which they will give an account. That is obvious from the context, and besides, who else could they be? What other leaders could he describe in this way? Since they have this role and weighty responsibility, he says make their work a *joy!* This is a most important passage, but we must be careful how we apply it. To apply it to a six-month-old Christian who is discipling a two-month-old Christian, and to equate the six-month-old with the leader described in this passage would be a misapplication of Scripture, and might be hazardous to the spiritual health of both! This does not, however, give the younger disciple license to rebel against the one trying to help him. God blesses humility and opposes pride in all situations. It is just that in such cases we should think more in terms of peer relationships and less about someone being over someone else.

To the sometimes rowdy Corinthians, Paul wrote words they no doubt needed:

> You know that the household of Stephanas were the first converts in Achaia, and they have devoted themselves to the service of the saints. I urge you, brothers, to submit to such as these and to everyone who joins in the work, and labors at it (1 Corinthians 16:15-16).

The word "submit" in verse 16 is from *hupotasso* in the Greek. It is also a strong word, as its usage in James 4:7 would indicate: "*Submit yourselves*, then, to God. Resist the devil, and he will flee from you" (emphasis added).

This passage in 1 Corinthians 16 shows the natural ordering of leadership relationships in a developing church. The earlier converts became the early leaders, as would be expected, and should be submitted to as leaders. Also, all the others who "joined in the work" (almost certainly, *as* leaders, given the meaning of *hupotasso*) should be submitted to as well. This pattern is very natural in any organization. Those on the "ground floor" gain the most experience, and naturally lead the less experienced ones who come in later. Levels of leadership develop in this manner, as experience and knowledge dictate who is best equipped to lead.

Some people have tried to escape the clear teaching of this passage by appealing to verse 12 in the same chapter (1 Corinthians 16) regarding the unwillingness of Apollos to follow the urging of Paul. However, any appeal which sets one scripture in contradiction to another is a very suspect appeal to begin with! The issue in this verse was not *whether* Apollos was going to do what Paul asked, but only *when* he was going to do it. We must also keep in mind that we are talking about two very influential leaders with different responsibilities that had to be taken into consideration. Timing in discharging ministry responsibilities is always a big issue. Comparing this situation with submission to leaders in a congregation is comparing apples and oranges. On the other hand, the passage does show the correctness of discussing differing opinions with the right spirit and even working out compromises (regarding timing, in this case).

Dynamic Leadership

A number of passages from Paul's letters to evangelists demonstrate that Paul expected them to use authority in discharging their responsibilities. To give you the flavor of such scriptures, they are included here without comment but with emphasis added:

> As I urged you when I went into Macedonia, stay there in Ephesus so that you may *command* certain men not to teach false doctrines any longer (1 Timothy 1:3).

> *Command and teach* these things. Don't let anyone look down on you because you are young, but set an example for the believers in speech, in life, in love, in faith and in purity (1 Timothy 4:11–12).

> *Command* those who are rich in this present world not to be arrogant nor to put their hope in wealth, which is so uncertain, but to put their hope in God, who richly provides us with everything for our enjoyment. *Command* them to do good, to be rich in good deeds, and to be generous and willing to share (1 Timothy 6:17–18).

> Keep reminding them of these things. *Warn* them before God against quarreling about words; it is of no value, and only ruins those who listen (2 Timothy 2:14).

> In the presence of God and of Christ Jesus, who will judge the living and the dead, and in view of his appearing and his kingdom, I give you this charge: Preach the Word; be prepared in season and out of season; *correct, rebuke and encourage*—with great patience and careful instruction. For the time will come when men will not put up with sound doctrine. Instead, to suit their own desires, they will gather around them a great number of teachers to say what their itching ears want to hear. They will turn their ears away from the truth and turn aside to myths. But you, keep your head in all situations, endure hardship, do the work of an evangelist, discharge all the duties of your ministry (2 Timothy 4:1–5).

> The reason I left you in Crete was that you might *straighten out* what was left unfinished and appoint elders in every town, as I directed you (Titus 1:5).

> For there are many rebellious people, mere talkers and deceivers, especially those of the circumcision group. They *must be silenced*, because they are ruining whole households by teaching things they ought not to teach—and that for the sake of dishonest gain (Titus 1:10–11).

> These, then, are the things you should teach. Encourage and rebuke with *all authority*. Do not let anyone despise you (Titus 2:15).

Even a cursory reading of these passages should convince anyone that authority in the church is established by God. We could add to them passages about the authority of elders or of leaders in other roles, but these should suffice for our purpose of showing that leaders in the church definitely have authority.

The Extent of Authority

When Scripture speaks clearly, all of us have the authority to apply the Authority (Scripture) to people's lives. The challenges come when Scripture does not speak definitively on some matter, but decisions must be made. Who has the authority, how much do they have, and how should it be used?

Common Sense

Common sense and practical judgment are definitely required when the "book, chapter and verse" method does not provide specific instruction about a topic. In other words, leadership in the church is not only authorized to enforce obedience to specific biblical commands; it is also authorized to designate the practical elements required to carry out those commands. Decisions of all sorts have to be made for the church, including when to meet, where to meet, how to organize and other such extra-biblical (but not *anti-biblical*) issues.

Once these decisions are made by leadership, we must follow them. If not, chaos would rule. Therefore, even in these areas of judgment, leaders' decisions should be followed unless one of two conditions exist: one, you are asked to violate Scripture (Acts 5:29); or two, you are asked to violate your conscience (Romans 14:23). However, to appeal to the conscience as a reason for not submitting is a serious matter and cannot be used simply as an excuse to do your own thing![1]

A related point is that spiritual maturity brings with it a certain authority. A very mature Christian, even at lower levels of leadership, would exert more influence generally than would a young Christian. The reason is obvious: He has more knowledge and expertise to offer. But when we are discussing this type of knowledge authority in lower-level leaders, how binding is it? An important part of the answer concerns the impact made by the response of the follower.

Would he be the only one affected by his decisions, or would others be affected as well? If the impact were only on the person making the decision, that is much different than making a decision which affects many people. Therefore, in one case, the input might be viewed by the leader more as advice, while in the other case, he would view it as more binding. Sensitive leadership and humble followership will protect all of us.

A Biblical Precedent

In determining the authority of different levels of leadership in the church, including the possible authority of a discipler, Moses and Jethro have valuable insights which remain helpful to us centuries later. Read carefully Exodus 18:13–26. Different levels of leadership were appointed by Moses at Jethro's suggestion. If they had different levels of leadership, then by necessity they had different levels of authority. The higher the level of leadership, the higher the level of responsibility; and the higher the level of responsibility, the higher the level of authority. Leaders of tens dealt with their ten, meeting needs and solving every problem they could. If they reached an impasse, they went to the leader over them for help, which would have been a leader of fifty.

If this leader could not solve it, he appealed to a leader of a hundred, and next to a leader of a thousand, and ultimately to Moses. Leaders at lower levels took care of as many situations as possible before appealing to a higher-level leader. The same principle must be applied in the church. The lead evangelist and the elders are not the ones to call first (nor second nor third, usually). It is not because they are not concerned, but because ignoring the principle of working through the various levels of leadership has deleterious consequences: It leaves leaders stretched too thin, making them ineffective, and it leaves their followers unsatisfied (or worse). Sheer numbers alone dictate that Jethro's solution is the only one which can possibly work in any larger group. So to complete the thought, a leader of even a small group must be allowed the authority to lead that group. Otherwise, leaders already having more responsibility will be overwhelmed with needs and details.

Let's Avoid Overreactions—Please!

The above material from *Discipling* should help us understand the overall subject of authority in the church much better. Correctly understanding the issue of authority in any relationship or set of relationships is not only important to the effective functioning of any organization, it is *emotionally* vital—yea, essential. The word *authority* itself produces heightened feelings, concerns and reactions in most of us. In our pre-Christian days, we have run amok with those having authority over us, often in very painful ways. The human tendency to enjoy the limelight and the control that goes with it is all too prevalent. While we quickly recognize that tendency in others, truthfully, it is a temptation for any of us who lead.

In our movement of churches, we have had to struggle with a paradigm shift in our view of leadership and the authority that accompanies it. The earlier days of our movement were unquestionably too authoritarian. Authority was viewed primarily as positional in nature, not dissimilar to the kind found in the military. The higher the position, the greater the authority; and very often in practice, the higher the position of the leader, the less care the leader actually took in the exercise of his or her authority. It should have been quite the opposite, as the principle of James 3:1 clearly indicates. The wrong use of authority is nearly always accompanied with insensitivity and/or harshness, and harshness carries with it more ramifications than we can possibly imagine. Our view of authority affects, and maybe determines, our view of God, especially in the case of younger and weaker disciples.

In addition to our movement's authoritarian mindset with its attendant abuses, God's name and the Bible were sometimes invoked to uphold that authority. The view that God specifically put everyone in the authority positions that they held, that they were in fact "God's anointed," was unquestionably espoused in many quarters. Thus, being authoritarian in heart and demeanor was one mistake we made, but dogmatically affirming God's blanket approval for anything leaders did was likely a worse mistake.

This recent reevaluation of our views of authority is certainly colored by our former emphases and abuses. One real danger is that we will allow the pendulum to swing too far, causing us to shy away from the practical need for authority and from the biblical injunctions for exercising the right kind of authority. One thing that I hope will help us to avoid this overreaction is to better define and understand the different types of authority, which we have already discussed in some detail.

Positional authority has to be handled very carefully, to be sure, and it must be said that this type of authority is not the principal type conveyed in the New Testament, even in the practice of Jesus (to whom all authority had been granted). A comparison of John 13:13 and John 15:15 will surely demonstrate that point. In the first verse, Jesus said to the Twelve that he was their Master and Teacher (showing them to be servants and students). In the second, he said that he no longer wanted them to think of their relationship with him as Master-to-servant, but as friend-to-friend, because they were sharing in the Father's business together. Of course, he is still the Master, but he doesn't call attention to that as a way of making people obey him; rather, he encourages his disciples to think about their relationship with him in terms of friendship.

Our leadership roles may vary, along with the authority which is inherent in them, but relationships are yet another thing. The idea that role determines relationship is a bad idea, but a common one. It grew out of the assumption that our closest personal relationships should be reserved for those at similar levels of leadership. Again, the military model rears its head. Relationships between disciples should always move in the direction of *peer* relationships, just as they should in a family. The goal of godly parenting is to develop maturing relationships with our children that are age-appropriate at each stage, with the ultimate aim of exchanging our parent's hat for a friend's hat. That same goal must define our relationships in the kingdom. Our roles may be different, but our relationships must become that of peers, of friends. As sinners, we are all on level ground at the foot of the cross, and we cannot ever forget that.

With our former experience of feeling the heavy hand of positional authority and the *dictated* unity it emphasized, we now have to be willing to *forge* unity, avoiding the real tendency to run toward independence and even autonomy. Surely we must avoid that tendency like the disaster that it is. Having been raised in churches that prided themselves on having autonomous congregations, I am absolutely certain that I never want to go back to that unbiblical system.[2] Too many in our movement have overreacted, and if they were to stay on that track, they would end up in places that work against the very unity for which Christ prayed and died. Thankfully, most leaders have moved past that overreaction and are realizing the huge need for remaining a united movement of *discipling* churches. Just as individuals need other individuals in their lives for purposes of discipling, so congregational leaders also need relationships with other congregational leaders to stay healthy and growing.

What is the overall concern that prompts the inclusion of this material in the book? Simply stated, the human tendency to overreact is very real, and if we have experienced the exercise of abusively applied positional authority in the past, that ushers in a strong temptation to swing the pendulum to the opposite extreme. We can so overreact to that abuse that we move away from the right kind of authority and move toward an independence that is prideful and disunifying. My appeal is for reconsideration, but not reaction. Authority is God-ordained, and without it, chaos reigns. Harsh leadership is bad leadership, but independent leadership rather than interdependent leadership is also bad leadership.

We are a brotherhood, not a loosely connected group of churches that eschew the development and practice of the authority of influence. We are our brothers' keepers and they are ours. That means that we seek the input of other leaders and take that input seriously, and are very willing and anxious to provide the same support for others. Whatever the failures of our movement, they have often been more failures of implementation than principle. Let's deal with these failures and hang on to the principles that have produced, in spite of the abuses in application, some pretty amazing accomplishments in planting and building churches all over the world. God's provision of leadership is truly a blessing in our lives. The order he has established in the universe and in his church are both logical and powerful. May we trust his authority by trusting the authority he has ordained in his kingdom, and may we all, leader and follower alike, remain clothed with humility.

End Notes:
1. See Appendix Six: *Matters of Conscience: A Deeper Look*, page 249.
2. Gordon Ferguson, *Prepared to Answer*, (Spring, Texas: Illumination Publishers), Chapter 9: "Restoration Churches," pages 113–135.

Chapter Four

Leadership Styles

Introductory Caution

This is one of those chapters that starts one way and ends up another, so be prepared. Some readers will really like the first part and others will probably dislike it and wish I had left it out. However, the readers who disliked the first part will really like the last part, and the ones who loved the first part may well hate the last part. I hope most readers will like both parts. Please read the whole chapter before reaching your conclusions about the material *and* its author! I guarantee you will not find it boring.

Leadership Styles

In the Business World

One of the most helpful business books I have ever read, especially because of its application to our movement prior to our upheaval in 2003, is *Primal Leadership* (Harvard Business School Publishing, 2002). The book was produced by a consortium of writers led by Goleman, Boyatzis, and McKee. Goleman is perhaps best known for his research and writings about the importance of leaders possessing and applying emotional intelligence, a subject that receives much attention in *Primal Leadership*. The authors and their team analyzed data in a predetermined and systematic fashion from nearly five hundred global companies and organizations in order to measure their effectiveness. To determine which personal leadership capabilities produced outstanding performance within these organizations, they grouped capabilities into three categories: purely technical skills, such as accounting or business planning; cognitive abilities, such as analytic reasoning; and traits showing emotional intelligence, such as self-awareness and relationship skills.

Stated more simply, the CEOs of companies have to know their "business," which depends on the nature of the company they lead; they have to have reasonably high intelligence (IQ); and they have to possess good emotional intelligence (EQ). The authors used the term "primal leadership" to define the traits that they believed to be of *primal* (first) importance in leading. Their conclusion was that the exercise of emotional intelligence is primal, in two senses: It is both the original and the most important act of leadership. Even if leaders get everything else just right, but fail in this primal task of guiding the emotions of their employees in the right direction, nothing they do will work as well as it could or should.

In the early part of the book, six leadership styles are described and rated as to their effectiveness. Four of them are said to create the kind of resonance that boosts performance, while two others are said to be the *dissonant* styles, reserved for exceptional situations and even then to be applied very sparingly and very cautiously.

Leadership Styles in the International Churches of Christ

Not surprisingly, all six styles can be found in the Bible and in our movement. However, prepare yourself for a shock as we examine these styles and how they have been applied within our movement in its first two decades or so (dating back particularly to the decades of the 1980s and 1990s when the Boston Church of Christ and Los Angeles Church of Christ held heightened influence). Although the authors rate each style as to its effectiveness, I am purposely going to list the styles in random order to allow you to reach your own tentative conclusions about which styles we once used most.

One style is described as the *affiliative style*. A leader utilizing this style builds relationships personally with those under his or her leadership and also helps them build peer relationships with one another in the organization. The emotional needs of people in the organization are valued more highly than work goals. Another style

Dynamic Leadership

is termed the *pacesetting style*. You can likely guess what this style encompasses: Goals and achievement (often of the short-term variety) are the mainstays of this style, and it is usually employed by a leader who is himself a pacesetter. The authors note that such leaders often have a lack of empathy that makes them fairly oblivious to the rising distress of the people asked to achieve the leader's goals. A third style is called the *coaching style*. This approach could also be called *mentoring*, as the leader focuses on helping individuals develop their abilities and reach their own personal goals. The fourth style is the *commanding style*, favored by leadership that seeks tight control of any situation and monitors it studiously. Those under this kind of leadership have no doubts about who is in charge. A fifth style is the *visionary style*, similar to the coaching style, but applied to the organization as a whole. The visionary leader consistently keeps the long-range possibilities of the organization on the hearts and minds of those in all levels of the organization. The final leadership style is *democratic*. As the term suggests, this approach uses team leadership at various levels to help determine the directions of the organization.

How would you rank the use of these six styles by the prominent leadership of our movement during most of our history (excluding the post-2003 years)? Take the time to rank them before reading further. (Waiting, waiting, waiting . . .) I have asked a number of ministry staff groups to rank our past use of the six styles, with very consistent results. Although some variations have occurred in ranking between styles one and two, the same two are always ranked at the top. At least leaders understand how we have led and been led, even if we don't fully understand the effectiveness (or lack thereof) of our leadership approaches. The ministry groups I surveyed have consistently ranked our predominant leadership styles in this order:

1. Commanding
2. Pacesetting
3. Visionary
4. Coaching
5. Affiliative
6. Democratic

How did you rank them?

The sobering fact is that the authors of *Primal Leadership* described the commanding and pacesetting styles as the dissonant styles that should be used very sparingly and cautiously. And yet for many years, our movement's leaders focused on the two most potentially dangerous styles. That fact was highly alarming to me when I first read the book (pre-2003), but it does help explain the intense reactions many of our members had toward their ministry staff leaders back when the firestorm broke into flame. They felt that they had been led in ways that damaged them, and one can hardly disagree with their conclusion. I think it's fair to say that on some level, nearly all of us—leaders and nonleaders alike—have experienced this kind of damaging leadership from someone "over us" in the church. Would to God that those dissonant styles had been used cautiously and sparingly, rather than boldly and freely! I recommend reading *Primal Leadership* for further exploration of the six leadership styles, along with a great deal of interesting and helpful information about leadership in general. As I said, it is one of the best business books I have ever read, particularly in terms of its relevance to our movement's past leadership approaches.

The Military Model

This rather shocking section will be followed by the further explanation that while these facts were generally true, they were not universally true. (I hope my saying this will help you read it without being either defensive or overly critical regarding the issues addressed.) Surprisingly, it took me at least a year after reading the book to ask a question that begs to be answered: "*Why* have we held to the commanding and pacesetting models so tenaciously?" The answer (which is now obvious to me, but wasn't at the time) is that our movement's primary leadership approach was a military model— the very term the authors use to further describe the commanding style of leadership. I don't think it is too difficult to ascertain just why that happened. Our most influential past leader, Kip McKean, was raised in a military setting by a father who had been a career military officer of an extremely high rank. I won't delve into that point further, but suffice it to say that our leadership model has been more like a military model than any other model.

Several years ago, while I was serving as a consultant for the ministry leadership group of one of our larger churches, I asked a group of leaders why they thought we have held so strongly to the military model of leadership. I also asked this group to list evidences of how the military model was manifested in our past church structure and environment, and also asked the ministry brothers in my home church for the same input. Here are some of the evidences mentioned by these two groups:

1. A hierarchical leadership, with a well-defined chain of command.
2. A high degree of discipline demanded of individuals, with corrective discipline often applied in case of lapses—often delivered in group settings.
3. Anyone who did not obey leadership unquestioningly was treated with impatience at best and strong disapproval at worst.
4. The mission was clearly valued over the needs of individuals. Leaders (includingnon-staff leaders) were required to make some significant sacrifices for the good of the mission. Matthew 6:33 was our mainstay passage in enforcing these requests.
5. However, rank had its privileges. In other words, a "lieutenant" (lower-ranking staff member) would be given his marching (moving) orders with little say in the decision, while a "colonel" was included in the decision and had more possibility of the right of refusal.
6. A strong emphasis on conformity (which effectively shut people down).
7. A sense of patriotism was honored and rewarded, to the point that a type of blind, unquestioning loyalty often resulted.
8. An "us-versus-them" mentality, which evidenced itself in a number of divisions: staff versus nonstaff; our church versus other denominations; our congregation or ministry group versus sister congregations or ministry groups . . .
9. Applied in extreme, "they" (whichever *they* they were!) were viewed somewhat like opponents (armies fight enemies, after all). In a military milieu, everyone tends to be viewed as either ally or enemy—they are either *with* us or *against* us. And in a related application, even our allies were sized up as strong or weak. (Could they help with the mission or not?)

10. Adapt and overcome no matter what the price tag—even when things hurt you or seem unfair. (In the military, lower-ranking members have absolutely no ability to influence or change policy.)

11. A distrust or resentment of those up the ranks (and on the other side, often little sensitivity shown toward those down the ranks).

12. An emphasis on opportunities for promotion, which fueled selfish ambition and a competitive atmosphere.

13. The educational or training backgrounds of the officers played into the pecking order and helped to determine who was valued most.

14. The higher up the leadership ladder you moved, the less in touch you were with what people at lower levels were facing and feeling.

15. "Military brats" and "kingdom kids" are terms applied in similar ways, sometimes negatively and sometimes neutrally (simply depicting the children of people in either organization).

16. The term "Christian" was viewed as being a bit ordinary and weak, but the term "disciple" was similar to the Marines' appeal to "the few, the bold, the brave."

17. Public relations efforts for the purpose of attracting recruits and reenlistments were highly promotional, focusing entirely on the positives and putting on the best face possible. (Some respondents even used the term "spin doctors.")

18. The purpose of military is war! This mindset affects the way you view casualties: Send them to the MASH unit for rehabilitation (especially those of higher rank), but move on with those who are still standing. (This doesn't square well with the weak being indispensable; see 1 Corinthians 12:22.)

19. Three foundational articles of our early movement, written by Kip McKean, exemplified the military mold perfectly: "Revolution Through Restoration I, II, III."[1]

God's Cure for Leadership Ills

Family First!

What shall we say to these things, to borrow Paul's terminology in Romans 8:31? Here are some of my observations, about the results that the military style of leadership yielded within our churches; observations about the fallout afterward; and observations about righteous and unrighteous responses we've had to our own past. First, here is a brief section I wrote in *Golden Rule Leadership* to address the military model issue:

> The New Testament has many descriptions and designations for what we commonly call "the church," and each has special meaning. Besides the term church, God's people corporately are called the kingdom, the body of Christ, a temple or building of God, a field, the bride of Christ and the family of God. Interestingly, some have a tendency to view the church in two other ways that the Scripture does not develop: as an army, out to spiritually conquer the world, and as an athletic team. While it is true that metaphors are used in connection with these two concepts, the Bible does not call the church an army or an athletic team. The athletic mindset ministers more to our pride and competition than to the spirit. I think that the military perspective runs deeper than we might think, making a significant impact on our mode of operation in trying to evangelize the world. A country's military branch actually de-emphasizes relationships to insure the completion of the mission, no matter what the personal cost to any individual or family. But the military is not a Spirit-driven organization and does not exist, as does the church, to specifically help the weak, the sick, the helpless and the lost. Fundamentally, every resource of an army is put toward capturing and conquering the enemy. Every resource of the church is designed to heal and to build. We are about building families that build villages that impact nations. We need to be very careful about how we view the church overall. The family analogy is the one most needed in guiding our thinking about golden rule leadership.[2]

Beware Generalizations!

As you read all of this, keep in mind that not all of our leaders followed the military model, and some only followed parts of it. Generalizing about leadership styles can lead to raised blood pressures, mob mentality and unrighteousness—and away from both Scripture and common sense. That was one of the fallacies of the infamous letter of 2003 that I mentioned earlier in this book. It was written in a way that implicated every leader, and I don't want to be guilty of doing the same thing here. Having said that, I do believe that we once had far too much military-style leadership operating in virtually all levels of our leadership. It characterized us in general, although there were many wonderful exceptions. But who among those of us who were leaders during those earlier years can claim that we never practiced some degree of military-style leadership? Much of the kind of authoritarian leadership that I questioned and even came to despise, I have practiced myself in some ways at some times (to my shame).

Motivations—How Could This Have Happened?

There are reasons that we acquiesced to this model. When I look back, I remember how the results were unlike anything I had ever seen: thousands of people baptized; scores of churches planted around the world; countless Christians inspiring us all by rising to the call to "go anywhere, do anything, give up everything" for the sake of the gospel. All of us wanted to make a difference in time and eternity, and the results we saw caused many of us to look past too much of the methodology. I don't think I did it with bad motives as a whole, and most other leaders could say the same thing. We didn't sit up late at night trying to invent ways of hurting people, but we did hurt many. And we also did many things to help people (which should never be forgotten or go unappreciated).

Another reason I didn't question more things earlier was my conviction that the best leadership is authoritative without being authoritarian. Studies in parenting effectiveness have demonstrated this point. An authoritative parent is definitely in charge, but they employ good communication and relationship skills with their children. However, an authoritarian parent is a "my way or the highway" type who practices only one-way communication and places no real emphasis on relational issues. The problem is that the two styles are similar in some ways, but totally dissimilar in the results they produce. Sometimes it's tough to tell the difference right away. And so, when it came to our churches' leadership, I was not discerning enough fast enough to raise the red flag soon enough! That observation is not meant as an excuse, but only an explanation. Hindsight is always twenty-twenty.

Hurt Goes Both Ways

Keep in mind that we leaders also experienced things that hurt us, from those who led us and from those whom we led. When the firestorm hit in 2003, I thought a lot more about how I had hurt others than about how I had been hurt. Unfortunately, many of my fellow leaders focused on how they themselves had been hurt, and it severely damaged or destroyed them spiritually. I cannot blame anyone for what I did wrong as a leader. I did it—period! I accepted the responsibility for what I did, repeatedly repented of my sins (both privately and publicly), learned my lessons as best I could, and moved on to better things. Is that not the biblical path? Where is the justification for continuing to point fingers (as leaders *or* followers) and continuing to develop bitter roots that kill our own soul and the souls of others? Maybe you can get justification for that from Satan, but you will never get it from God. Following Jesus simply doesn't allow it. Read 1 Peter 2:13–3:12 and see what you come up with.

Bitterness Destroys; Grace Heals and Strengthens

No matter what you've been through, maintaining a victim mentality will indeed destroy your righteousness. The first Bible Talk I ever attended (as an observer) was on a university campus, led by a single college student whose spirituality was most impressive to me as an older minister. He had a sincere, gentle spirit about him, but courageously laid out the biblical message in an admirable way. Experiences like that one drew me like a magnet into the discipling movement (as I called it then), although it took me a few years. After his graduation, he married a wonderful young disciple, whose spirit was just as refreshing as his. They had what seemed to be the ideal marriage. On a recent trip to their home state, I was told that they are now divorced. Hearing that news shocked and depressed me. We had started a friendship back in that campus Bible Talk that meant something special to me. His influence on me was profound, even though our times together were few and far between over the years. What happened? I don't really know, but what I do know is that he was a frequent contributor to a certain website where bitterness was fertilized incessantly by former church members who refused to handle hard times and hurts God's way. Bottom line, bitterness may enter our hearts through different avenues, but once inside, it is only a matter of time before it destroys our own hearts. I have watched this process over and over in the past few years. Satan must be rejoicing.

You might be thinking, "Wait just a minute, Ferguson! You don't understand my situation. I've been hurt, and hurt badly!" I am moved quickly to respond to statements like that by saying, "I'm truly sorry, I really am." But I am also moved to follow that statement up by saying, "Join the club—the human club, and then the Jesus club." The human club is a large one indeed, because we have all experienced hurts at the hands of others, but the Jesus club is a very small club, comprised only of people who have chosen to respond as Jesus did (and *does*, by the way). Am I critical of the military model of leadership described in this chapter? Yes. But do I also understand the environment that produced it and the good that occurred all over the world in spite of many types of sins by the leadership? Yes. If I could redo those years, would I do things a lot differently? Yes. If I could just remove those years from my life, would I do that? Absolutely *not*! God has always worked his will through sinners. He has no other choice.

What does he expect of us sinners? That we do the best we know and keep striving to learn and become better in every way; in other words, to be disciples of Jesus: followers and learners. Will we make mistakes and hurt people? Let's get real here. The person I have hurt most in this life is the one I love most: my wife. But she will tell you that I came from a very dysfunctional home and did the best I knew in our earlier days of marriage, and that over the years I have also kept striving to learn and become better in every way. And by her grace and God's grace in my life, I have come a long, long way. Yes, I still have a long way to go, but I've come a long way. As the old saying puts it: "I'm not what I ought to be, but thank the Lord I'm not what I used to be."

Some years ago, I was walking around my basement praying. The week before had been a bad one for me (for reasons I no longer remember). As I prayed, I confessed that I had been a mess the week before, and I promised to work really hard in the new week and make up for the bad week. I remember exactly where I was in the room when I said that, because I stopped in my tracks and said aloud, "That's really bad theology, Ferguson." No one can *make up* for anything in the past. Even if that new week I was entering went really well, it still would have contained quite enough of its own sin. That's the "reality show" that we all live in every day, every week, every month, every year, for our whole life.

What shall we do with our bad days, weeks or months? I discovered an approach to prayer that day in my basement that I think is not only practical, but also biblical. I started most of my prayer times long after that day with this approach: "Lord, here is what happened yesterday—the good and the bad. For the good, I thank you so much. For the bad, all I know to do is confess and repent and then learn from it. So, my plan for today is to learn from both the good and the bad of yesterday, shut the door on yesterday and set out on my journey with you today determined to make this the best day I can, by your grace." If you are unable to process your past like that, you are in a heap of trouble.

Is not Paul saying basically the same thing in Philippians 3:15–16 that I said in my prayer? After describing some lofty goals in his own life, he then gets practical with these words: "All of us who are mature should take such a view of things. And if on some point you think differently, that too God will make clear to you. Only let us live up to what we have already attained." I'm not as good a leader today as I will be next year, but it's not next year yet. What I am today, I am, and I have to be content with living up to what I have attained at this point. And guess what? The people under my leadership are going to have to be content with that as well—it's the best I have to offer. Can you follow that principle for your leaders' sake? Can you follow that same principle, for your own sake? Can you give others grace and can you give yourself grace? If not, you are *cooked*—no way out. If you cannot accept mercy and if you cannot give mercy, I pity you. We are all a bunch of sinners trying to get to heaven and help each other get to heaven, and that's going to require enormous amounts of grace from God and from one another.

Nineteen Reasons—Stumbling Blocks or Stepping Stones?

In this chapter, I listed nineteen evidences of our military model of leadership in the past. For you and for me, that list contains either nineteen reasons to be bitter or nineteen reasons to learn and grow spiritually and not make those same mistakes in the future. It is not what happens to us that ultimately matters; it is how we *process* what happens to us that matters. We need to learn from our mistakes, but what then? We will make some new ones! We are sinful human beings. This life is not heaven, nor will it ever be. The challenges of life, including all sins you commit and that others commit against you, will either be stumbling blocks or stepping stones. The old bumper sticker said, "Life is tough—and then you die." That's true, isn't it? The real issue is how you handle life *when* it's tough. Will it be Satan's way or God's way? Those are the only two choices we have, and we have to make that choice on a daily basis, usually many times a day. Jesus said that there are two paths: The narrow path is difficult in the short run, but is the only choice in the long run; the wide one seems deceptively easy in the short run, but is deadly in the long run. If we hang in with God, no matter what happens to us in this life, the long run will be unimaginably wonderful and wonderfully long.

The evolution I wrote about in the introduction has occurred once again, hasn't it? In talking about a bad style of leadership, we have ended up at the cross once again. It's interesting how that will keep happening over and over, if we allow it to happen. The Latin word for cross is crux. The crux of the matter is not man's leadership style, although I deem it important enough to write a chapter with the title. The real crux of the matter is the cross—God's leadership style. That is the style I want to *employ* in my own leadership and to *experience* as I follow others, but no matter what people may do, God is still my leader, and yours. Whatever he causes or allows in my life, he already has my permission. Otherwise, life will make me bitter. But if God really is the architect of my life, I can handle whatever design he develops in my life. You can too—but the question is: Will we?

End Notes:

1. These three articles, detailing the history of our movement from 1979 to 2003 as perceived by McKean, were written in 1992, 2001 and 2003, respectively. (The word "revolution" in each of the titles, combined with the writing approach and content, all show clearly the military emphasis of which we speak.)

2. Gordon Ferguson, *Golden Rule Leadership*, pp. 18–19, reprinted with permission of Discipleship Publications International.

Chapter Five

All Leaders Are Builders for God

Building by Preparing Others

> It was he who gave some to be apostles, some to be prophets, some to be evangelists, and some to be pastors and teachers, to prepare God's people for works of service, so that the body of Christ may be built up until we all reach unity in the faith and in the knowledge of the Son of God and become mature, attaining to the whole measure of the fullness of Christ. Then we will no longer be infants, tossed back and forth by the waves, and blown here and there by every wind of teaching and by the cunning and craftiness of men in their deceitful scheming. Instead, speaking the truth in love, we will in all things grow up into him who is the Head, that is, Christ. From him the whole body, joined and held together by every supporting ligament, grows and builds itself up in love, as each part does its work (Ephesians 4:11–16).

The large majority of congregations in our movement of churches have united in what is officially called the "Plan for United Cooperation." The purpose of this plan is to provide a structure for regional and international cooperation among our family of churches around the world. We are coordinated by delegates who are commended by the brothers in their regions of the world to help address the most relevant issues and provide recommendations and direction. To further assist in meeting these needs, nine service groups have been selected by the delegates to offer recommendations to the delegates in their particular areas of responsibility. Three of these—the Evangelist Team, the Elder Team and the Teacher Team—are viewed as a type of overall leadership group to help provide direction in a number of areas. The evangelist group was originally called the "Church Builders," but the designation was later changed—to my delight. If evangelists are the only leadership group focused on building the church, we are in a very dangerous and unbiblical place. The purpose of all leadership roles is to help implement the Great Commission (which we will address more specifically later in this chapter).

To be church builders, we have to carefully follow God's principles of building. Church-building principles are simply the biblical principles that make a healthy spiritual body, because just as a healthy physical body reproduces, so a healthy spiritual body (the body of Christ, God's family) will also reproduce. One of the most fundamental building principles is found in the passage at the beginning of this chapter. Leadership in the church is God's plan and his gift to the church. In Ephesians 4:11–16, we find what God's purposes of leadership are. As we study this passage in detail, we quickly notice that several types of leaders are mentioned here, and additional types are mentioned in other passages. This means that no one type of leader is sufficient to accomplish what God wants accomplished through his leaders. This point has already been discussed in chapter 2 in some detail as we studied spiritual gifts. Not only are there many types of gifts, there are many roles under the "leadership gift" category. The overall purpose of leadership is to mature the body of Christ, and the maturation process is described in clear terms.

Paul begins in verse 12 by saying that leadership is to prepare God's people for works of service (translated "works of ministry" in some versions). This means that leaders are to train others to serve rather than simply serving them. How simple, and yet how profound! The large majority of people who consider themselves Christians view the work of leaders as meeting their needs, and that concept is not absent in our fellowship of churches. Leaders are servants, but their service has as a major focus the equipping of others to serve. Is that not precisely what Jesus did with the Twelve? And he did it so effectively that they spread the gospel around the world in spite of the huge challenges involved in accomplishing it. Even if we had ten times the number of leaders we now have, the plan of God would not be altered in the least. No disciple of Jesus could ever be described as mature without being a servant of others. This principle is foundational, and is stated in the last part of this verse as the body of Christ being built up.

Verse 13 informs us that building up the church has maturity as its goal, measured by unity in the faith and in our knowledge of the Son of God—to the point that it may be said that we have attained to the whole measure of the fullness of Christ. Wow! God has some amazingly high standards for his family, and therefore for the leaders in his family. It would be very tempting to take the course taken by most religious people and just say that such biblical statements are ideals and not actual standards. But we are going to have to take a deep breath and fall to our knees in prayer and beg for help. No wonder so few find the narrow path of which Jesus spoke!

What does the New Testament have to teach us about unity in the faith?

First, Jesus prayed that we would have *complete* unity in the faith: "May they be brought to complete unity to let the world know that you sent me and have loved them even as you have loved me" (John 17:23). Next, Romans 15:5 speaks of having a "spirit of unity among yourselves as you follow Christ Jesus." That suggests likemindedness, a desire to be unified. That's the starting place for sure—a serious intent to be pursued, by whatever means it takes to get there. Paul elaborates further on this concept in 1 Corinthians 1:10 in these words: "I appeal to you, brothers, in the name of our Lord Jesus Christ, that all of you agree with one another so that there may be no divisions among you and that you may be perfectly united in mind and thought." Not surprisingly, Paul's final comment on the subject (as the NT books are arranged chronologically) is in Colossians 3:14, about having love as the final touch in reaching the complete unity for which Jesus prayed: "And over all these virtues put on love, which binds them all together in perfect unity." With that, the cycle of the pursuit of unity is completed.

How do we arrive at the knowledge of God's Son that Ephesians 4:13 mentions? Knowledge is a bit more difficult to understand than the term "unity." 1 Corinthians 8 mentions knowledge in a negative sense several times, which means that knowledge alone is not the knowledge of Ephesians 4. No wonder Paul also mentioned several times that he prayed for the disciples to have knowledge and to continue growing in it. One such passage, Colossians 1:9, helps us understand the path to the right kind of knowledge: "For this reason, since the day we heard about you, we have not stopped praying for you and asking God to fill you with the knowledge of his will through all spiritual wisdom and understanding." Understanding means that we grasp Christ, not just facts about him. Wisdom means that we grasp what being his disciple means—to follow him and imitate him, always asking in all seriousness, "What would Jesus do?" One of my favorite passages (for several reasons) is Romans 15:14: "I myself am convinced, my brothers, that you yourselves are full of goodness, complete in knowledge and competent to instruct one another." Genuine knowledge of God's Son changes us, filling us with goodness and making us others-focused—like Jesus.

Being like Jesus leads naturally to the next phrase in Ephesians 4:13: "attaining to the whole measure of the fullness of Christ." Within this phrase is one of the most staggering concepts in the New Testament, the fullness of Christ. Colossians 2:9 informs us that the fullness of God dwelt in Jesus, meaning that the complete picture of God could be seen in him. Without that flesh and blood demonstration, I don't think men could see the bigger picture of who God is. Remarkably, the church is described as the fullness of Christ three times in Ephesians (1:23; 3:19 and 4:13), the natural implication being that men cannot get the complete picture of Christ without seeing him dwell in flesh and blood in every generation within his people. So this is a major role of the church, and an almost shocking role at that!

To make the point perfectly clear, the Israelites in the Old Testament could not gain a complete understanding of God simply from reading the Law—they needed to see a flesh and blood God (in the form of Jesus). People today cannot gain a complete understanding of Christ simply from reading the New Testament; they need also to see a flesh and blood Jesus in the form of his body, the church of his disciples. No wonder Paul said he was in birth pangs until Christ was formed in the Galatian Christians (Galatians 4:19)! Unless we are that demonstration, the world will never really see Jesus. *Amazing!* Just stop and think about how God chose to communicate the gospel to man. He didn't choose to drop leather-bound, gold-edged Bibles from heaven. He knew that the gospel had to be communicated by humans, because those receiving the message had to see it in writing *and* in lives. Although the Bible alone is sufficient to reveal the content of the truth to man, in order to grasp its power we must read it both in black and white (pages) *and* in black, white, red and yellow (people). Leaders, are we grasping this point? Our jobs are more challenging than we might have imagined!

Once we reach this level of maturity, wonderful results follow, as described in Ephesians 4:14–16. One, false teachers and false teaching will not affect us—we will know what we believe and why we believe it. Two, we will speak the truth to one another and to the lost, but we will do it in a loving manner that opens hearts instead of closing them. Three, we will grow up spiritually in all areas, meaning that our weaknesses will no longer make us lopsided disciples. Four, mature disciples will be committed to being ligaments to keep the body of Christ united. We must have ligaments at every possible level: small groups, churches, regions in larger churches, leadership (on staff and volunteer; and leadership must be connected both with other leaders and with the people they lead), and finally, we need ligaments between congregations. When we think of congregational ties, we normally think of the leaders being connected (and we should), but our members are more connected intracongregationally than we are sometimes aware, and that's good—it's all good, yea essential, for developing and maintaining a unified and mature body.

Five, the church will grow both spiritually and numerically as each member is meaningfully involved in the works of ministry—using their gifts for one another's good and for God's glory. I spent many years as a minister in churches that were characterized by having a minority do a majority of the work and give a majority of the money. When I first became a part of a discipling church, it seemed to me that virtually every member was as involved and committed as any other (just as Paul said that it should be). In more recent years, I would say that we still have a majority meaningfully involved in the work of the ministry, but it's a smaller majority. That must change, because lukewarmness is both deadly and contagious. Ephesians 4 makes it abundantly clear what our goals as leaders are for the church, and we must begin with preparing God's children to do what they were designed to do.

Building Carefully

What, after all, is Apollos? And what is Paul? Only servants, through whom you came to believe—as the Lord has assigned to each his task. I planted the seed, Apollos watered it, but God made it grow. So neither he who plants nor he who waters is anything, but only God, who makes things grow. The man who plants and the man who waters have one purpose, and each will be rewarded according to his own labor. For we are God's fellow workers; you are God's field, God's building.

By the grace God has given me, I laid a foundation as an expert builder, and someone else is building on it. But each one should be careful how he builds. For no one can lay any foundation other than the one already laid, which is Jesus Christ. If any man builds on this foundation using gold, silver, costly stones, wood, hay or straw, his work will be shown for what it is, because the Day will bring it to light. It will be revealed with fire, and the fire will test the quality of each man's work. If what he has built survives, he will receive his reward. If it is burned up, he will suffer loss; he himself will be saved, but only as one escaping through the flames.

Don't you know that you yourselves are God's temple and that God's Spirit lives in you? If anyone destroys God's temple, God will destroy him; for God's temple is sacred, and you are that temple (1 Corinthians 3:5–17).

When churches or movements of churches go through a firestorm, you can be sure of one thing: Something has been amiss in the building process. The fires of testing leave no doubt about the quality of our work. In the past, whenever I moved from one church I had been leading to another one, or from one ministry group to another in the same congregation, I always gave a certain parting admonition. I shared with the group that my work among them was about to be tested and shown for what it was, and I closed my lesson with this statement: "Therefore, don't mess up!" I have seen some leaders who appeared to be a little hurt if the ministry they left flourished after their departure. Not me. I rejoiced, because it proved the quality of my work. I was only hurt if it didn't go well after I left, because that also reflected upon my leadership, just not in a good way.

As leaders, we either point people to ourselves or to Jesus. That is an undisputable truth. In reading what Paul said in 1 Corinthians 3, to whom did he point people? Clearly, he gave God all the glory and took none for himself. O God, multiply this kind of leader, and multiply it exponentially! Mold us all into that type of leader, no matter what crucible we each must go through, and please do it as soon as possible! My mind is racing in two directions right now, thinking of leaders (mostly past leaders) so full of themselves that they sicken(ed) me (and surely God), and also thinking of leaders whose example humbles me just by picturing their hearts, their demeanor, their imitation of Christ. The bad part is that I have been both types, and to some extent, I am still capable of being both. That is an embarrassing admission, but it's true. As I often say in preaching about Romans 1–3 and the universality of sin, the best of us is a mess. Pride is the only disease that makes everyone sick except the person who has it!

Leaders are both praised and criticized. We should be at least somewhat grateful for the criticism, because it keeps the praise from inflating our pride too much. Being self-aware and in touch with our own heart is not easily achieved, according to Jeremiah 17:9: "The heart is deceitful above all things and beyond cure. Who can understand it?"

I heard about one preacher, an older man, who was more in touch with himself than most. After preaching what must have been a great lesson, a woman approached him after he came down from the podium and said breathlessly, "That was the greatest sermon I have ever heard you preach!" He replied simply, "Yes, Dear, Satan has already told me the same thing."

What's my point here, and why am I pursuing the pride issue? Read that 1 Corinthians 3 passage again. How many leaders have you heard say the kinds of things Paul said about himself—and really mean it at the deepest level? How often do you say those things about yourself and really mean it? Leaders have a great responsibility in how we build, and the only real clue Paul gives us in this passage is that we must genuinely rely on God and not ourselves—by pointing our people to Jesus and not to ourselves. What else do you see in the passage about how to build carefully? I can't find any list of ministry-building principles and procedures, or anything remotely akin to those things. All I can see is that if we are really relying on God and not on ourselves and the wisdom of men, God will bless what we build. That leaves us with a seemingly simplistic antidote for avoiding firestorms, and the solution for seeing God's family grow and prosper. In a word, it's *humility*.

> All of you, clothe yourselves with humility toward one another, because, "God opposes the proud but gives grace to the humble." Humble yourselves, therefore, under God's mighty hand, that he may lift you up in due time. Cast all your anxiety on him because he cares for you (I Peter 5:5–7).

Do you really believe what Peter said there? We have all seen prideful leaders have some amazing results, have we not? What kind of results were they—short-term or long-term? The question is best answered in asking how the people under their leadership fared when the firestorms burst into flame. Some exceptions can always be found, when poor leaders convert some people who make it long-term, but in that case, people make it in spite of their leader, not because of them. Our upheaval of 2003, and other, smaller-scale crises since then, have seriously thinned the ranks overseen by people who led in worldly ways. Most of our leaders who have survived to the present were either already humble leaders, or they were refined in good ways by the fires.

Two final thoughts regarding this passage we have been examining: One, I am not decrying ministry-building principles and procedures. I am a pragmatist who likes structure, expectations and systematic ways of doing things. But I refuse to miss the implications both of what Paul wrote—and what he *didn't* write. You can have all the ministry-building techniques you want, but if you don't have the genuine humility in church-building described in 1 Corinthians 3, you will be limited in what God is able to accomplish through you as a leader (perhaps severely limited in the long term). Two, I included 1 Corinthians 3:16–17 in this chapter for a reason, although you might have expected me to end with verse 15. Verses 16–17 speak of destroying the church ("God's temple" in this analogy). In context, he is actually talking about the negative impact of continuing to have worldly views of leaders and leadership. That fact alone is more than a little sobering. A related thought from the Old Testament is just as sobering: "One who is slack in his work is brother to one who destroys" (Proverbs 18:9). Paul is sounding a strong alarm about worldly leadership, and the Proverb writer is sounding a strong warning about not taking the need to build for God seriously. Leaders cannot be blessed by God if they have worldly mindsets and are following worldly building principles. But mark it down: Neither can leaders be blessed by him if they are not really dedicated to building the church, spiritually and numerically. Neither building carefully nor building in the name of Christ is optional. God help us to build carefully, but may he also help us to take intense personal responsibility for the *need to build*.

The Building Blueprint

Then Jesus came to them and said, "All authority in heaven and on earth has been given to me. Therefore go and make disciples of all nations, baptizing them in the name of the Father and of the Son and of the Holy Spirit, and teaching them to obey everything I have commanded you. And surely I am with you always, to the very end of the age" (Matthew 28:18–20).

I have no idea how many sermons I have preached from this text containing what we call the Great Commission. If this subject was the last thing on Jesus' mind before he ascended to heaven, I'm all ears. I keep finding more and more lessons in these words. Calling the Great Commission a blueprint is not just utilizing a catchy word. I think it grasps exactly what Jesus' words directly say and indirectly imply. Like most of the Master's teachings, it is fairly simple to understand, although greatly challenging to consistently put into practice. Let's examine at least the primary contents of this amazing blueprint for world evangelism.

It begins with fully trusting, following and imitating him to whom all authority in the universe has been given. We have already elaborated on this concept enough for our present purposes. Next, the blueprint continues with helping spiritual babies to be born—in all nations. By God's grace, our family of churches has started churches in many nations, but we have far to go in reaching the majority of people in those nations. Huge amounts of money and manpower will have to be dedicated to this task, in ever-increasing measure. I'm grateful for all that has been done, but we have to keep our focus on reaching more and more people in more and more cities.

Jesus says that we are to make disciples, not just church members. When Paul planted the church in Thessalonica, he practiced this principle well, stating that "our gospel came to you not simply with words, but also with power, with the Holy Spirit and with deep conviction" (1 Thessalonians 1:5). I can remember a time when finishing a study series with a non-Christian by "counting the cost" provided them with a serious cost to count. We often explained to the person that we were going to play the devil's advocate and try to talk them out of being baptized, which meant that they would have to have enough conviction and urgency to convince us to baptize them. We were fully engaged in purposefully making disciples, not "getting baptisms." However, in time, an ungodly focus on numbers led some of us in the opposite direction—we began trying to talk people into being baptized, and we often succeeded, but too many times their response was based on our urgency and not theirs. Increasing fallaway rates were definitely connected to that change in our cost-counting approach and the mindset behind it.

In the second edition of *Prepared to Answer*, I elaborated on my concerns about churches who teach an incomplete repentance. Repentance is often taught as a turning away from doing wrong things, without the aim of turning to do right things—notably in becoming representatives of Christ and doing his bidding on planet earth. Since teaching is how we bring people to Christ, it must be noted that we cannot teach what we do not know. Hence, the need to really study and learn ourselves remains a task of paramount importance. Paul is my greatest biblical hero, next to Christ, for a whole host of reasons. One reason was his amazing example of wanting to keep studying and learning all of his life—even as he awaited execution while in a Roman prison. He asked Timothy for two things to comfort him when in this situation: a cloak to keep him warm and his parchments to keep him growing (2 Timothy 4:13)! I am trying hard to imitate his example through having a heart to keep learning. If nothing else, it keeps the brain from getting old before it should!

Finally, in making spiritual babies for God, baptism is obviously a part of the plan. I filled many pages in *Prepared to Answer* with details about all aspects of this subject, so I will limit what I write here. Suffice it to say that baptism is a part of the broader subject of discipleship. Since a disciple is a learner and a follower of Christ, baptism must be experienced by someone who has learned what the Bible has to say about the subject and is willing to accept it. Further, he must make a decision to be a true disciple, not just seek to have sins forgiven. In being baptized into Christ, a person is signing on to be a disciple, to make Jesus the Lord of his life all of his life. Baptism is not an end within itself, but the means to an end. It is an act based on a decision to repent by stopping the wrong practices in one's life and replacing them with biblical practices. What are those biblical practices? That question leads naturally to the next major part of our blueprint.

The newly baptized disciple has a life goal clearly defined by Jesus in Matthew 28:20, being taught to obey everything Christ commanded. As we make disciples, we have the huge task of helping these new disciples to continue growing for a lifetime as they live Jesus lives. The text doesn't say simply to teach them all that Christ commanded; it says teach them to obey it. All parents know the vast difference between simply teaching something to their children and teaching them to obey what has been taught. This part of the Great Commission is clearly the most challenging part of the blueprint—by far! Teach to *obey* and teach to *obey everything* commanded by Christ.

Whew—that's a lifetime endeavor for disciple and disciple trainer!

An intriguing question is in order. In teaching a prospective disciple up to the point of conversion, how is this best done—in a group setting or in a private setting? The answer to that one is pretty much a "no-brainer," isn't it? In a private setting, we can personalize the study and really get into a person's heart and life with the Scriptures. Given that this personalized approach works best in the easier part of the disciple-making process (conversion), wouldn't it be logical to assume that this approach is also the best way to carry out the harder part, the disciple-maturing process? The term "discipling" is the ideal term to describe this process, as we put "one another" Christianity into practice. The full title of my longer book (now out of print) on this subject is *Discipling: God's Plan to Train and Transform His People*. That title encapsulates what Jesus calls for as we make and mature disciples.

One essential part of teaching obedience to "everything" Jesus commanded is to avoid assumptions. We cannot assume that we or anyone else is without blind spots. It is far too easy to become selective in our own lives, emphasizing some things as important and other things as simply optional. Additionally, we can get comfortable with some sins in our lives and in the lives of others. While we cannot afford to become legalistic nitpickers, we cannot afford to become complacent with attitudes and actions that belong in the devil's realm. Sentimentality may be commonplace, but it is misplaced when found in the kingdom of God. How about you? What is your biggest challenge right now in obeying all things Jesus commanded? Will you go after changing it? Will you also go after helping others face their challenges and overcome them?

There is much in the Great Commission that we need to see, understand and live out. It begins with a huge amount of trust in Jesus. Next, it takes a determination to be our best for God if we intend to help others know him. Finally, it takes quite a sacrifice of our time, our prayers and our tears. How much do we love God, and how much do we love our neighbors? Let's give him and them all we have, with the special help of Jesus, and both our world and God's world will be changed for eternity! Praise Jesus that he ended the description of our joint mission with this precious promise: "And surely I am with you always, to the very end of the age."

Part Two
Leadership Roles

Chapter Six

The Role and Function of Elders

Elders: Why Do We Need Them?

In the normal life of any mature church, the training, selection and appointment of elders is expected. For many years, our movement could have been described as a "youth movement." Today, as our churches (and leaders!) have matured, we are more interested in this process than ever before. We see our need for elders as a vital part of church leadership, and in a real sense, we are "playing catch-up." Incidentally, starting out as a youth movement is not a negative thing, or even surprising, since the young (and young at heart) are often more open to considering new concepts. Most movements of almost any type begin with the youth.

I believe that the early church also started as a youth movement (especially with young apostles), but unlike us, they converted former synagogue leaders who could be appointed as elders rather quickly. That phenomenon most likely explains how Paul and Barnabas could plant churches on their first missionary journey, and in revisiting the same churches on the same journey, appoint elders in each church. We read about this relatively short process in Acts 14:21–23:

> Then they returned to Lystra, Iconium and Antioch, strengthening the disciples and encouraging them to remain true to the faith.... Paul and Barnabas appointed elders for them in each church and, with prayer and fasting, committed them to the Lord, in whom they had put their trust.

The Bible has more to say about the roles of elder and evangelist than any other leadership role. Because the role of elder is such a vital one to the health of the church, and because there is much to study, I am devoting two chapters to the topic. In this chapter we'll focus on the role and function of elders; in the next chapter, we'll delve into qualifications, selection and appointment. My purpose in writing in such detail is to provide reference material that leaders can return to time and again as they train, select and appoint elders in their churches.

Most of what the Bible has to say about eldership is straightforward and easily explained. However, some of it is not as easy to deal with and has become somewhat controversial among Bible students. Some of the controversial aspects are long-standing, due either to the possible ambiguity of some biblical wording, or to insufficient biblical information available that would enable us to reach definite conclusions. Certain of these controversial aspects have received much more recent attention within our movement. This fact has been borne of our desire to appoint more elders while facing the challenge of biblical qualifications that appear to be stringent enough to rule out many mature leaders who might otherwise be candidates.

Many of these disputable areas were commonly discussed in the churches I grew up in—churches that usually had appointed elders. Therefore, my perspectives on the subject have been developed in more than one religious setting, over a period of at least four decades. In the end, I can only offer my best judgment in these more disputable areas, and you will have to study what I say in addition to studying what others have taught—all done with an open Bible in hand, for it alone is the ultimate authority.

Elders: Who Are They?

The Bible calls for elders to "direct the affairs of the church," according to 1 Timothy 5:17. However, the precise meaning of that passage must be given more attention, and we will return to it later in the chapter. All leadership in the church must function in harmonious teamwork, including the ministry staff, the eldership, leadership groups, the Board of Directors and all other designated leadership roles. The purpose of our study is not only to instruct and inform—it is to inspire. 1 Timothy 3:1 says: "Here is a trustworthy saying: If anyone sets his heart on being an overseer, he desires a noble task." Although being an elder is often a demanding task, it is a noble task in the sight of God and the church. May God inspire our brothers to aspire to such a shepherding role! We need to develop a biblical understanding of this noble task by looking at what the New Testament says about the elder's function, from several perspectives.

Definitions

First, note the specific terms used to describe elders. The term "elder," from the Greek *presbuteros*, denotes an older person. It is used in passages like 1 Timothy 5:1 and 1 Peter 5:5 simply to describe a person of older age. Of course, that ushers in the question of who is *older*. While the answer would be somewhat relative based on life expectancy in a given culture and based on the demographics of the group in question, it is interesting to note that Timothy was considered youthful by Paul (1 Timothy 4:12). Assuming that Timothy was at least twenty when Paul first met him (Acts 16:1ff), he would likely have been in his mid-thirties when Paul wrote 1 Timothy. The majority of elders I have seen appointed have been at least forty, but I have seen a few appointed in their thirties. Overall, the Bible shows that the elder role was to be filled by an older person who could use his wisdom gained by experience to provide security and direction for the flock of God.

Then we have the designation for this role indicated by the Greek word *poimen*, ordinarily translated "shepherd" in the newer versions. Inexplicably, in Ephesians 4:11, the NIV translates this word using the older English term "pastor." Not only is the translation inconsistent within the NIV, it is misleading. Most denominational churches speak of their minister or preacher as being their pastor, although biblically, the term *pastor* describes an elder. The shepherd had two primary functions: to lead the flock in the way it should go; and to watch over the flock to keep any from straying, getting lost or being attacked.

A third term used to indicate an elder is "overseer" (from the Greek *episcopos*). This word was translated "bishop" in the older versions, and because this word conveyed the idea of a hierarchal leader in many churches when these versions were translated, it too is very misleading. The verb form of the Greek word is translated to mean looking after someone and taking care of their needs. For example, in Matthew 25:36 we read, "I was sick and you looked after me," and in James 1:27, "look after orphans and widows in their distress." To be an "overseer" involves an examination of, and a provision for, the needs of the church.

Biblical Mentions of Elders

As we examine the biblical function of elders, let's look at the New Testament passages that simply mention the elders, without elaborating further about their role.

> The disciples, each according to his ability, decided to provide help for the brothers living in Judea. This they did, sending their gift to the elders by Barnabas and Saul (Acts 11:29–30).
>
> Paul and Barnabas appointed elders for them in each church and, with prayer and fasting, committed them to the Lord, in whom they had put their trust (Acts 14:23).
>
> Some men came down from Judea to Antioch and were teaching the brothers: "Unless you are circumcised, according to the custom taught by Moses, you cannot be saved." This brought Paul and Barnabas into sharp dispute and debate with them. So Paul and Barnabas were appointed, along with some other believers, to go up to Jerusalem to see the apostles and elders about this question (Acts 15:1–2).
>
> When they came to Jerusalem, they were welcomed by the church and the apostles and elders, to whom they reported everything God had done through them. Then some of the believers who belonged to the party of the Pharisees stood up and said, "The Gentiles must be circumcised and required to obey the law of Moses." The apostles and elders met to consider this question (Acts 15:4–6).
>
> Then the apostles and elders, with the whole church, decided to choose some of their own men and send them to Antioch with Paul and Barnabas. They chose Judas (called Barsabbas) and Silas, two men who were leaders among the brothers. With them they sent the following letter: "The apostles and elders, your brothers, To the Gentile believers in Antioch, Syria and Cilicia: Greetings" (Acts 15:22–23).
>
> As they traveled from town to town, they delivered the decisions reached by the apostles and elders in Jerusalem for the people to obey (Acts 16:4).

> From Miletus, Paul sent to Ephesus for the elders of the church (Acts 20:17).
>
> The next day Paul and the rest of us went to see James, and all the elders were present (Acts 21:18).
>
> Paul and Timothy, servants of Christ Jesus, To all the saints in Christ Jesus at Philippi, together with the overseers and deacons (Philippians 1:1).
>
> Do not neglect your gift, which was given you through a prophetic message when the body of elders laid their hands on you (1 Timothy 4:14).

Elders: What Do They Do?

The series of passages examined next contain the specific biblical directives to and about elders, and reveal much about their role and function.

Acts 20:28

> "Keep watch over yourselves and all the flock of which the Holy Spirit has made you overseers. Be shepherds of the church of God, which he bought with his own blood."

In this passage, Paul is giving direction to the elders in Ephesus. In Acts 20:17, we are told that Paul called for the Ephesian elders to meet him in Miletus. In these two verses, we find all three terms used in reference to the same role (which we usually just call "elder"): elder, overseer, and shepherd. The importance of the elder role is seen in several ways: the description of Paul's personal relationship with them; the description of their responsibilities in the church; and in the fact that the elders were the only type of church leaders Paul called to meet him (and surely a church like Ephesus had many leaders and types of leaders). They apparently were expected to be the primary protectors of the flock, based on what Paul said in the verses that followed:

> "I know that after I leave, savage wolves will come in among you and will not spare the flock. Even from your own number men will arise and distort the truth in order to draw away disciples after them. So be on your guard! Remember that for three years I never stopped warning each of you night and day with tears" (vv. 29–31).

Ephesians 4:11–12

> It was he who gave some to be apostles, some to be prophets, some to be evangelists, and some to be pastors and teachers, to prepare God's people for works of service, so that the body of Christ may be built up."

Here Paul mentions elders as shepherds (translated "pastors" in the NIV). This mention ushers in an interesting and important consideration of another role, that of *teacher*. Here in Ephesians 4:11, the terms "pastors" and "teachers" are closely connected, and may refer to dual aspects of the same shepherding role. A single definite article in Greek links the two terms, and thus the phrase may be describing a single category of leader—a pastor/teacher—although this is not agreed upon universally by Bible scholars. No doubt there were (and are) elders who were gifted as teachers, just as there were evidently elder/evangelists as well. 1 Timothy 5:17 mentions elders who also taught and preached—hence, perhaps an elder/teacher/evangelist. I have served in all three roles, sometimes one at a time, sometimes two at once, and sometimes all three at the same time. At this stage of my life, I am serving only in the teacher role officially, although I still do many things that could fall into the other categories of elder and evangelist. I will say more about what it means to be serving in an *appointed* role later, a topic of importance. Suffice it to say that in Ephesians 4, along with the other offices mentioned, the pastor/teacher (or elder/teacher) is to serve in a training and equipping role for the church.

1 Timothy 5:17–22

1 Timothy 5:17–22 is perhaps the most significant passage in the New Testament describing the role and function of elders. It is pregnant with meanings, applications, and statements that raise questions.

> The elders who direct the affairs of the church well are worthy of double honor, especially those whose work is preaching and teaching. For the Scripture says, "Do not muzzle the ox while it is treading out the grain," and "The worker deserves his wages." Do not entertain an accusation against an elder unless it is brought by two or three witnesses. Those who sin are to be rebuked publicly, so that the others may

take warning. I charge you, in the sight of God and Christ Jesus and the elect angels, to keep these instructions without partiality, and to do nothing out of favoritism. Do not be hasty in the laying on of hands, and do not share in the sins of others. Keep yourself pure.

Let's break this passage down into a few key sections:

"The elders who direct the affairs of the church"

First, we have the statement that the elders direct the affairs of the church. What does that mean? The basic meaning of the Greek term *proistemi* is simply to lead or manage, and most other versions translate it thusly. Here, the NIV has an unusual translation of the term, once again showing the translators' approach to be often interpretative instead of more literal. This Greek term is used eight times in the New Testament, translated by the NIV in Romans 12:8 as "leadership;" in 1 Thessalonians 5:12 as "over you;" and in 1 Timothy 3:4, 5, and 12 as "manage" (applied to both elders and deacons managing their families well). Older versions such as the King James Version and the American Standard translate the term in 1 Timothy 5:17 as "rule." The KJV is known for its focus on church hierarchy in its translations, for it was translated in the midst of a very "high church" era in the history of Christianity. The problem with the phrase "direct the affairs of the church" or the term "rule" is that they leave the impression that elders are the sole leaders in charge of leading the church. That is neither biblically defensible nor practically effective. Perhaps the best simple translation of this term when applied to elders would simply be "leads" and "leads well." That would reduce its authoritarian feel and yet allow for a leadership style that fits into all that we studied about servant leadership previously. A servant leader is still a leader, and a leader with authority (as we have already defined authority).

No leader or group of leaders in any organization should make all of the decisions for the organization in isolation. I will have more to say on that subject in a later chapter about team leadership, but the idea that the elders or other leaders in any single role should make all of the decisions is a poor idea. The CEO of a company may in one sense "direct the affairs" of the company, but how does he do it? If his brain is functioning at all, he leads through others who function in key roles according to their expertise, who are also equipped to make decisions within those roles. Those who delight in making all of the decisions themselves are missing some pieces in the area of good judgment. No one person has enough perspective to make all of the right decisions, and the same may be said of any group comprised of leaders in only one type of role. I recall hearing an elder in fairly recent times saying that in the past, the evangelists made all the decisions, and now the elders make them. I cringed when I heard that, and of course I addressed my concerns directly with him. Leadership is about far more than simply making decisions. And the best decisions are going to be made by taking more than one perspective into consideration. That is why I will always argue strongly for team leadership. Elders have an important and even somewhat predominant role in the church, but they are not bosses and should avoid leaving such an impression through their words or demeanor.

"The elders...are worthy of double honor, especially those whose work is preaching and teaching."

What is double honor? Contextually, it is being supported financially. Verse 18 makes that point so clear that I am amazed anyone could possibly argue to the contrary (although some have). Elders can be financially supported and serve on a ministry staff. They don't have to be, but they can be. Having an elder or elders on staff provides an additional perspective and helps avoid the deadly "us-versus-them" conflicts that can arise in church leadership groups. Whether the elders in a congregation are on staff or not, they should frequently meet together with staff members. Note also that the text mentions the idea of dual roles: elder/ evangelist and elder/teacher. Those serving in dual roles would most likely be financially supported, but men who only serve in the elder role could certainly also be supported. Further, those in dual roles would in some ways be better equipped to "direct the affairs of the church," simply because they have a broader perspective. The idea that in the early church, evangelists planted churches and then elders led the churches is not only biblically indefensible, it is practically ineffective. Of course, if the elders were of the evangelist/elder combination, that would be a different matter entirely.

"Do not entertain an accusation against an elder unless it is brought by two or three witnesses."

The voice of one malcontent is just that—one voice (not two or three), and the voice of a critic, at that. The principles of Proverbs 18:17 and Matthew 18:15–18 should also come into play here. Anyone having a problem with an elder should first go to the elder, brother to brother or sister to brother, and try to work out the problem. An elder still is a brother, and deserves to be treated as such before the issue is escalated. If that attempt fails, then other leaders will need to get involved. The directions in 1 Timothy 5 are addressed to Timothy, an evangelist. Paul does not detail here how the evangelist and other leaders should work together in such situations, but it is clear that the leaders should work in harmony. The point Paul seems to be making is that elders have a high calling and are not above being called to account for their lives and example. But there is a right way to go about making an accusation, and there is a right way for other leaders to handle it, which is described in the passage itself.

"Those who sin are to be rebuked publicly."

Elders who sin (literally "are sinning") are to be rebuked publicly. Of course, it should be kept in mind that Paul started the chapter out with these words: "Do not rebuke an older man harshly, but exhort him as if he were your father." Taking into account the tense of the verb *sin*, Timothy is being instructed to carry out the rebuke for those who continue in their sin.

Then we have another question: How public is the rebuke? Is it a rebuke among the leaders or before the whole church? The text doesn't give us an absolute answer to the question, but common sense, in conjunction with the progressive nature of discipline detailed by Jesus in Matthew 18, would suggest that we start with the former and end with the latter if the elder does not repent. If the elder does not change, removal from the eldership would be next; removal from the church would be the final step. Actually, the stage at which an elder is removed would depend upon the nature of the sin, his willingness to repent, and how public his sin has been. If he were rebuked publicly and repented with true brokenness, the issue of his influence with the flock would have to be taken into serious consideration to determine whether he should remain an elder. I have seen such situations go both ways. In complicated situations like this, I highly recommend getting input from other leaders outside your own congregation.

"I charge you . . . to keep these instructions without partiality, and to do nothing out of favoritism."

Human nature being what it is, an evangelist may have a closer relationship with some elders than others. He may share the same perspectives with one elder more than another. An evangelist is not above showing favoritism or partiality. Remaining impartial in all situations is the acid test of a leader's character and leadership ability. In the midst of our times of upheaval after 2003, some of our church leadership groups were accused of being like an "Old Boys' Club." In some cases, I think those accusations were spot-on accurate. There is a fine line between showing support and appreciation for a leader because of past work, and showing favoritism and sentimentality. If this were not a strong temptation, Paul would not have mentioned it to such a trusted coworker as Timothy. None of us is exempt. Some of us are really good at avoiding conflict with certain people or certain types of people, and really poor at avoiding conflict with others! That is why we so desperately need teamwork and the unbiased perspectives of outsiders.

"Do not be hasty in the laying on of hands"

Leaders (Timothy, in this case) are warned against showing poor judgment by appointing elders too quickly. First impressions and early impressions are often shown to be inaccurate with the passing of time. Elder-training sessions are invaluable tools in helping us avoid making mistakes in appointments. Such sessions should never consist primarily of having more mature leaders teaching lessons to those in training. These sessions should also allow for a lot of interaction among the elder candidates as topics are covered that raise discussions and differing opinions. Group interaction is vital to such training. In the next chapter, we will examine the qualifications of elders. In those lists are qualities, good and bad, that we should examine in someone's character and life before appointing them. It is far easier to appoint than to "dis-appoint," so by all means be careful and calculated. Don't rush the process.

James 5:14

James 5:14 is a fascinating verse describing a somewhat perplexing function of elders. James writes:

> Is any one of you sick? He should call the elders of the church to pray over him and anoint him with oil in the name of the Lord.

Of course, the need for prayer is undisputed, but anointing with oil is the cause of varying interpretations. Three interpretations of this passage have been offered most frequently. One view is that the oil is medicinal in nature, and it was used for that purpose in the first-century setting. The Good Samaritan dressed the wounds of the hurt person with "oil and wine" (Luke 10:34). However, oil was used for first-aid purposes, not for healing of more serious illnesses, making this interpretation unlikely. Also, prayer was said to do the healing, not the oil. A second view is that anointing with oil was ceremonial in nature, accompanying a miraculous healing through the gift of healing in the early church. It was so used in Mark 6:13, and mention of miraculous healing "in the name of Jesus" is found in Acts 19:13. This passage depicts a failed attempt at healing by the sons of Sceva (a very humorous passage!), but they were likely imitating the apostles.

The third view is that the oil symbolically stood for the special favor and blessing of God. God's leaders in the Old Testament were often anointed with oil simply to show God's approval of their appointment (Exodus 29:7; 1 Samuel 10:1; 1 Samuel 16:3). Thus, in James 5, oil may just symbolize the blessing of healing from God. The oil does not heal, but the Lord (who hears the prayers of elders in a special way) does, and the oil is a symbol of this blessing. I believe that this third view is most likely correct, and I have practiced this action on many occasions. When I pray over people (with my hands on their head or shoulders), I tell them that this action is not a guarantee of healing, but a sincere attempt to simply follow God's directions in faith. And although some whom I have anointed with oil (I use olive oil, since that would have been the type of oil used in the first century) were not healed physically, they were blessed spiritually. Others were healed physically in amazing ways.

Years ago, a young woman in a congregation outside the US developed a life-threatening brain tumor. She was newly married, her life just beginning in so many ways. As a visiting elder, I anointed her and prayed over her just before she went back to the doctor for another examination. Shortly afterwards, she and her husband attended a church conference, and while they were there, she received an urgent call from her doctor. He said that something had gone wrong with the X-rays they had just taken, and he urged her to come in for more tests as soon as she could. The doctor's concern was that the X-rays no longer showed the tumor. Many years and two beautiful children later, the doctors have never found any more evidence of a tumor. I have witnessed other similar experiences, as have other elders, yet we also have stories that did not turn out with physical healing. All elders can do is follow God's directions in this passage and put their faith in God as they pray.

The two verses (James 5:15–16) also mention forgiveness of sins and the confession of sins. It is natural for a person who is very sick to be particularly conscious of sin and eager to get it off their conscience. This would be especially true in a setting like James describes, when elders are present to minister to them. Therefore, when anointing a sick person, I have always read this passage and asked them if they have any sins they feel like they need to confess and get off their hearts. That is a good part of the whole process. Another lesson we glean from verse 16 is that confession of sins to one another should be a part of normal spiritual life. "Be in the habit of confessing" would be a good translation of the verb. In other words, although confessing when we are sick and in the presence of elders is natural and good, we shouldn't wait until we are in that situation! We should all confess our sins regularly to fellow disciples—a practice that provides us with another compelling passage about the need for discipling in each of our lives.

1 Peter 5:1–4

> To the elders among you, I appeal as a fellow elder, a witness of Christ's sufferings and one who also will share in the glory to be revealed: Be shepherds of God's flock that is under your care, serving as overseers—not because you must, but because you are willing, as God wants you to be; not greedy for money, but eager to serve; not lording it over those entrusted to you, but being examples to the flock. And when the Chief Shepherd appears, you will receive the crown of glory that will never fade away.

By the time Peter wrote these words, many years had passed since his Pentecost sermon in Acts 2, and now he was an elder as well as an apostle. As an elder, he was writing to other elders, understanding their particular challenges from personal experience. Peter addresses several things about the role of elder. Note that just as in Acts 20, all three terms for the elder role are used here: elder, shepherd, and overseer.

Peter admonishes elders to fulfill their role by really caring for the flock, not out of duty but out of desire. Further, their motives must be pure: a desire to serve others, free from a worldly desire for money. This would suggest that some elders were in fact supported by the church as a part of the leadership staff. It is possible that elders were the only type of leaders supported, for that matter. We are not told. Verse 3 warns against exerting what I would call "position-only" leadership. About forty years earlier, Peter had been in the inner circle of men who heard Jesus' words about servant leadership in Matthew 20:25–28, and he had not forgotten that lesson. Peter's exhortation to be examples to the flock defines leadership in its simplest terms: leadership leads! Before the Hebrew writer penned Hebrews 13:17, urging the church to obey leaders and submit to their authority, he wrote 13:7: "Remember your leaders, who spoke the word of God to you. Consider the outcome of their way of life and imitate their faith." Leaders lead by example.

Elders: How Should We View Them?

In seeking to learn as much as we can about the role and function of elders, we should consider two additional passages. Although they do not mention elders specifically, they can be applied to elders because they talk about our overall attitude toward leadership. Both passages have much to say about how we should view and respond to leaders (including elders).

1 Thessalonians 5:12–13

> Now we ask you, brothers, to respect those who work hard among you, who are over you in the Lord and who admonish you. Hold them in the highest regard in love because of their work. Live in peace with each other.

Leaders, including elders, should be respected and held in the highest regard for their work. Whose responsibility is it to teach the church to view and treat leaders in this way? Primarily, it is the leaders' responsibility, as awkward as this might seem at first glance. But another analogy can help remove the awkwardness: Whose responsibility is it to teach children to respect their parents? Primarily the parents'! In both cases, extended family also does their part. This is the plan of God, but respect must be taught, and not simply demanded. As it is taught, we must note that Paul says that leaders are over the members in the Lord, and they will at times give *admonishment* as leaders. Combining this passage with 1 Peter 5, which we just examined, we see that the words "under," "over," and "admonish" are all used. These are not negative words, nor do they represent negative concepts, although all of them can be applied in wrong and sinful ways. As a leader, I have the responsibility to lead righteously, keeping these concepts in mind, and as a follower, I also have the duty to recognize my leaders' responsibility to lead.

In saying that leaders are primarily responsible for teaching church members to respect and appreciate them, we have to add that all members of God's spiritual family should help each other respect leaders. The church in Phoenix appointed a new elder in 2009. This brother had been in the church for a long time and had always treated the elders with respect and appreciation. When he was approached about the possibility of becoming an elder, he was willing to serve but made a disturbing observation. He said that he remembered the time when elders were held in high esteem, and he was somewhat shocked now by the lack of respect shown to the elders by some (dare I say many?) church members. I believe he was thinking about how freely some Christians criticize leaders in our present environment. Such critics need to be taught and challenged by leaders and fellow Christians alike. Unfortunately, we live in a society where criticism of all types of leadership is totally accepted. We would do well to be reminded that God considers it a serious offense to speak negatively of any leader, including those of our government:

> Remind the people to be subject to rulers and authorities, to be obedient, to be ready to do whatever is good, to slander no one, to be peaceable and considerate, and to show true humility toward all men (Titus 3:1–2).

Hebrews 13:17

The next passage that doesn't mention elders but obviously includes them is Hebrews 13:17:

> Obey your leaders and submit to their authority. They keep watch over you as men who must give an account. Obey them so that their work will be a joy, not a burden, for that would be of no advantage to you.

I have already addressed this passage in some detail in chapter 3, so I won't repeat that material. However, I will add an additional thought or two on what it means to obey your leaders. It means more than simply obeying specific biblical lessons that they teach. You cannot limit your obedience to leaders only if they produce "book, chapter and verse" biblically. The Bible is not a law book, with directions for every possible situation or need. More than anything, it is a set of principles, which means that leaders have to provide the practical ways for applying those principles to the lives of disciples. That isn't too much of a surprise, is it?

When you study what the Bible says about vitally important subjects like marriage and parenting, how many specific "how to's" do you actually find? Not many. I think God left those specifics up to us for many reasons, one of which is to allow us to apply his principles in appropriate ways in cultures that are always changing. We have to discover ways of recognizing and applying biblical principles, and in my opinion, the most efficient way to do that will always be discipling. Parents and older siblings teach younger children in the family how to do just about everything they learn to do. Isn't that discipling in its purest form? Do you really think you can improve on that plan? To be sure, books, classes and seminars on the subjects of marriage and parenting are also very helpful. But I'm a "both/and" man—I believe in those other strategies *and* in discipling—because I need all the help I can get, and I want to give others all the help I can as well.

Leaders have to provide specific direction and help in a number of areas. When is the church going to meet; where are they going to meet; how many times do they need to meet in a week; in what format should they meet; I could go on and on. Can leaders exercise poor judgment in providing advice, or go too far with what they ask people to do? Of course—just as parents can make mistakes in parenting their children.

So, knowing that we can (and will) make mistakes, what should we do? Should we let fear rule, and do nothing? Leaders have many responsibilities, and they will be greatly hindered if their every decision is analyzed, picked apart and judged by critical members. Leaders need to be trusted and followed. They also need feedback from those whom they lead, and those who give the input should realize that not all input can be put into practice. Decisions have to be made for the good of the entire group, and that means that any given decision aims to meet the needs of the majority and may not perfectly meet the needs of each individual. The minority who may not be helped as much by a particular decision have to recognize the weighty responsibility that leaders bear, and respect and follow their leaders' decisions. Hebrews 13:17 cannot be taken lightly, if God is to be pleased and the church blessed.

May God help us to view and respond to elders and other leaders in a biblical manner. And may we all recognize how much we may have been influenced by people who think nothing of criticizing leaders—people who are careless with their words, or even deliberately destructive. We need to keep 1 Thessalonians 5:12–13 and Hebrews 13:17 on our hearts, and encourage the people who have the willingness and courage to lead us. Let's make their work a joy and not a burden, as God directs.

Chapter Seven

Qualifications, Selection and Appointment of Elders

Character Qualification of Elders?

Let's begin this section by quoting the two main passages in the New Testament that list the qualifications elders are to have.

> Here is a trustworthy saying: If anyone sets his heart on being an overseer, he desires a noble task. Now the overseer must be above reproach, the husband of but one wife, temperate, self-controlled, respectable, hospitable, able to teach, not given to drunkenness, not violent but gentle, not quarrelsome, not a lover of money. He must manage his own family well and see that his children obey him with proper respect. (If anyone does not know how to manage his own family, how can he take care of God's church?) He must not be a recent convert, or he may become conceited and fall under the same judgment as the devil. He must also have a good reputation with outsiders, so that he will not fall into disgrace and into the devil's trap (1 Timothy 3:1–7).

> The reason I left you in Crete was that you might straighten out what was left unfinished and appoint elders in every town, as I directed you. An elder must be blameless, the husband of but one wife, a man whose children believe and are not open to the charge of being wild and disobedient. Since an overseer is entrusted with God's work, he must be blameless—not overbearing, not quick-tempered, not given to drunkenness, not violent, not pursuing dishonest gain. Rather he must be hospitable, one who loves what is good, who is self-controlled, upright, holy and disciplined. He must hold firmly to the trustworthy message as it has been taught, so that he can encourage others by sound doctrine and refute those who oppose it (Titus 1:5–9).

In our discussion of the qualifications of elders, we are going to treat character qualifications and family qualifications separately. Regarding the use of the term "qualifications," some have suggested that we use another term, such as "qualities." I assume that the intent of the change in terminology is to help us focus on the general tenor of a person's life and avoid making these "qualities" some sort of a legalistic checklist. Although I am not out of harmony with that purpose, I don't think much of value is accomplished in changing the terminology. For example, suppose that a man is not at all greedy—in fact, he is quite generous and hospitable—and yet he gets drunk with regularity. Does his spirit of generosity somehow offset the problem of drunkenness? Obviously, all humans are stronger in some areas than others, but can an elder be seriously weak in one of the things listed in these passages and still be qualified? I think not. He will be perfect in none of them, but he must be reasonably strong in all of them. Therefore, I am going to use the familiar term *qualifications*. I suspect that the fairly recent emphasis on changing terminology was brought about by a desire to lessen the emphasis on what appears to be a very high standard (almost impossibly high, some would say) for the elder's family. We will discuss those particular issues in detail later in the chapter.

Too many items appear in these lists to examine each one in an in-depth manner. Therefore, we will list all of them and comment on only one of the character qualities that needs a closer examination. We will address the family issues in the most detail. The following lists are divided into several general categories, allowing for some obvious overlap.

Personality and character qualities:

- Temperate
- Self-controlled
- Hospitable
- Disciplined
- Not violent, but gentle
- Not quarrelsome
- Not overbearing
- Not quick-tempered

Spiritual qualities:
- Not a recent convert

- Loves what is good
- Holy
- Upright

Reputation:

- Good reputation with outsiders (or else he may fall into disgrace)
- Respectable
- Above reproach
- Blameless
- Not given to drunkenness
- Not a lover of money
- Not pursuing dishonest gain

Teaching skills:

- Able to teach
- Holds firmly to the trustworthy message (thus able to encourage others by sound doctrine and to refute those who oppose it)

Leadership skills (as demonstrated by his family):

- Husband of but one wife
- Manages his own family well
- Sees that his children obey him with proper respect
- His children believe, and are not open to the charge of being wild and disobedient.

Summing up, the biblical qualifications dictate that the elder be an older, experienced, spiritual brother with children who positively reflect his family management ability. Further, he must be a reputable man even among outsiders, and one who clearly possesses an ability to lead the way and to effectively teach others to follow his lead.

The one character quality I do want to comment on is found in Titus 1:7. Here the NIV says that an elder is "not overbearing." The word in Greek is *authadēs*, which carries the meaning "self-pleasing." The NASB translates it as "self-willed." The Greek term is based on two other terms, *autos*, meaning self, and *hedone*, meaning pleasing. Perhaps it is obvious that *hedone* is the root for our English word "hedonism." *Authadēs* is found only here and in 2 Peter 2:10, where the NIV translates it as "arrogant," while the NASB sticks to the term "self-willed." But notice in the context of 2 Peter 2:10 what the arrogant or self-willed person does: "This is especially true of those who follow the corrupt desire of the sinful nature and despise authority. Bold and arrogant, these men are not afraid to slander celestial beings." Being self-willed is obviously a very dangerous characteristic.

How does a self-willed person act, and why does this quality disqualify him from serving as an elder? Stated simply, he is inflexible and will fight tooth and nail to get his way. He will often also have a temper problem, although he sometimes is characterized by a relatively quiet stubbornness. He cannot be a team player, and should never be put in any type of leadership group. I've been in groups with a few people who had this character flaw, some of whom were outspokenly unyielding, while others were more quietly stubborn and resistant. Both are self-willed and an absolute blight to any group to which they belong, particularly when the group is by definition a spiritual group. I unhesitatingly give you this advice: Don't ever appoint anyone to any leadership role who even tends in this direction, and if you already have, remove them. If you have ever been in a leadership group with such a person, you know exactly what I am talking about; if you haven't, consider yourself blessed—and pay close attention in the future to what is written in this paragraph. All leaders have strong opinions; how they handle their opinions is the ultimate issue. End of sermon!

Family Qualifications of Elders

This topic has been studied quite a lot in the recent history of our movement, most likely in a desire not to disqualify anyone from serving as an elder that God's word actually qualifies. Reexamining traditional views is a good idea, especially in areas where the consequences of our conclusions can have a decided impact on the church—positively or negatively. Since we are dealing with matters of judgment and challenging interpretation issues, in which good brothers have some differing viewpoints, these suggestions are in order: Dogmatism must be avoided, no matter how strong our opinions. We should strive to maintain an open mind as we consider ideas that may be new to us. As long as a good case can be made for either side of an issue, surely we are not going to incur God's displeasure by taking one side or the other. Having said that, let's proceed to deal with three basic family qualifications.

Marriage History

We will begin with the elder candidate's marriage (or marriage history). He is to be "the husband of but one wife" (1 Timothy 3:2; Titus 1:6). A literal translation of the Greek text is "a one-woman man." What does this mean? Several possibilities have been espoused by various writers.

Interpretation 1:

The most conservative interpretation of the passage would be that no man could serve as an elder (or deacon, 1 Timothy 3:12) unless he met the following requirements: In the first place, he would have to be a married man. Next, he could not be either widowed or divorced, whether or not he had remarried. Thus, he would have to have been married one time and one time only, and his wife would have to be living in order for him to be qualified. He could not serve if he had ever divorced, regardless of the reason for the divorce and whether it took place before or after he became a Christian.

Interpretation 2:

A less strict interpretation would be that no one could serve in these roles if he had been divorced while he was a Christian, even if the divorce were based on biblical grounds. This interpretation would allow a person to serve as an elder if he had been divorced prior to becoming a Christian, as long as he had never been divorced after becoming a Christian.

Interpretation 3:

An even less strict approach would be to allow a man to be an elder as long as his present marriage was biblically allowable. In other words, if a man had been divorced for biblically justified reasons (even as a Christian), he could still serve as an elder. Biblical grounds for divorce would be either of these two situations: a desertion by a mate who either never became a Christian or who became a Christian but fell away and became an unbeliever again (1 Corinthians 7:15); or a divorce based on sexual unfaithfulness (Matthew 19:9). So if he had been divorced—even as a

> Christian—due to his mate's sexual unfaithfulness or her desertion of him and God, he could still serve as an elder, assuming he met the other qualifications. I think that this most liberal interpretation may be too questionable for the majority of disciples to accept, although it could perhaps still be argued logically.

Examining the Interpretations

It seems to me that whatever any of us did prior to becoming a Christian is not the issue. In other words, if we are going to hold a man accountable for his marriage failures before becoming a Christian, should we not also hold him to all the other qualifications (temperance, sobriety, discipline, etc.)? Singling out the marriage issue as the only qualification that must be met in a man's pre-Christian experience does not seem reasonable. Let's say we have two men who would like to become elders in a church. The first man had been a thieving, womanizing alcoholic before he became a Christian; however, he married and never got divorced. He and his wife both became Christians and dramatically cleaned up their lives. The second did not lead a particularly wild life in his non-Christian days, but got married and divorced before he was baptized; after becoming a Christian, he remarried and built a great family with a Christian wife. According to the strictest interpretation of the phrase "one-woman man," the first man could be qualified to serve as an elder, but the second would be automatically disqualified because of his pre-Christian divorce. Does that reasoning make sense? It would seem most logical and biblical to say that God is looking for a godly man to lead his spiritual family, regardless of what his past may have held. A radically changed life can often have the most influence for good anyway.

What then is the most likely meaning of "one-woman man?" A consideration of first-century culture is relevant. A young man growing up in the Roman Empire experienced sexual temptations of many kinds (the same could be said of young men in most twenty-first-century cultures). Going to the pagan temples and having sex with the priestesses was the order of the day. It was common practice for men to continue to have sex with priestesses even after marriage. In view of that ungodly sexual atmosphere, any married man who remained faithful to his wife would have provided an example that stood in stark contrast to most other men. Hence, it is likely that being a "one-woman man" meant simply that a man had been faithful to his wife after becoming a Christian.

This brings to mind a similar phrase in 1 Timothy 5:9, which deals with the marriage history of widows. The passage requires a widow supported by the church to be a "one-man" woman. Does that mean that she had been married only once before being widowed? The NIV simply translates this phrase, "has been faithful to her husband." If this rendering is accepted, the same thing is being required of the widow as the elder and deacon—each must be faithful to their mates after becoming Christians.

If this is not the correct interpretation, and the more rigid interpretations are applied, some strange conclusions would follow. For example, one man may have slept with scores of prostitutes (which the temple priestesses were), while avoiding the marriage altar. Another man may have avoided the prostitutes as a young man, but entered an ill-advised marriage that ended in divorce. If the first man later married, he could still be considered a "one-woman man" who could be appointed an elder if he was otherwise qualified. If the second man later remarried, he was not a "one-woman man" and could never become an elder, even if he met the other qualifications.

To me, such interpretations miss the point of the spiritual and character qualities God requires, and are no more than legalistic rules. A mature friend of mine made this statement during the challenges of 2003: "As a movement, we have had impossibly high qualifications for elders and unbelievably low qualifications for evangelists." His statement certainly contains some truth, although I hope it was intended as a hyperbole. (Don't get offended, evangelists!) Therefore, I am open to a reexamination of my long-held views regarding elder qualifications. I am not open to lowering the spiritual standard for men who serve in this role, but it seems to me that this spiritual standard is not about past history. It is about current spirituality.

Thus, my personal conclusion regarding marital history is this: A man can be appointed an elder if, since becoming a Christian, he has been faithful to his one wife. If he divorced before becoming a Christian, he is not automatically disqualified from consideration. If he has been divorced as a Christian for biblical reasons, he may still be qualified—but that decision must be carefully weighed by people who know him well and by how his congregation views his qualification to serve. The most important question is: Is he currently faithful to his wife? Has he upheld the highest marital morality as a Christian? Obviously, as with all complex issues, you are going to have to study and wrestle with these issues for yourself.

One other related issue is sometimes raised regarding marriage and family history qualifications. What if an elder's wife dies (or his children)? Does that tragedy disqualify him? I certainly wouldn't argue that it should. The qualifications are designed to show that his character and experience have prepared him in the sight of God and man to serve as a shepherd. The death of a wife or children does not affect character and expertise. In the event his wife dies, he may choose to resign simply because he needs time to grieve or feels that he is not going to be effective enough to serve without her help. But that is a personal choice issue, not a biblical issue.

What about a man being appointed who is already a widower? I have never seen it done, but I wouldn't rule it out as a possibility. Admittedly it might be more questionable in the minds of some, but we would all have to ask ourselves why. Is it because we have never considered the possibility and are simply uncomfortable with a new consideration? Is it because we are a bit too legalistic in our views of the qualifications? Good questions to ask ourselves. This situation is not nearly as pertinent to us as is the real possibility of older men losing their wives while serving as elders. On that issue, I would not want to lose the service of good elders simply because they no longer had a living mate. To me, that would be a legalistic approach I couldn't accept. On the other hand, I could easily accept an elder's personal decision to resign after becoming a widower.

Qualifications for Wives of Elders?

The question mark in this heading is there for a reason: It is not certain that the New Testament contains qualifications for the wife of an elder. In 1 Timothy 3:8–13, the qualifications of deacons are listed. In the midst of that passage, we find the following verse: "In the same way, their wives are to be women worthy of respect, not malicious talkers but temperate and trustworthy in everything" (1 Timothy 3:11). Who are the wives (or women) being addressed? Three possibilities exist: Only the wives of deacons are being addressed; or both the wives of elders and deacons are being addressed, through a parenthetical statement inserted at this point by Paul; or Paul is describing women deacons (deaconesses), a separate but related role. Arguments can be made for and against each of these interpretations; we'll explore them one by one.

> **Interpretation 1:** The passage concerns wives of deacons **only**.
>
> The first interpretation is the strongest one from a strictly contextual standpoint. However, assuming that the elder's role is at least as important as the deacon's, and assuming that his wife will usually be more involved in helping him to carry out his role than the deacon's wife will be with his, we are left wondering why Paul would have made such an omission.
>
> **Interpretation 2:** The passage concerns wives of elders **and** deacons.
>
> Interpretation 2 would be the most practical, logical approach. Paul does at times drop parenthetical statements into his writing that seem at first glance to be somewhat out of context. (See Romans 5:15-17; 1 Corinthians 9:20-21; Galatians 1:1; 1 Timothy 3:5.)
>
> **Interpretation 3:** Paul is describing female deacons (deaconesses).
>
> On the other hand, the wording of verse 11 begins very similarly to verse 8, which addresses the deacons. This interpretation is supported by the observation that the word translated "wives" here can also be translated "women." Translation is therefore a matter of judgment based on context. In Romans 16:1, Phoebe is called "a servant of the church in Cenchrea." The translation "servant" comes from the feminine form of the Greek word sometimes translated "deacon." However, the term is used most often for a servant generally, not in specific reference to appointed deacons. Most would question the existence of a biblical role of deaconess based upon the scant evidence of these two verses.

Which interpretation is the best? I believe evidence is strongest for Interpretation 1 or 2. If interpretation 2 is not accepted, does the Bible say anything about an elder's wife? The idea of an elder/shepherd comes first from the Old Testament, where the term is used nearly 150 times. One of the best-known verses in the Old Testament along these lines is actually found in Proverbs 31:23, in the midst of a passage describing the wife of noble character. It reads: "Her husband is respected at the city gate, where he takes his seat among the elders of the land." Although I decidedly lean toward accepting Interpretation 2 (Paul is describing the wives of both elders and deacons), the most lofty description of a wife's mature spiritual character is found in Proverbs 31, where the wife of an OT elder is described. On a purely practical basis, an elder's wife is either an asset or detraction to his ability to carry out his shepherding role. If her spiritual character does not match his, his appointment should be seen as questionable. However, if she obtains the help she needs to make changes, he could and should be appointed.

Bottom line, the wife of any leader plays a crucial role in his ability to serve and lead in the church and in their ability to function and serve as a couple. The primary questions to be asked about an elder candidate's wife are these: Is she spiritual? Is she respected? Can she keep a confidence? Can she be trusted? Is she a strong support to her husband? I'm sure other good questions could be added, but it is essential that an elder have a spiritually qualified wife.

The Children of an Elder

Without question, the elder's qualifications enter their most controversial scenario when we discuss their children. Two verses deal with this particular qualification:

> He must manage his own family well and see that his children obey him with proper respect. (If anyone does not know how to manage his own family, how can he take care of God's church?" (I Timothy 3:4–5).

> An elder must be blameless, the husband of but one wife, a man whose children believe and are not open to the charge of being wild and disobedient (Titus 1:6).

The controversial interpretation issue is how to interpret the Greek word *pistos*, translated "believe" in Titus 1:6.

Pistos is used more than 60 times in the New Testament. In the large majority of those occurrences, pistos is translated by the word "trustworthy," "reliable" or the equivalent, rather than as "believer." However, a closer examination of the passages shows that we can easily be comparing apples to oranges if we aren't careful. Strictly speaking, *pistos* is used 67 times in the New Testament— translated 57 times by the word "trustworthy" or a similar term and only 10 times as "believing", "believe" or "believer." At first glance, it would appear fairly conclusive that *pistos* in Titus 1:6 is most likely *not* requiring that an elder's children be Christians. However, this is where the apples to oranges comparison can come into play.

There are two basic issues involved. One is the fact that many times, *pistos* is not actually referring to human beings, but rather to *concepts or to deity* (God or Jesus); and even when the word does refer to humans, it refers to them before they could have been called Christian believers.

- The word is found 12 times in the gospel accounts before it could be applied to Christians. For example, *pistos* is found twice in Luke 16:10, translated as "faithful" in the NASB: "He who is faithful in a very little thing is faithful also in much; and he who is unrighteous in a very little thing is unrighteous also in much."
- The word is used about 10 times to refer to nonpersons ("trustworthy sayings," for example). "Here is a trustworthy saying that deserves full acceptance: Christ Jesus came into the world to save sinners--of whom I am the worst" (1 Timothy 1:15).
- *Pistos* is used 15 times in reference to deity (God or Jesus). "But the Lord is faithful, and he will strengthen and protect you from the evil one" (2 Thessalonians 3:3).
- Taking into account that several of the occurrences of *pistos* (including Titus 1:6) could arguably be interpreted in several ways, the remaining usages of *pistos* (those which refer to humans) are almost equally divided between indicating a Christian believer, as opposed to just a trustworthy person. Here are examples of each type:

> Don't let anyone look down on you because you are young, but set an example for the believers in speech, in life, in love, in faith and in purity (1 Timothy 4:12).

> Moses was faithful as a servant in all God's house, testifying to what would be said in the future (Hebrews 3:5).

All of that shows that the evidence is not overwhelming either way, and the context alone must determine the correct translation.

The second statistical issue to consider is how *pistos* is applied in 1 and 2 Timothy and Titus (the Pastoral Epistles), where it occurs 17 times. These are the books in which Paul gives the lists of elder qualifications. In 1 and 2 Timothy, our term is translated 8 times as "faithful," "reliable" or "dutiful" (1 Timothy 1:12; 1:15; 3:1; 3:11; 4:9; 2 Timothy 2:2; 2:11; 2:13). It is translated 6 times in the sense of "believing" and "believer" (1 Timothy 4:3; 4:10; 4:12; 5:16; 6:2). In Titus, pistos is used 3 times, two of which are indisputably in the sense of "trustworthy" or "reliable" (Titus 1:9; 3:8). The third is the passage in question (Titus 1:6).

In all three of these books, a closer examination of these passages shows the following:

Of 17 instances of *pistos* found in the Pastoral Epistles, 11 refer to persons. Of those 11, only 4 clearly do not use the term in the sense of "believer," and Titus 1:6 is the only usage whose interpretation is unclear. Thus, the ratio is either 6 to 5 or 7 to 4 ("believer" to "reliable"), depending on how Titus 1:6 is viewed. Therefore, the numbers alone would favor "believer" in the Pastorals, but not overwhelmingly so.

We are left with three plausible interpretations of Paul's meaning in Titus 1:6.

> **Interpretation 1:**
> *Pistos* means "faithful" in a general sense. An elder's children are to be "faithful" in the sense of being trustworthy, reliable, obedient and respectful to their father, but not necessarily in relation to faith in God or being faithful to God. This would be more parallel with Paul's elder qualifications in 1 Timothy 3:4: "his children obey him with proper respect." Thus, the contrast in Titus would not be between "believing" and "unbelieving" children, but between "faithful, dutiful" children and "wild and disobedient" children.
>
> **Interpretation 2:**
> *Pistos* in this context indicates a younger child who believes in God and Jesus in contrast to one who does not believe in God or Jesus. Matthew 18:1-6 refers to little ones (young children) "who believe in me." This child may have a "childlike faith" that responds to God in a manner appropriate to his age. This child has an obvious spiritual bent which reflects on the parent's heart. Therefore, a prospective elder need only have children that have an age-appropriate faith, who show every sign of becoming a Christian at the appropriate age and level of maturity.
>
> **Interpretation 3:**
> *Pistos* refers to a child who has made Jesus Lord of his life, repented of his sins and been baptized into Christ. The word pistos is used of "believers" (i.e., Christians) in this sense many times in the New Testament, several times in the Pastoral Epistles. This view would require that the children of the prospective elder must be baptized believers. What about the fact that this qualification is not listed in 1 Timothy 3—does it make sense that men could serve as elders in Ephesus who would not have qualified to be elders in Crete? Since there were already elders in Ephesus

> where Timothy was, this might explain the difference in Paul's writings. Perhaps Timothy was being told how to *treat* elders (and many other types of people, in context), while Titus was being told how to *appoint* them.

Regardless of which view is accepted, questions and potential problems remain. Conversion is a supernatural act of God, not simply a product of good parenting (John 1:12–13). Questions on this subject are going to be probing and sometimes troubling, but they should be asked and given due consideration. Can even the best Christian fathers *guarantee* that their children will become and remain Christians? The free moral agency of all people comes into play here. Obviously, potential dangers exist in dealing with all of these issues, one of which is shifting the emphasis and scrutiny from the spiritual character of the man to that of his children as the overriding criterion for selection.

If we accept the more traditional, conservative view requiring an elder's children to be believers, questions arise in certain cases. Must one or all of an elder's children be baptized before he is qualified to serve? If the oldest child has already become a Christian and the younger children appear to be headed in the same direction, the one believing child would seemingly qualify him, although some would disagree on that point. But according to Genesis 21:7, having one child qualifies you as having *children*, for the plural includes the singular. Using the same principle from Genesis 21:7, you could argue for regarding an elder as having believing *children*, even if only one child has become a baptized believer. A related issue arises when children are baptized at an early age (twelve or thirteen years), at which point their faith has probably not been tested in a significant way. Thus, a man could become an elder when his child is baptized at twelve years old, only to have to resign several years later if the child becomes unfaithful in the high school or college years.

Another common question based on the conservative view of having believing children is this one: What about an elder whose children become unfaithful to God after they leave the elder's home (and direct influence)? Two extremes should be avoided in answering this question, it seems to me. If the child leaves God and the church rather quickly after leaving home, his newfound freedom has only provided the opportunity to show what was in his heart already. Such a quick departure from the faith should disqualify the elder. On the other hand, if an elder's child remained faithful for a number of years and then fell away, that would be another matter. At some point, the responsibility for a person's spiritual choices comes to rest upon the (grown) child alone, and not on their father. Like many such scenarios, I believe this one is a judgment call, and the elder's own conscience in the matter has to be taken into consideration. I know some men who have intellectually agreed that they could remain an elder when an older child (who was married with their own family) has left the church, but their own emotional concerns about their influence has led them to resign anyway.

What is the best approach to follow regarding these views? Unquestionably, the best possible scenario would be for a man's children to be adults and regarded as tested believers who are living as strong disciples. However, making this a hard-line requirement would be questionable for a number of reasons. It would seem best to consider each elder candidate on a case-by-case basis, with a main focus on being sure that a potential elder's family shows good evidence that he has managed his family well and brought his children up "in the training and instruction of the Lord" (Ephesians 6:4).

After dealing with areas of judgment that are less than crystal clear, it would be good to remind us all of what I said earlier in this chapter. In areas of judgment, where good brothers have differing viewpoints, dogmatism must be avoided, no matter how strong our opinions. We should fight to retain an open mind as we consider ideas that may be new to us. As long as a good case can be made for either side of an issue, surely we are not going to incur God's wrath by taking either side. Each of us, leader and nonleader alike, is going to have to dig into the Scriptures to develop our own convictions. These are not easy matters to determine with certainty, so we had best be prepared to state our opinions, and then be prepared to have those opinions tested by those who have come to different conclusions. Most likely, this process will be ongoing until the Lord comes!

Selection and Appointment of Elders

The Selection Process

In studying this topic, it needs to be stated at the outset that the Bible is not as specific about this process as we may have thought.

Evidently, God wanted to leave quite a few details to us, allowing us to adapt to different situations that might arise. With that in mind, an examination is in order regarding the New Testament examples and principles that apply to the process. Acts 6:1–6 provides us a good starting place.

> In those days when the number of disciples was increasing, the Grecian Jews among them complained against the Hebraic Jews because their widows were being overlooked in the daily distribution of food. So the Twelve gathered all the disciples together and said, "It would not be right for us to neglect the ministry of the word of God in order to wait on tables. Brothers, choose seven men from among you who are known to be full of the Spirit and wisdom. We will turn this responsibility over to them and will give our attention to prayer and the ministry of the word."
>
> This proposal pleased the whole group. They chose Stephen, a man full of faith and of the Holy Spirit; also Philip, Procorus, Nicanor, Timon, Parmenas, and Nicolas from Antioch, a convert to Judaism. They presented these men to the apostles, who prayed and laid their hands on them.

An obvious question (and need) developed in the Jerusalem church—how to provide for two types of widows within the fellowship. The responsibilities of the apostles' role made it important for them to select others to take care of this vital need. (It's not that the apostles were "too important" to serve in this way, but they had other responsibilities that they'd been especially appointed to carry out.) They decided that the task would take seven men who were spiritually qualified to serve. The church selected the seven men and presented them to the apostles, who then appointed them for the role. Acts does not detail the exact process they used in selecting these men, but it is clear that the church took part in the process at the direction of the apostles.

Acts 15:1–22 is another significant and applicable passage to our topic. Due to the length of the passage, I will include only the verses most pertinent to our consideration.

> Some men came down from Judea to Antioch and were teaching the brothers: "Unless you are circumcised, according to the custom taught by Moses, you cannot be saved." This brought Paul and Barnabas into sharp dispute and debate with them. So Paul and Barnabas were appointed, along with some other believers, to go up to Jerusalem to see the apostles and elders about this question. The church sent them on their way, and as they traveled through Phoenicia and Samaria, they told how the Gentiles

had been converted. This news made all the brothers very glad. When they came to Jerusalem, they were welcomed by the church and the apostles and elders, to whom they reported everything God had done through them.

Then some of the believers who belonged to the party of the Pharisees stood up and said, "The Gentiles must be circumcised and required to obey the law of Moses." The apostles and elders met to consider this question. . . .

Then the apostles and elders, with the whole church, decided to choose some of their own men and send them to Antioch with Paul and Barnabas. They chose Judas (called Barsabbas) and Silas, two men who were leaders among the brothers (vv. 1–6, 22).

In this case, the church needed to clarify how the Gentiles were to be treated in the kingdom. Leaders from Antioch were selected and appointed by the Antioch church to go to Jerusalem to work out the solution. Once in Jerusalem, the elders and apostles met to make those decisions. Then in verse 22, the church was brought into the process, and they helped select the men who delivered the details of the decision to the various congregations. Similar to the situation in Acts 6, the churches in Antioch and in Jerusalem helped select leaders for given roles, as decisions were made about how to meet the current needs.

The Appointment Process

In the New Testament, we find it mentioned a number of times that God appointed leaders (1 Corinthians 12:28; 1 Timothy 1:12; 2 Timothy 1:11). In all of these cases, we are not told exactly how men were involved in these appointments. Apostles appointed elders in churches that they had planted recently (Acts 14:23). Titus was given the charge to appoint elders in the towns to which he was ministering (Titus 1:5). Timothy's role in Ephesus gives us some important insights as well. The church already had elders when Timothy came to lead the church, for Paul met with these men in Acts 20 long before 1 Timothy was written. Yet Paul gave Timothy the same basic list of qualifications that Titus was given (1 Timothy 3:1–7). Although he was not told specifically to appoint elders, it is clearly implied in 1 Timothy 5:22 by the wording the "laying on of hands."

The laying on of hands denoted either the appointment of leaders or the conferring of supernatural gifts by an apostle. Compare the following two verses to see an example of each of these actions:

> Do not neglect your gift, which was given you through a prophetic message when the body of elders laid their hands on you (1 Timothy 4:14).
>
> For this reason I remind you to fan into flame the gift of God, which is in you through the laying on of my hands (2 Timothy 1:6).

It would appear most likely that Paul had laid his hands on Timothy in order to confer miraculous gifts, and the elders had laid hands on him to appoint him as an evangelist. It seems clear that the evangelists did the appointing of elders in the first-century setting, although the church was or could be involved in the process of selection.

When we first appointed elders in the Phoenix church, we tried to apply the principles found in the epistles. Here is what we did: First, we preached three sermons on the biblical role of elders, the elder's family, and the selection and appointment process. Afterwards, we handed out printed outlines of the lessons, and also posted them on the church website. Then we had a meeting, open to anyone in the congregation who wished to attend, where we answered any questions people still had about eldership.

The church members were asked to participate in the selection process in the following ways:

- We asked them to pray that God would guide the whole process.
- We asked them to study the biblical qualifications of elders.
- We invited them to suggest names of men that they believed to be biblically qualified and judged to be good shepherds of the flock. (Forms were provided for this and an end date given for their submission.)

After this, the evangelists were very involved in making the final decision about who was to be appointed an elder. The remainder of the process of selection and appointment was as follows:

- The existing congregational leadership group, comprised of the evangelists and mature nonstaff brothers, met to consider the names recommended (which took some hours).

- The men who seemed to be biblically qualified were contacted and asked if they wanted to be considered as elder candidates.
- The final group of elder candidates was selected and informed of their selection, and then the church was informed of the names.
- The members were invited to register any concerns that they may have had about any of those whose names were put forward.
- An elder training class was started immediately, with two goals in mind: to determine which of the elder candidates should be appointed first; and to provide further training for all of the candidates.
- Finally, the first group of elders was appointed by the evangelists as soon as it seemed appropriate (several months after starting the training class).

The selection and appointment of elders is a crucial yet complex topic, without easy answers. The Bible does not spell out clear answers on every question, and so we must do our best to make decisions based on sound theology and biblical interpretation. This chapter has not answered all of the questions that could be addressed—perhaps it's brought up questions you didn't know you had!—but I hope I have provided enough information to be genuinely helpful. Where we lack explicit command or explanation in the Bible, may God guide us all to make the best possible decisions with the information we have. Seeking input from mature leaders outside your own congregation is highly recommended as a part of the process. God designed the church to be overseen by mature leaders, and may he guide us as we seek out, train and appoint such men.

Chapter Eight

Evangelists: Who They Are and What They Do

Who Are Evangelists?

Biblical Mentions of the Term

Within our movement of churches, most of the biblical examination of leadership roles has been focused on the role of elder, with the study of the deacon role in second place. Much less attention has been given to studying what the Bible says about the roles of teacher and evangelist. Obviously, given the prominence and preeminence of the role of evangelist in our churches, much has been taught from a practical vantage point about their role, but the teaching has not been nearly as focused on what the Bible says about them. When we have gone to the Bible for direction about the evangelist, we have tended to assume more than we have actually established from a careful study of Scripture. Therefore, an examination or re-examination of this particular role is in order, and the same may be said of the role of teacher. (We will examine the role of teachers in chapter 10.)

I would imagine that many readers already know that the popular term "Christian" only appears in the New Testament three times. (Perhaps you remember feeling surprised when you learned that fact!) But you may be more surprised to learn that the term "evangelist" is also found only three times, in spite of our emphasis on using this term almost exclusively to describe this particular leadership role. These three occurrences are Acts 21:8, Ephesians

4:11 and 2 Timothy 4:5.

The first example refers to Philip, who began his distinguished career as a member of the Seven in Acts 6, where he was chosen to serve tables. In Acts 8, we find him functioning as an evangelist, taking the gospel to Samaria after the scattering of disciples from Jerusalem following the death of Stephen. After Philip was sent by the Spirit to preach to the eunuch, he next "appeared at Azotus and traveled about, preaching the gospel in all the towns until he reached Caesarea" (Acts 8:40). We read nothing more about him until he is mentioned in the Acts 21:8 passage, which reads: "Leaving the next day, we reached Caesarea and stayed at the house of Philip the evangelist, one of the Seven." He was still in Caesarea, and was still called an evangelist, but the text may imply that he was best remembered for being one of the Seven chosen to serve tables (or more likely to oversee this service, given the size of the Jerusalem church at the time). I would surmise that disciples of Philip's day saw more value in being a servant than in being a leader (unlike in ours!).

Certain questions arise about this evangelist. Was he still serving in this role while permanently based in Caesarea, or was he traveling to other places, with Caesarea serving only as his home base? Was he called Philip the evangelist because of past service—but no longer serving in this role? I raise these questions because most religious writers define an evangelist in the New Testament as one who traveled from place to place establishing churches. Paul would be the premier example of someone in this role, for he was the ultimate church planter. Interestingly, Paul is not called an evangelist in the Bible, nor does he refer to himself as such. He does say in 2 Timothy 1:11 that he was "appointed a herald and an apostle and a teacher." But no one would argue that he was not also an evangelist, based on the work that he did.

The second biblical mention of the term "evangelist" reads, "It was he who gave some to be apostles, some to be prophets, some to be evangelists, and some to be pastors and teachers" (Ephesians 4:11). Nothing is said here about the exact definition of the evangelist role, and the two roles mentioned prior to it are considered by most scholars to be temporary—limited to the first-century "miraculous age." However, it must be noted that the work of all types of leaders mentioned here had to do with maturing the church. Please keep that in mind as we delve more deeply into the topic.

The only biblical material that approaches a definition of the role of the evangelist is found in the three letters written to the evangelists Timothy and Titus. The third and final use of the term is found in 2 Timothy 4:5: "But you, keep your head in all situations, endure hardship, do the work of an evangelist, discharge all the duties of your ministry."

The question raised by some about this statement is what, exactly, constitutes "the work of an evangelist." Is Paul simply reminding Timothy to keep his focus on doing the work of an evangelist while performing the other duties he carried? Or do all of Paul's instructions to Timothy and Titus within the Pastoral Epistles have to do with their duties as evangelists? What cannot be questioned is that both Titus and Timothy were evangelists and that they were being directed by Paul to do a variety of things relating to maturing the church (the second part of the Great Commission). Some have argued that these other duties were in fact pastoral in nature, and were to be performed by an evangelist until other mature leaders were available to assume them.

At least some biblical evidence could be cited for that assumption. For example, Titus was directed to deal directly and strongly with divisive people (Titus 3:10). This was not a case to be run through the process of church discipline described in Matthew 18, for divisive people are smooth talkers who "deceive the minds of naive people" (Romans 16:18). Divisiveness is best handled by mature leaders—by Titus, in this case. However, as Titus was given directions about appointing elders, he was given this qualification for an elder: "He must hold firmly to the trustworthy message as it has been taught, so that he can encourage others by sound doctrine and refute those who oppose it. For there are many rebellious people, mere talkers and deceivers, especially those of the circumcision group" (Titus 1:9–10). And so we see that although Titus was to deal with divisive people, he was also to appoint other mature leaders to help in this matter. Based on what Paul said in Acts 20 to the Ephesian elders, the protection of the flock against divisive leaders was one of the primary responsibilities of elders. I think this explains why he called for the elders and not other leaders on that occasion. I am not comfortable with the rather bold assumptions some make about the Acts 20 passage, escalating the role of elder beyond what is actually said in the text. To assume that this passage "proves" that elders were the primary leaders of the church is, in my opinion, jumping to a convulsion, not a conclusion. Paul's purpose determined who he asked to meet with.

At any rate, the main issue in our discussion is whether the work outlined for Timothy and Titus was intended to be their permanent work or their temporary work as they raised up other mature leaders to assume it. That also brings up the question of whether they were to raise up these leaders to *assume* the duties of maturing the church or to *share* with them in this vital work. Said another way, was the evangelist only to work in the field of evangelism, the first part of the Great Commission, or was he also to carry out the second part of the Great Commission—that of teaching the disciples to obey (with a stronger focus on the first part)? Most teachers and writers, within and without our movement, would say that the evangelist's focus should be primarily (perhaps exclusively) on the evangelistic front. Paul, the greatest church planter in history, would be a poor example of that premise, it seems to me. He invested much time and energy helping the churches to mature, as evidenced by his own example and by what he said in passages like Acts 20 and Ephesians 4.

Regardless of where we come out on these issues, some assumptions are going to be made. I don't think the Bible is totally clear in defining just how each of the leadership roles works, or how they must interrelate in function with one another. And of course, if God left it somewhat unclear, he did so for a reason. My own assumption is that each church has to make the best use of the leaders that they have, and God allows us the latitude to do so.

In Phoenix, my home church, when we first appointed elders (five of them), they were a good deal more mature than our evangelists. Therefore, the elders were the most prominent in decision-making for the church. To be a part of what might be described as a "top leadership group," a person should be mature and stable both emotionally and spiritually. (This group in Phoenix is called a "leadership team," which helps to lessen the impact of our worldly training and subsequent tendency to think "authority" instead of "responsibility.") When these elders were appointed, I was one of them, becoming an elder/evangelist. Our other evangelists did not meet the maturity and stability requirements.

In time, the leadership team evolved into a combination of three elders, three evangelists and one teacher (me). I liked that combination better, because it provided us with broader perspectives. At present, due to my teaching ministry traveling schedule, I am no longer a part of the leadership team, but it remains a combination of elders and evangelists. Although I have spoken and written against the idea that having a leadership team comprised of different types of leaders creates a "balance of power," such a combination does form a "balance of perspectives," which is very important.

Common Claims and Assumptions

The definition and duties of an evangelist are described in one way by most religious writers, and perhaps in somewhat of a different way in Titus and 1 and 2 Timothy, which some prefer to call the "evangelistic epistles." While it is debatable whether the duties described in these books were meant to be temporary or permanent, the description provides us with the most detailed information found in the Bible. As we examine the defined duties, one thing is obvious: Titus's and Timothy's role definitely included the maturing of individual churches. Just how long an evangelist stayed in a particular church is not stated, nor can it be inferred with certainty. But his responsibilities in helping churches mature is unmistakably clear, and not unexpected, based on Ephesians 4:11–16.

Should a person who serves in one church for a number of years still be called an evangelist (and appointed as such)? The use of terminology for roles is likely more important to us in our day than it was to those who preached the gospel in the first century. In our modern world, we seem to have a harder time distinguishing between role and position, function and title. All church leadership should be described in terms of role and function, not in terms of office, position or title. Nonetheless, if we are to decide whether a "located preacher" can be rightly called an evangelist, or whether that term should be reserved only for those who plant new churches, the Bible should guide that decision.

Many people have used the writings of the early church fathers to illuminate their understanding of the evangelist role, and to show that the role vanished over time. Those early writers had some things to say that we would agree with and other things to say that we would not accept. Thus, we end up quoting what we agree with and dismissing that with which we disagree. That makes me uncomfortable, because the beauty is in the eye of the beholder, so to speak, leaving the "beholder" (us as individuals) as the authority. I would rather just stick with the Bible on this topic and all others.

It doesn't take long to depart from biblical truths, whether in the second century or the twentieth and twenty-first centuries (and our movement provides ample evidence of that truth).

We have noted that most biblical scholars believe, based on certain assumptions made from the biblical account and from early church history, that evangelists were basically church planters—traveling preachers like Paul and his friends. After they planted a church, they trained and appointed others (primarily elder/teachers or elder/preachers), who were then left to lead and mature the church. Church history does provide some supporting evidence for this scenario, but as we saw in chapter 6 of this book, the Bible itself doesn't make these assertions in nearly as clear-cut a fashion as do modern scholars and writers, at least in my opinion. Acts 20 has been used as proof positive that elders became the main leaders in established churches. That passage is important in this consideration, but using it to establish a *pattern* is quite a stretch.

In an effort not to be overly one-sided, I want to include at least a summary of what another teacher wrote about this subject. In Andy Fleming's *New Testament Paradigm of Ministry and Ministry Roles*,[1] he wrote the following regarding roles in the first-century church, which is similar to what other teachers have written:

> It would seem that in a similar way to how spiritual gifts (*charismata*) were initially manifested miraculously for the purpose of modeling "speaking and serving" (*diakonia*) to build up the church, these different ministry roles listed in Ephesians 4:11 were not only given to establish the church universally but also given as gifts by Christ to model "service" (*diakonia*) and thereby set the standard for the training up and eventual appointment of local elders-overseers and deacons. It would also seem to follow that parallel to the cessation of partial prophecy, partial knowledge and tongues "when the perfection comes" (1 Corinthians 13:9–10), the immediate need for these specific roles (apostles, prophets, evangelists, shepherd-teachers) would also pass as the local churches (body of Christ) reached "unity in the faith and in the knowledge of the Son of God, and become mature, attaining to the whole measure of the fullness of Christ" (Ephesians 4:13). Therefore, a mature congregation led by capable elders/overseers and served by qualified deacons would be fully able to fulfill God's plan as described in the next three verses of Ephesians 4.

So what are we to make of these observations by respected scholars inside and outside our movement? For starters, that the term "evangelist" can be most accurately applied to church planters. Nearly all conservative churches, including those within the Restoration Movement (the Christian Church and Church of Christ), use the term in that way and in that way only. Those in Restoration churches call their local preachers either "preachers" or "ministers" almost exclusively, and evangelical churches use these terms plus the term "pastor" (we've already established that biblically, "pastor" is another word describing an elder). Have we appointed evangelists in our movement in a way that harmonizes with this definition of evangelists as church planters? Certainly. Have we also appointed evangelists in our movement in a way that doesn't align with this definition? Again, the answer is yes. However, that doesn't provide the total picture, in my mind.

With those thoughts in mind, let's examine more specifically the role of the evangelist as described in the Bible.

What Do Evangelists Do?

Based on 1 and 2 Timothy and Titus

It is relatively simple to deal with the qualifications and duties of elders, because we have two distinctive lists of qualifications. Additionally, we can turn to many other passages that mention the elders specifically. This is not the case with evangelists. There are no similar lists of qualifications, and as stated in the introduction to this chapter, the term itself is found only three times. Even in those three cases, the evangelist's work is left largely undefined. However, in looking at 1 and 2 Timothy and Titus, the work of these evangelists is described in some detail. In the following section, I will list each of the passages from these three letters defining the duties of evangelists, with the particular duty summarized in one sentence. I strongly suggest reading each of the references in your Bible as you proceed.

> 1 Timothy 1:3–4: Command people teaching false doctrines to stop.
>
> 1 Timothy 1:18–19: Follow Paul's instructions in order to keep faith and a good conscience, unlike those who have shipwrecked their faith.
>
> 1 Timothy 2:1–2: Follow Paul's urging regarding the content and direction of prayers.

1 Timothy 2:8–15: Instructions for both men and women in their worship and life roles.

1 Timothy 3:1–15: Instructions regarding the qualifications of elders, deacons and wives.

1 Timothy 4:1–7: Point out to the brothers the truth, as contrasted to the Gnostic teachings of people who are following demons, and train yourself to be godly.

1 Timothy 4:11–16: Command, teach, set an example in life and doctrine, and devote yourself to public reading of Scripture and to preaching and teaching.

1 Timothy 5:1–2: How to treat older men and women, and younger men and women in righteous ways.

1 Timothy 5:3–16: How widows should be cared for by their family and by the church.

1 Timothy 5:17–22: How to treat elders of the church, in both good and challenging circumstances.

1 Timothy 6:11–16: Flee from materialism and pursue righteous living, fighting the good fight of faith.

1 Timothy 6:17–19: Command the rich how to view and use their money for God.

1 Timothy 6:20–21: Guard the gospel and avoid godless talk and false teachings.

2 Timothy 1:6–8: Fan into flame God's gift in order to avoid timidity and fear and to embrace the gospel and the suffering that goes with it.

2 Timothy 1:13–14: Keep the pattern of sound teaching as heard from Paul, and guard that with which you have been entrusted, with the help of the Holy Spirit.

2 Timothy 2:1–7: Be strong in grace, and train reliable men to teach others, while remaining focused on the task and working hard at it.

2 Timothy 2:8–9: Remember Christ as the foundation of the gospel.

2 Timothy 2:14–16: Remind and warn the people about teaching false doctrines and arguing, presenting yourself as one who correctly handles the word of truth.

> 2 Timothy 2:22–26: Flee the sins of youth and pursue righteous living, while avoiding arguments and quarrels by responding to critics righteously and calmly.
>
> 2 Timothy 3:14–15: Continue in the truths of the Scripture learned at a young age, for they lead to salvation through faith in Christ.
>
> 2 Timothy 4:1–5: Preach the Word; correct, rebuke and encourage, with patience and careful teaching, for men will turn away from the truth to embrace myths.
>
> Titus 1:5–9: Straighten out what is unfinished and appoint elders in every town.
>
> Titus 1:13–14: Rebuke those who espouse false doctrines, especially Jewish myths.
>
> Titus 2:1–6: Teach sound doctrine; teach older men and women and young men how to live righteous lives.
>
> Titus 2:7–8: Set an example and teach with integrity and seriousness.
>
> Titus 2:9–10: Teach slaves how to respond to their masters, thus making the teaching about God attractive.
>
> Titus 2:15–3:2: Teach, encourage and rebuke with all authority, and remind the people how to respond righteously toward authorities and all men.
>
> Titus 3:8: Stress how believers are to devote themselves to doing good.
>
> Titus 3:9–11: Avoid Jewish controversies and deal strongly with people who are divisive.

Concluding Thoughts Regarding These Passages

As I stated earlier, these two men we call evangelists had clearly defined responsibilities to help churches mature. Little or nothing is said about them leading an evangelistic charge, which we will say more about in the next section. The letters to these two first-century evangelists focused on how to build up a congregation in the right way. As I also stated previously, modern Christians are likely more concerned about terminology for our leaders, particularly our preachers, than were the leaders in the early church. However, Paul did not hesitate to refer to overseers (elders) and deacons by these descriptive terms (Philippians 1:1). We don't need to avoid the use of specific terminology, whether it is found in the Bible or developed later, as long as we are thinking about function and role instead of position and title. Jesus said to call no man "teacher" (Matthew 23:10), and yet he placed "teachers" within the church (Ephesians 4:11). Obviously, he is talking about the wrong and right use of terminology—the wrong was using terminology to exalt mere men into positions with titles; the right was using that same terminology to describe function and role.

Let's Get Practical!

Based on the Need for a Prophetic Voice

If we were to adopt the conclusions of many scholars, and have elders or elder/teachers lead mature churches, what results would likely ensue? Depending on the personality of the elders or teachers, it is possible that the church could become less visionary and evangelistic. The church needs a prophetic voice to lead it—the kind of voice that an evangelist is usually best equipped to provide. Whatever you call the person who most often occupies the pulpit, his role must include helping the church to bring others to Christ, however that is best accomplished. Without question, he has to be an effective speaker and good motivator. The average elder is simply not equipped to lead large churches. However, if an elder is also an evangelist type, capable of leading the charge, then that is another matter.

One of the puzzling things in the New Testament is that it never mentions any leader directly motivating disciples to share their faith with the lost. However, the early Christians spread the gospel in a way that has not been duplicated since their generation. Two possible scenarios might explain this absence. One, the church was so healthy and happy that they did it naturally. That's a nice thought, but I have never seen a church (even the happiest and healthiest) where the majority of the members were automatically and consistently self-motivated to share their faith. The second scenario is that the greatest two commands in Matthew 22:36–40 and the Great Commission in Matthew 28:18–20 were so etched into the DNA of the early church that the New Testament writers presupposed that all Christians knew that this was an expected emphasis by the church leaders.

Maybe there are other plausible explanations for the absence of direct teaching to evangelize, but these seem the most likely to me. At this juncture, let me ask you a question: Do you stay motivated to share your faith without some reminders from others, and perhaps even some accountability? I don't. I wish I could say otherwise, but I can't. And I don't think I am an unspiritual, uncaring disciple, nor do I think that I am much different from most disciples. I really want to do the things that Jesus would do if he were back on earth, and seeking and saving the lost was at the top of his agenda when he was here in the flesh.

So which of the two alternatives mentioned here do you think is most likely? Could it not have been both in some combination? When I am feeling most fulfilled as a disciple, sharing comes easily. But I also deeply appreciate the challenges to evangelize, given in a spiritual manner. As stated earlier in the book, I am a "both/and" man. Happy disciples share more naturally about finding "the pearl of great price" (Matthew 13:44–46), but being motivated and given direction by leaders adds to the effectiveness.

How does all this apply to evangelists? I think quite a lot. The inspired writers focused on the way in which the church matured into a loving family of God, for that was the true foundation through which effective evangelism could take place (consider John 13:34–35). With this in mind, there can be no doubt that any evangelist saw evangelism as one of his foremost duties, if not his primary emphasis.

I have learned many important lessons in the writing of this material and through past discussions on the subject. One such lesson is that all of us in the church need some clear teaching about what evangelists are to do in our congregations. Evangelists need to lead an evangelistic charge, and the elders and other shepherd types need to counsel and strengthen the flock. Obviously there will always be some overlap in these roles, but we cannot afford to be *fuzzy* in the distinctions that should exist in this area. My view of how elders and staff should work together has always been that the elders would handle the problematic situations in the church, thus freeing up the evangelists to lead the charge in seeking and saving the lost. That distinction has not always been followed well, but it is time to make a change and make it clear to the church so that their expectations of the evangelists are correct. Too many evangelists have become mainly shepherds and administrators, but they need to regain their focus and their prophetic voice.

Evangelists are the ones whose gifts most closely align with having a prophetic voice, and I have not seen any church become what the New Testament says it should be without the leadership of someone who has such a voice. I'm speaking here of someone with deep convictions who has the courage of those convictions to fearlessly call us to accept the God-inspired challenges given in his word. Maybe it is only my pragmatism speaking here, but I think churches must have leaders who exhibit those qualities that we most naturally associate with the evangelist role. Cannot we have a both/and approach in defining evangelists? Can we not define them as church-builders who plant churches *and* who continue to lead churches (churches that continue planting yet more churches, or planting ministry groups in new parts of their area)? That would be my vote, since that is all that I have seen to work effectively. While I would encourage us to be less traditional in our terminology for leadership roles, I want to be in a congregation where the man in the pulpit has a prophetic voice and the motivational ability to help me stay focused on both *serving* people and *saving* people.

Based on Qualifications and Duties of Ministry Staff

My ministry life over the past two decades has been spent serving in several roles: elder, evangelist and teacher. As one given the responsibility of discipling other staff members (always younger than me!), I have given a lot of thought to what the qualifications and responsibilities of the staff should be, in very practical terms. Of course, most of these staff persons were recognized as evangelists, although some of them were still more in the training stage. So, asking and answering the following questions will provide a path for examining these practical areas. What qualities should we seek in our ministry staff people? What should leaders in these roles bring to the table? The qualities that follow are not listed in any particular order of importance, but they are all significant.

It begins with a *desire* to be in the ministry, as is required of those desiring to become elders in 1 Timothy 3:1. I have no doubt that virtually all who go on staff do so originally out of a genuine desire to lead in a full-time capacity. If that desire wanes sufficiently for whatever reasons, evangelists become clergymen. Their fireplace is still there, but the fires have gone out. They have lost their zeal to evangelize and to lead others to evangelize. When duty replaces desire, such leaders qualify for the designation of "hired hands" (John 10:12). In such cases, we must do all that we can to help the desire to be rekindled, but if the efforts to do so are unsuccessful, the staff person should be terminated. In churches that employ husband and wife teams, as we do in Phoenix, this desire has to be present on the part of both husband and wife. The Bible doesn't demand that we have both men and women on staff, but it allows that choice, and I personally wouldn't want it any other way. Half or more of the members of every church are women, and for many reasons, women should be the ones working most closely with other women. Being on the church's supported staff allows them the time to devote themselves to leading the other women.

I originally thought about this next quality when describing what type of person should be on the top leadership team of a church. However, it is applicable to any church-supported staff person, although they may need help and time to arrive at this level of maturity. The quality of which I speak is a compound: spiritual and emotional stability and maturity. Each of these words is important. Being spiritually stable is a part of becoming spiritually mature. The same may be said of being emotionally stable and mature. Real leaders are steadfast and unafraid in the midst of the storms of leadership. They cannot be "up, down and all around." Those of us who are more emotional will have more challenges in these areas, to be sure, but it is all about possessing self-control—a fruit of the Spirit (Galatians 5:23). I have seen a number of men and women on the ministry staff of churches that lacked such self-control, but I have never seen any of them remain on staff unless they became much more mature and stable.

Next, those on staff must be team players. They have to consistently be open and honest with all other leaders, yet flexible in the decision-making process. They must also be good examples to the believers, which include at least the following ways:

- An overall high level of spirituality.
- A strong, observable work ethic.
- Genuine love for people, shown by mixing and mingling with lots of people in lots of different settings.
- Strong family dynamics within their own family—in both marriage and parenting.

- Evangelistic in heart and in practice.
- Proficient in administration and organization.
- Educated sufficiently in Bible, and in general (which makes them relatable to different kinds of people).
- Developed people skills—they know how to build relationships, resolve issues between people, and generally just "pull people in" relationally.
- A "gift" of leadership, which shows up in the following ways:
  - Good communicator in public and in private—direct enough and sensitive enough to be both understood and trusted.
  - Strength of character and personality—their strength of convictions must clearly outweigh any tendencies to be sentimental, be a people-pleaser, or avoid conflict.
  - Motivational and inspirational—they "connect" when they are speaking to people individually and collectively. They are easy to listen to and can hold the attention of an audience well.
  - They motivate by their own "life force," which is sensed in many ways by those whom they lead.
  - They must noticeably affect the atmosphere of any group they are in, making it more positive and more exciting.

This list is not meant to completely describe the staff person's qualities and responsibilities, but it does provide us with at least a good summary. It must be noted that no ministry person has the whole package and will have varying degrees of strength and ability in the different areas. However, some of these qualities are more vital than others and cannot vary as much as other qualities might. One thing is certain: In our present climate, deficiencies and weaknesses will be evaluated more critically by the average member than in the past. (So pick your weaknesses well!)

In addition to the criteria for ministry staff members (present or future), the following questions are also relevant as we make decisions about hiring and retaining staff. I list these considerations in light of the current atmosphere produced by our movement's recent history. Further, the answers to these three questions are absolutely essential in considering whether a staff person can remain in a specific role after his church or ministry group has undergone any type of serious upheaval. (Incidentally, human nature being what it is, we likely have not undergone our last upheaval.)

1. Do they really "get it" in terms of what the leadership sins of our past system were, how they personally practiced them, and how these systemic sins affected the average member?
2. Given who they are, can they make the changes needed in their leadership style and approach? In other words, how strong is their "default button"?
3. Finally, will the people whom they led in the past still follow their leadership, or is the damage too deep for the person to continue in the same role? Stated another way, do people have enough confidence in the leader to enable them to remain at the helm of the ship?

Final Observations

We began the chapter by studying the biblical mentions of the term "evangelist." We then progressed to a brief examination of common claims and assumptions, which contained more debatable conclusions (no matter how dogmatically they are stated by some). Then we proceeded to consider the specific duties of two evangelists in the Bible as described in the three letters written to them. That material is biblically based and thus certain in application, regardless of the time frame of the service rendered. From that point, we entered the world of pragmatism and common sense, first by considering the practical implications of the type of leaders needed to produce a healthy and growing church. Finally, we examined the character, qualifications and responsibilities of churches' paid ministry staff. Excepting the section containing "common claims and assumptions," the remainder of our study rests on the solid ground of biblical evidence or on time-proven pragmatic observations based on common sense and experience.

The most uncertain aspects of the study are to me twofold: First, the issue of whether evangelists have a one-dimensional role as church planters, or a two-dimensional role that involves either planting or staying (or doing both in the course of their careers). Second, I have reservations about our use of terminology. Just as we seem to be stuck on using the term "elder" for those who could just as accurately be called "shepherd" or "overseer," so we are also stuck on the term "evangelist" for those who could just as accurately be called "preacher" or "minister." The exclusive use of the term "evangelist" is much more questionable than using the term "elder" exclusively, since the definition of the evangelist's role is less certain. I don't think what we are doing is wrong, but varying our terminology for both elders and evangelists would be a good idea, and would certainly help us to view them as roles and functions rather than as offices and titles. It could also help lessen the temptation to have questionable motives in desiring those roles. For those reasons, I strongly recommend embracing variations in terminology for both elders and evangelists.

Regardless of what we have called uncertain aspects of the evangelist's role, what is certain is that they are sorely needed, both biblically and practically. Like any other role, our view and practice of this one can be faulty (and has been at times). However, I would never want to be a part of a congregation that was without a strong evangelist (by whatever term) who was essentially the face and the voice of the leadership for the church. He serves in one role of leadership, and is a part of a team of leaders serving in other roles alongside him, but his role is essential. I love to preach, but I love to be preached to, and I will always need it. May God bless our evangelists to keep their prophetic edge as they call us all higher for him!

End Notes:

1. For full article, access http://www.redaxo.european-bible-school.org/files/shifting_paradigm.pdf)

Chapter Nine

The Appointment of Evangelists and Others

Our Historical Background: The Good and the Questionable

The appointment of evangelists in the brief history of the International Church of Christ has been a well-established tradition. And yet I have never heard a biblical lesson on the subject of the appointment process or read any article in which our practice was examined carefully from the Bible. Although I am comfortable with much of what we have done in this realm, I am uncomfortable with other aspects of it. Since I am not aware of a specific study having been done on the topic, and since the event can be accompanied by certain attitudes that are in fact unbiblical, it is appropriate that we devote a chapter to an examination of the appointment process.

A historical background is important to our understanding of how we arrived at our common practices in appointing evangelists. Although we have appointed some to be elders or to serve in other roles, from our earliest days as a movement, most of our focus has been on appointing evangelists. From my early experiences (dating back to the mid-1980s), here are my perspectives regarding our practices. Men who went on the ministry staff of churches began in the role usually designated "intern," which was seen as an early training phase of ministry. As time passed and they gained experience, they were either appointed as evangelists, or at the least, no longer called interns. Men who remained in the ministry without being appointed evangelists usually felt like they somehow didn't measure up to others who had been appointed. This led to a number of awkward situations.

Therefore, the goal of all men on staff was to be appointed as an evangelist, because it signaled a man's maturity in ministry, and perhaps more importantly to some, also showed him to be a success in the eyes of his peers and of those who had trained him or were training him in ministry. This moment was in a real sense a reward for achievement, which in my experience was often measured in terms of being able to "grow" his ministry—or said another way, to "crank" baptisms. Although our leadership structure had elements of corporate America and the military model mixed in with the biblical model, the military model too often predominated. (See chapter 4 for a review of these terms.) Therefore, being appointed as an evangelist was similar to a soldier graduating from Officer's Training School and being promoted to the level of an officer. (I have even heard people describe the appointment approvingly in exactly that way.) For people prompted by a fair amount of worldly ambition, appointment became a prized accomplishment, and it was therefore used as a motivation by those with the authority to appoint. Surely there were many men appointed evangelist who rose above such base motivations, but I'd say that this observation applied to too many situations, particularly based on what I saw during my earliest days in Boston.

A different, and higher, level of motivation also came into play: namely, the belief that being appointed an evangelist somehow garnered more power from the Holy Spirit to lead, and that church members would be more trusting and respectful of a "fully trained" evangelist, and therefore more likely to follow (and be effective and fruitful). I observed many appointments during my sixteen years in Boston, and would (regretfully) judge that a fair number of those men had questionable aspects mixed into their motivation (and I was one of those men, to be perfectly candid). I'm sure a number of men were appointed whose motivations remained untainted by selfish ambition, perhaps especially those who were sent out to plant churches. The church planters were often younger and less experienced than other men who had served on staff longer, and some of these older men were never officially appointed. As I said earlier, awkwardness was never absent in this arena.

Certainly there were exceptions to the worldly aspects of the atmosphere I have described, and some people (and churches) rose nobly above these common tendencies, but those of us who were in the middle of it all cannot dismiss the unsavory aspects of the practice. As with many practices within our movement in the past, good *things* were done in wrong *ways*, and the wrong ways most often involved motivation. At this present phase of our history, the challenge is to distinguish between wrong things and wrong ways. We cannot afford to quit doing right things out of fear of making mistakes or out of confusion over the difference between wrong things and wrong ways.

With this background in mind, the purpose of this chapter is to examine afresh the practice of appointing evangelists (and other leaders). My conclusion, as you will see in reading this chapter, is that while I believe that our common practice is *allowable* biblically, I do not believe the biblical evidence clearly supports our former (or current) practice, and it certainly doesn't *mandate* it. In other words, appointment is something that can be done even if the Bible is not clear about aspects of either the role or the appointment process. However, purposes and motivation must be clearly spiritual and not worldly. It is my concerns on those points that prompt the writing of this chapter. With this introduction in mind, let's consider some of the key areas of the subject.

The Biblical Mentions of Evangelists

To reiterate, the Bible mentions evangelists three times: Acts 21:8, Ephesians 4:11, and 2 Timothy 4:5. In the first of these, Philip is called an evangelist, one who began his distinguished career as a member of the Seven in Acts 6, chosen to serve tables. The apostles appointed him for this role. The Bible does not say whether he was later officially appointed as an evangelist. He may simply have been called an evangelist by virtue of his evangelizing. In the Ephesians passage, it says that Christ "gave" some to these various roles. The NIV in Ephesians 1:22 translates the same Greek word (*didomi*) "appointed." It reads: "And God placed all things under his feet and appointed him to be head over everything for the church." The Greek term *didomi* means simply "to give." It is found hundreds of times in the New Testament and translated by a dozen or more common words—none of them suggesting a technical appointment process. In 2 Timothy 4, Timothy is simply told to do the work of an evangelist. Both of the letters to Timothy and to Titus are very descriptive of their work, but not much is said about some aspects of the role or about the appointment process itself.

The Terminology Related to Appointments

If the term *evangelist* is only used in the three passages examined briefly above, what can we learn from terms relating to appointments in the New Testament? I am listing here some key passages that use some form of the word *appoint*, and I have emphasized the word in each example. You will see that many different terms were used interchangeably, and whether they were used to describe some "official" type of appointment can be determined only by the context itself.

> He *appointed* twelve—designating them apostles—that they might be with him and that he might send them out to preach (Mark 3:14).

Here the word *appointed* comes from the Greek term *poieō*, which means "to make" or "do," and is translated into about thirty words in the NASB, but is only used in our sense of "appoint" only this one time. It is found many times in the New Testament and is not a technical term.

> After this the Lord *appointed* seventy-two others and sent them two by two ahead of him to every town and place where he was about to go (Luke 10:1).

The Greek term translated "appointed" here is *anadeiknumi*, and this term is only found one more time in the New Testament—in Acts 1:24, where it is translated *chosen*.

> Then they prayed, "Lord, you know everyone's heart. Show us which of these two you have *chosen*" (Acts 1:24).

> "You did not choose me, but I chose you and *appointed* you to go and bear fruit—fruit that will last. Then the Father will give you whatever you ask in my name" (John 15:16).

> And in the church God has *appointed* first of all apostles, second prophets, third teachers, then workers of miracles, also those having gifts of healing, those able to help others, those with gifts of administration, and those speaking in different kinds of

tongues (1 Corinthians 12:28).

For God did not *appoint* us to suffer wrath but to receive salvation through our Lord Jesus Christ (1 Thessalonians 5:9).

I thank Christ Jesus our Lord, who has given me strength, that he considered me faithful, *appointing* me to his service (1 Timothy 1:12).

And for this purpose I was *appointed* a herald and an apostle—I am telling the truth, I am not lying—and a teacher of the true faith to the Gentiles (1 Timothy 2:7).

And of this gospel I was *appointed* a herald and an apostle and a teacher (2 Timothy 1:11).

... but in these last days he has spoken to us by his Son, whom he *appointed* heir of all things, and through whom he made the universe (Hebrews 1:2).

These seven verses use the Greek term *tithemi*, which is translated as "appoint" or "appointed," and its most basic meaning is to "place," "lay," or "set." In the NASB, the word is translated with more than thirty different terms or brief phrases.

... and that he may send the Christ, who has been *appointed* for you—even Jesus (Acts 3:20).

Then he said: "The God of our fathers has *chosen* you to know his will and to see the Righteous One and to hear words from his mouth" (Acts 22:14).

"Now get up and stand on your feet. I have appeared to you to *appoint* you as a servant and as a witness of what you have seen of me and what I will show you" (Acts 26:16).

These three verses use the Greek term *procheirizō*, which is translated as "appoint" or "chosen," and its most basic meaning is "to determine." In the NASB, the word is translated "appoint" or "appointed" all three times.

Paul and Barnabas *appointed* elders for them in each church and, with prayer and fasting, committed them to the Lord, in whom they had put their trust (Acts 14:23).

> What is more, he was chosen by the churches to accompany us as we carry the offering, which we administer in order to honor the Lord himself and to show our eagerness to help (2 Corinthians 8:19).

In these two verse, *cheirotoneō* is the Greek term translated "appointed," and it is found only in these two passages.

> This brought Paul and Barnabas into sharp dispute and debate with them. So Paul and Barnabas were *appointed*, along with some other believers, to go up to Jerusalem to see the apostles and elders about this question (Acts 15:2).

In Acts 15:2, the Greek term translated appointed is from the word *tassō* and means "to draw up in order," or "to arrange." In the NASB, it is translated in the following ways (with the number of times noted): appointed (2), designated (1), determined (1), devoted (1), established (1), set (1).

> The reason I left you in Crete was that you might straighten out what was left unfinished and *appoint* elders in every town, as I directed you (Titus 1:5).

> Every high priest is *appointed* to offer both gifts and sacrifices, and so it was necessary for this one also to have something to offer (Hebrews 8:3).

In these two passages, the Greek term translated "appoint," "appoints," and "appointed" is *kathistemi* and means "to set in order" or "appoint." In the NASB, it is translated by nine different terms.

After examining all of these passages, including those that specifically say that some were appointed to various roles, how was the appointing done? That leads to a few passages that may shed light on the subject in terms of what was at least occasionally done. When people were chosen for special roles, they were sometimes sent out to fulfill those roles in a way that might be described as ceremonial—done with a ceremony. Some would say that simply asking someone to serve in a role and then publicly announcing it would be equivalent to appointing the person. It would be difficult to argue that such a process would not be an appointment. Appointments can be carried out that way, and indeed they often are, particularly when naming people to serve in certain ways (for example, as children's ministry leaders or youth leaders or ushering coordinators). But for examples of a more ceremonial approach, see the following passages:

Appointments and Ceremonies

> They presented these men to the apostles, who prayed and laid their hands on them (Acts 6:6).
>
> When Simon saw that the Spirit was given at the laying on of the apostles' hands, he offered them money (Acts 8:18).
>
> In the church at Antioch there were prophets and teachers: Barnabas, Simeon called Niger, Lucius of Cyrene, Manaen (who had been brought up with Herod the tetrarch) and Saul. While they were worshiping the Lord and fasting, the Holy Spirit said, "Set apart for me Barnabas and Saul for the work to which I have called them." So after they had fasted and prayed, they placed their hands on them and sent them off (Acts 13:1–3).
>
> Do not neglect your gift, which was given you through a prophetic message when the body of elders laid their hands on you (1 Timothy 4:14).
>
> Do not be hasty in the laying on of hands, and do not share in the sins of others. Keep yourself pure (1 Timothy 5:22).
>
> For this reason I remind you to fan into flame the gift of God, which is in you through the laying on of my hands (2 Timothy 1:6).

What can be learned from these passages? In Acts 6:6, the Seven were commissioned by the apostles to do the work (of serving tables) with prayer and the laying on of hands. At least Stephen and Philip received miraculous powers from this laying on of the apostles' hands, given their later roles as prophets or evangelists, although the laying on of hands to confer such powers could have occurred at a different time. This passage is often viewed as the first example of "deacons" (servants) being appointed in the New Testament. It was certainly a process of selection by the church and a recognition that these men had been so chosen by their fellow members in the Jerusalem church.

In Acts 8:14, the apostles came to Samaria from Jerusalem for the purpose of laying on hands to impart the miraculous gifts of the Spirit. Philip had these gifts himself, but evidently could not pass them on to other believers. Only the apostles could do that. This doesn't appear to be any type of appointment to a role, but a procedure wherein people received the miraculous gifts that were needed in the early church before written New Testament scripture was available to guide the church.

In Acts 13:1–3, Barnabas and Saul (Paul) were first mentioned as prophets and/or teachers, and then sent off to do mission work by other leaders with prayer, fasting and the laying on of hands. Certainly this was an appointing or commissioning to fulfill a role, but it was not an appointment that made them something that they were not already. This type of event was a common way of commissioning people for a specific task or assignment.

In 1 Timothy 4:14, we learn that Timothy had the elders lay hands on him, and in 2 Timothy 1:6, we learn that he also had Paul's hands laid on him. It is most likely that Paul laid hands on Timothy in order to confer spiritual gifts upon him (especially prophecy), and the elders had most likely commissioned Timothy to fulfill a certain role or task. Both things appear to have been done at the same time, in a single event or ceremony. This is the closest thing to an evangelist appointment process that we find in the New Testament, and it may be that, but the Bible doesn't explicitly state this. In our movement, evangelists have nearly always appointed evangelists, a precedent that affords another example of how elders have not been viewed and used in some of the ways we see in Scripture—at least perhaps until more recent times.

In context, 1 Timothy 5:22 is found in a section addressing elders, so Paul is telling Timothy not to be hasty in appointing elders. Laying hands on them is another way of referring to their appointment. Unless the combination of 1 Timothy 4:14 and 2 Timothy 1:6 is the example of how an evangelist is to be appointed, we have no such example biblically. Regarding leadership roles generally, Ephesians 4:11 says that Christ appoints them. How he uses men in that process is not as clear. We have no precise example showing us how prophets were appointed, or even if they were *officially* appointed. (Interestingly, in Jeremiah 1:5, Jeremiah was appointed by God to be a prophet to the nations while still in his mother's womb, and something similar is said of Paul in Galatians 1:15–17.)

In a passage remarkably reminiscent of Ephesians 4:11, we read:

> And in the church God has appointed first of all apostles, second prophets, third teachers, then workers of miracles, also those having gifts of healing, those able to help others, those with gifts of administration, and those speaking in different kinds of tongues (1 Corinthians 12:28).

This could mean simply that Jesus appointed leaders in the sense of providing those leadership roles for the church. The apostles were appointed by Jesus, but the process is not described at all. We have no example of a teacher being appointed, so again we have nothing definite about the process. The same may be said about other roles in the list, including administrators. Are administrators to be appointed in a ceremony, or is announcing that they now hold that role equivalent to an appointment?

The most definite roles to which people were appointed in a ceremony were elder and deacon, if Acts 6 is taken as an example of a deacon appointment. Titus was told to appoint elders in every church in Crete, and Timothy was in essence told to do the same. Both evangelists were given qualifications for elders, and Timothy was given qualifications for deacons. While the letters to these two men provided them with many directions as evangelists, there were no instructions about appointing other evangelists. This seems clearly different than what was said about appointing elders and deacons. I don't believe that this means that it is wrong to appoint evangelists—or administrators, or leaders of children's ministry, or a whole host of other roles in the church, whether the roles are mentioned or not in Scripture. It just needs to be noted that no biblical injunction can be found that *demands* it. And so I say again that while appointment of evangelists is biblically allowable, it is not biblically mandated; however, it seems that appointments of elders and deacons are mandated.

What Are the Potential Positives and Negatives of Appointments?

Appointments, when done correctly, involve the simple commission to serve and the recognition that a person will be fulfilling a given role of service. Giving honor to those whom honor is due is a godly thing, especially when servants are honored for serving. It is encouraging to recognize those who have served or are going to serve in a needed way. Support, respect and appreciation are helpful to all who serve, whether they fill an "up front" role or work behind the scenes. I personally believe that those who serve behind the scenes may give God the most joy, and I say that as an "up front" person myself. But I too need to be appreciated and loved as I try to serve God by serving others. For these reasons, I am fine with the practice of appointing or recognizing servants of all types. And excepting my minor concern about our overemphasis on the term *evangelist*, I think it is fine to appoint evangelists (or ministers or preachers), in recognition that they have attained a certain amount of maturity in that role or are being commissioned to serve in that way. I would just caution us to look out for attitudes or procedures that cultivate mixed motivations in those being appointed (or desiring to be appointed). We must take very seriously what Jesus said in passages like Matthew 20 and Matthew 23.

I recently heard someone say that our leadership culture in the past produced something like a "celebrity status" for leaders. In many cases, it reminded me of the military model, for who can deny that rank had its privileges? Far too often, the higher up in the leadership hierarchy one rose, the more he was served by those under him. Somehow the meaning of being a leader got pretty twisted, and we leaders cannot allow that to happen again. Had we written a history book about ourselves some years back, entire chapters would have been devoted to those in the higher echelons of leadership, complete with glowing reports of their successes, and little or nothing mentioned of their defeats. By sharp contrast, when God wrote the history books of his people and their leaders, in both the Old Testament and New Testament, he described their weaknesses and failures vividly. Most of the top leaders (apostles) in the book of Acts received far less notice than Dorcas, the little widow who wove her love for people into the garments she sewed for them (Acts 9:36–42).

It is a fine thing to desire to serve as a leader. Spiritual ambition is a good thing. But keeping ambition spiritual and not allowing it to become worldly is not an easy endeavor. Even a casual reading of James 3:13–16 provides a sobering wake-up call on this topic. In my past church affiliation, I saw people leave our church because they were passed over when deacons or elders were appointed. Their reaction proved clearly that their being passed over was a really good decision—their ambition was for a title and recognition, not for being a humble servant. One of my favorite leaders I've ever known was George Havins, who has now graduated to glory. He served as an elder when I was the "lead evangelist" in San Diego years ago, but he stepped down from that role in an official capacity for the last years of his life. Yet he never missed a beat. Whether he was called an elder or not, he shepherded people wonderfully, and he served with all of his heart. He didn't care if he was noticed by men or only by God. If Hebrews 6:10 ever applied to anyone, it applied to George and his good wife Cleo: "God is not unjust; he will not forget your work and the love you have shown him as you have helped his people and continue to help them." George and Cleo will always be my heroes. I just want to imitate them in their humility and total lack of worldly ambition and pride. And I want to help all leaders, on staff and not on staff, to be like them.

As I have written this material, I realize (as you well may) that I have some baggage from the early experiences in my past. I don't want to allow my experiences with right things done wrong ways to drive my theology. At the same time, I don't want any traditions to drive it either. Bad theology, however it is derived, is still bad theology. I want to use my role and experiences and influence to help others think and study, even if they end up differing with me. On this subject of evangelists and evangelist appointments, I have vocalized some opinions in the past, without providing an adequate explanation for my opinions and conclusions. Therefore, I believe I owe it to those whom I love and work with to share this explanation. This chapter is not intended to be the last word on the subject, but at least it provides a beginning point for more in-depth study and the discussion I hope it will engender.

To summarize my view: I can with clear conscience appoint or commission people to roles, as long as we understand biblically what those roles involve, and also have the right purposes and motivations for such appointments. The issue of the heart is the issue, and the heart of the issue is the heart—in all things spiritual. And JOY is the means of keeping the heart in the right place: Jesus first, Others second, and Yourself last.

Any current appointment process would in some places best include an explanation to the church of what our past appointment practices have been, and why those practices have been somewhat sidelined in recent years during an unsettled state of the church. We have some mature leaders who are serving admirably in their roles and who are already evangelists in the eyes of those whom they lead—even though they haven't been officially appointed. They are doing the work, and doing it well. Should we now "double back" and appoint them officially? We could, or we could just recognize them for what they obviously have already become. In such cases, I would suggest asking them what they want to have done. I know some men who feel like the fact that they have been asked to fill the role (and have effectively carried it out) is equivalent to their having been appointed, so they would not opt for a ceremony. Others may want a more public ceremony, which is fine as well, as long as their motivations for wanting it are spiritually based. Some biblical teaching should precede or accompany our appointments, especially in churches where evangelist appointments have not occurred for a long time. For sure, we need to clarify for the church what the role of the evangelists is and what their focus is supposed to be, in order to correct some common misconceptions of the roles of ministry staff. All in all, if we can accomplish these things through teaching about appointments and roles, future appointments should lead to some very important victories for us all.

Are Appointments Necessary?

One final issue needs to be addressed, as suggested by the heading. Are appointments (however they are done, with or without a ceremony) *necessary*? Some leaders feel that their spiritual gifts alone make them an evangelist, elder or teacher. In such instances, they see any type of appointment as unnecessary, believing that God has appointed them by virtue of giving them certain gifts. I remember a number of former ministry staff men banding together in a group and giving themselves a very noble-sounding name. One of their oft-repeated assertions was, "Once an evangelist, always an evangelist." You can probably guess what the meetings of that particular group were like and what the end result of the group was. Right—sad, very sad.

If we start with the understanding that serving as an elder, evangelist or teacher is a matter of role and function, answering the question posed in the heading is far easier. I have been appointed as an elder in two places: Boston and Phoenix. When I left Boston, I ceased to be an elder because I was no longer serving in that role. It wasn't a case of "Once an elder, always an elder." When I got off the ministry staff in Phoenix and began traveling so much as a teacher,

I resigned as an elder, because I no longer had the time to shepherd the people as an elder must. Do I still have all of the qualities (gifts) that I used when serving as an elder? Sure, but I am no longer serving in that role, so I am not an elder. The same may be said about my former role as an evangelist. I am not serving in that capacity, although I use both my evangelist gifts and my elder gifts in my present teacher role.

Therefore, I think we would have to say that appointments of some type are necessary if we are to be recognized as an evangelist, an elder, a teacher, a deacon, an administrator, or whatever other role may be found in our church. If a person served at one time as the children's ministry leader, but does so no longer, how can he still be called a children's ministry leader? He may well still help out in the children's ministry, but someone else is now the appointed children's ministry leader. Is this not obvious common sense? You are not a teacher or an evangelist just because you have the gifts, any more than I am an elder just because I have the gifts and the experience. In order to actually serve in a specific role that is made known to the church or to a ministry group within the church, you should be clearly identified as such by the leaders of the group. Otherwise, confusion will exist. Declaring myself to be something that I have not been appointed to (with or without ceremony) is confusing. Leadership roles are just that—specific roles that should be recognized as such, as should those individuals who fulfill them.

The Conclusion of the Matter

If we keep our purposes and motivations in the right place, we can appoint disciples to various roles, whether the terms we use to describe them are biblical or not. I have no hesitation in appointing someone as a "youth minister" or a "children's ministry leader." Nor do I have any hesitation about appointing someone as an evangelist, in spite of my own uncertainty about the length of time that first-century evangelists served in one church, and the nature of biblical appointments. My concerns only have to do with keeping ambitions spiritual and not worldly, which may be reflected in how we use terminology to describe our functions and roles. Jesus wants us to hunger and thirst after righteousness, not for the recognition and praise of men. Serving him will always boil down to our own personal motivations for doing so. Beyond that, he gives us a great deal of latitude when it comes to form and function. Therefore, I often end up with the conclusion that many things along these lines are allowable, but far fewer actually mandated. For me, that is a comfortable conclusion that reflects a true freedom in Christ.

Chapter Ten

Other Leadership Roles

The Biblical Role of Deacons

As is the case with elders, Paul gave Timothy a list of qualifications for deacons (and possibly for their wives). He gave many of the same qualifications for deacons that he did for elders. This harmonizes with the general view that the deacon role is closely connected with that of the elder—that deacons support the elders by assuming tasks that take pressure off them. If we adopt that connection, then deacons are to help the elders in certain areas much as the elders are to help the evangelists in certain other areas. We have a perfect example of this principle in Acts 6, where the Seven were chosen to serve the widows, in order to offload this task from the apostles. Teamwork and load-sharing among leaders is vital and explains why the church must have leaders serving in a variety of roles.

Qualifications

> Deacons, likewise, are to be men worthy of respect, sincere, not indulging in much wine, and not pursuing dishonest gain. They must keep hold of the deep truths of the faith with a clear conscience. They must first be tested; and then if there is nothing against them, let them serve as deacons. In the same way, their wives are to be women worthy of respect, not malicious talkers but temperate and trustworthy in everything. A deacon must be the husband of but one wife and must manage his children

and his household well. Those who have served well gain an excellent standing and great assurance in their faith in Christ Jesus (1 Timothy 3:8–13).

In comparing the qualifications of deacons to those of elders, we find both similarities and differences in 1 Timothy 3. The following terms are applied to deacons and overseers (similar terms or meanings):

> **Respectable (vv. 2, 8):**
> - Not indulging in much wine (vv. 3, 8)
> - Not a lover of money (vv. 3, 8)
> - Above reproach (vv. 2, 10)
> - Husband of but one wife (vv. 2, 12)
> - Managing children and household well (vv. 4, 12)
> - Encouragement to serve (vv. 1, 13)
>
> **Mentioned of overseers but not deacons:**
> - Able to teach (v. 2)
> - Hospitable (v. 2)
> - Not a recent convert (v. 6)
>
> **Mentioned of deacons but not overseers:**
> - Sincere (literally, not *double-tongued*—v. 8)
> - Clear conscience (v. 9)
> - Must first be tested (v. 10)
>
> **Qualifications of a deacon's wife**
> (and perhaps the wife of an elder), or of a deaconess:
> - Worthy of respect (v. 11)
> - Not malicious talkers (v. 11)
> - Temperate (v. 11)
> - Trustworthy in everything (v. 11)

In addition to these qualifications, another type of qualification must also be taken into consideration. The deacon must also have the spiritual gifts commensurate with the specific tasks for which he is chosen.

Issues of Interpretation

As we have already studied, the term *deacon* comes from a Greek term (*diakonos*) that is translated a number of ways, but carries the basic meaning of "servant." All who serve the church in any capacity could be called deacons, but that would be somewhat confusing, due to the word itself. It is one of only a few words in the New Testament that were not translated but rather transliterated—brought from Greek into English and given an English ending. *Baptism* is another such word. In both cases, it would have been far less confusing if the words had actually been translated consistently. As it is, *diakonos* is most often translated as servant or minister, except in the cases where it is being used in the more specific sense of a designated role. The only place it is translated *deacon* besides in 1 Timothy 3 is in Philippians 1:1, which reads: "Paul and Timothy, servants of Christ Jesus, To all the saints in Christ Jesus who are in Philippi, including the overseers and deacons." An appointed deacon is one selected for a specific task who fulfills the qualifications and is thus appointed. Every Christian is a *diakonos* in the general sense, but most are not in the narrow sense.

One question that comes up frequently is whether or not deacons have to be married. Some would say that two classes of deacons are mentioned in the text—deacons in general (vv. 8–10); and those who are married (vv. 12–13). Others would say that a deacon being single or married would depend upon the ministry or task he is overseeing. The question is a logical one when you understand the differences between the elder's role and the deacon's role. Whereas elders direct the affairs of the church generally, the duties of a deacon relate to specific tasks—areas of service needed by the church that are in keeping with his spiritual gifts. The question of his marital status arises from practical considerations rather than from biblical ones, because the text seems pretty clear on the fact that he must be a married man with children (not required to be *believing* children). But on the practical side, many of the potential tasks done by deacons don't require a wife's involvement, whereas many of the tasks of an elder do. That is what prompts the question. Although my pragmatic side would lean to the side of requiring a deacon to be married for certain types of roles, and not married for other ones, my biblical side still leans toward the conclusion that deacons must be married with children whom they manage well.

Another issue of interpretation comes up when considering the verse regarding wives or women. In our study of elders, we have already dealt with the three possibilities, and I will not take up more space to reiterate what was said there.

The statement that deacons "must first be tested" (v. 10) is likely another way of saying what was said about elders in 1 Timothy 5:22—don't appoint them too quickly. Let them prove themselves in both a general way regarding their character and spirituality, and in the specific way that relates to the task for which they will most likely be appointed. In other words, if they are going to become a deacon of finance, make sure that they are capable in the financial arena, and also make sure that their spiritual maturity is such that they can handle these matters with complete confidentiality and faith.

Another question that will eventually arise is whether the deacon role is in fact a leadership role. In a general sense, all disciples are to lead by example. However, in the specific sense of appointed deacons, the role may be or may not be considered a leadership role, depending on the nature of the specific task for which a deacon was appointed. Some tasks would require interfacing and leading others (for example, children's ministry). Other tasks might be individually performed (for example, administrative tasks) and would not require a gift of leadership to perform that task well. In other words, all leaders are servants, but not all servants are leaders (including appointed deacons). For this reason, we should not assume that all deacons are automatically to serve in leadership groups of decision-makers. Other designated leaders who work with them will have to help determine their potential in this regard.

Practical Issues

Although the office of deacon is not specifically mentioned in lists of appointed roles (like Ephesians 4:11), they may be counted among "those able to help others" and "those with the gifts of administration" in 1 Corinthians 12:28. On purely practical grounds, those serving in the various ways mentioned in this verse could be appointed deacons if they were qualified. But in any case, deacons are generally viewed as being appointed for specific tasks and are not simply "deacons-at-large." Acts 6 would be the best example of this principle. Their qualifications, in contrast to those of elders, do not include managing both their family and the church. Further descriptions of the elder's role are absent in the case of the deacon's role. Therefore, although their designated task might be a church-wide task, they are not overseers of the flock as are the elders.

How are deacons selected? Using Acts 6 as a practical model, needed tasks should be identified by the key leaders of ministry groups or elders, and then the members of that ministry group should recommend qualified men to serve in those areas. Once such tasks are identified, recommendation forms can be made available to the church, and then the men recommended would be considered by the main leadership team of the church or ministry group in which the deacon will serve. The leadership team will have to make the final decision if more than one name is suggested for a role (which will almost always be the case). From there, the name (or names, if more than one deacon is being selected) will be taken back to the church or smaller ministry group in which they will be serving for final consideration. If no biblical objections are posed to the leadership group within a reasonable time period (commonly one to two weeks), the people being considered should be appointed (or recognized) in an appropriate manner.

The Biblical Role of Teachers

The first mention of teachers in the church (though many references to Jewish teachers of the law can be seen) was in Acts 13:1: "In the church at Antioch there were prophets and teachers: Barnabas, Simeon called Niger, Lucius of Cyrene, Manaen (who had been brought up with Herod the tetrarch) and Saul." It was in this setting that God responded to their worshiping and fasting by selecting Paul and Barnabas to send out on what we call the first missionary journey. It is interesting that the main leadership group there seemed to be made up of only two types, prophets and teachers. Nothing is said of elders or evangelists, but if the common definition of evangelist were accepted, Paul and Barnabas were sent out in that role. In the miraculous age, those occupying most of the key leadership roles must have received the gift of prophecy, certainly including evangelists and teachers. Otherwise, they would not have been able to teach and preach the Word (because the New Testament had not been committed to writing yet). This passage indicates that there were some leaders who were prophets *only*, whereas other leaders were apostle/prophets, evangelist/prophets or teacher/prophets. Whatever else may be said, the teacher role in Antioch was a significant one.

In 1 Corinthians 12:28 and Ephesians 4:11, we find that God appointed teachers as one type of leader in the church. Of course, in Ephesians 4:11, the reference may be to a joint role of a pastor/teacher, but that is debatable. However, in 1 Corinthians 12:28, the teacher role is definitely mentioned as a separate role. Prophets and teachers evidently comprised the primary leadership for the Antioch church when the church sent out Barnabas and Paul on the first missionary journey. Twice Paul said that he had been appointed a teacher (1 Timothy 2:7 and 2 Timothy 1:11). He never said specifically that he had been appointed an evangelist, which likely means that his work as an evangelist was encompassed within his apostle role (as one sent on a mission).

The gift of "teaching" is mentioned specifically in Romans 12:7, and is separate from the gift of "leadership" (Romans 12:8)—an interesting point. Certainly disciples can have more than one gift in that list, but they do not necessarily have to possess multiple gifts. Therefore, just as an inspired man could be a prophet *only*, a teacher could be a teacher only. Or he could have that gift in addition to other gifts, including the gift of leadership. 1 Timothy 5:17 mentions the elder/teacher or elder/evangelist types or elder/teacher/evangelist types, and Ephesians 4:11 may well mention the elder/teacher. Since the 1 Corinthians 12 passage was written prior to the Ephesians 4 passage, it may be that in time, most teachers also became either evangelists or elders, thus serving in a dual role, since teaching is a necessary component of both of these roles.

The Romans 12 passage, in listing the gifts of leadership and teaching separately, would lead us to the conclusion that teachers and deacons would share in common the *possibility* but not the *necessity* of being leaders in the normal sense of the word (though all lead in some way). In both instances, it would have to be determined on a case-by-case basis, and the people not having leadership gifts should not be placed in leadership groups as decision-makers. However, both teachers and deacons should have regular opportunity for giving input regarding their particular areas of responsibility. Acts 13 demonstrates that teachers can be (and were) included in key leadership groups, and if they have both the teaching gift and the leadership gift, they should be, for they add a valuable perspective. Any type of doctrinal discussion would need to include a teacher or teachers, even if no teachers were available who also had the leadership gift.

Hebrews 5:12 says that in a general sense, any mature Christian should be a teacher on some level (which is different than an appointed teacher). Some leaders have questioned whether there were leaders who were *only* teachers, or whether they were always evangelist/teachers (like Paul) or elder/teachers (like those mentioned in 1 Timothy 5:17). It would seem that Romans 12 settles that question. If the early church recognized some who were only teachers, rest assured that these men were not dry academics, unaccustomed to some level of influence in practical ministry, or else they would have been living a life unworthy of imitation (Hebrews 13:7).

In recent years, some have suggested that teachers are the solution to our movement's challenges, and they have downplayed the role of evangelists. But of course, in the past our churches have also downplayed or underestimated the importance of the role of teachers. Teachers do tend to look at the Scriptures from more historical and contextual perspectives, since that is their training, and this makes their contributions valuable and even vital. Wise leadership recognizes and uses all gifts that the Spirit gives as important and necessary to build a mature body, with all the parts working in harmony with one another, adding their various gifts for the good of the whole—but never viewing one role as superior to the other. All are important, or God would not have appointed them as a part of the overall leadership of his family.

The Bible does make a distinction between preaching and teaching, but does not define that difference. It is important to note that effective teaching is not the sole possession or responsibility of any one leadership role, but rather a necessary tool of every leader who has any role involving public proclamation or instruction. Evangelists, elders and teachers all share a common tool, but would be expected to exercise it in different settings, depending upon their role. All three of these particular roles are needed to build maturity in the church (Ephesians 4:11–16). Gifted teachers who become recognized in any leadership role are warned of a stricter judgment, which implies a serious responsibility that accompanies the role (James 3:1–2).

Perhaps the main distinction between preaching and teaching would involve the proclamation of the salvation message of good news to the lost, versus the systematic teaching of milk and meat to the saved. In that sense, preaching would belong more in the realm of carrying out the first part of the Great Commission, and teaching would fall more within the second part of the Great Commission—the maturation process. Preaching would thus be more the inspirational and convicting part of the process, and teaching would focus on conveying the depth of knowledge that brings maturity. However, as we have already seen in the Pastoral Epistles, the evangelist's role certainly includes helping the body of believers to mature.

In summation, teaching is a vital and essential function used by all leaders but uniquely distinguished as the more singular gift of some, whom we designate as teachers. However, just as evangelists and elders must exhibit the capacity to teach, so teachers much exhibit the capacity to inspire, convict and shepherd. No one, however much knowledge he may possess, has the right to make the Bible boring or inapplicable to the daily life of disciples.

Administrators and Other Roles

Administrators are likely the only other role mentioned in the Bible besides the roles that we have already discussed (elder, deacon, evangelist). 1 Corinthians 12:28 mentions specifically those with the "gifts of administration." Interestingly, the plural "gifts" may suggest that there are variations in types of administration needed, and all administrators may not have all of these various gifts. Practically, administrators are highly important to the function of the church, and due to their influence, they should be considered qualified not only based on their administrative gifts but also based on their having a recognizable level of spirituality. They are privy to much confidential information, which means that they must not only have integrity and the ability to handle private information appropriately, but must also be strong enough spiritually to handle the types of information with which they deal. As a person without an administrative gift, and yet who must function administratively in my teaching ministry, my respect and appreciation for administrators is at an all-time high! I have been blessed to work closely with some very capable and spiritual administrators, and I value their help and friendship more than I can describe in words. Administration is definitely a gift, and a gift from God to the church.

Regarding the inclusion of administrators in leadership groups, we may say the same things about them that we have said of deacons and teachers. Administrators may or may not have the gift of leadership, and thus they may or may not be a regular part of a decision-making leadership team. However, due to the financial knowledge of the church that they possess, they will need to be a part of many meetings. And if they have a leadership gift and a high level of spirituality along with their administrative gift, they will be a valuable part of various leadership groups. Administrators are a blessing from God—let us treat them as such.

When discussing administration, the subject of Boards of Directors inevitably comes up. Boards of Directors exist because of governmental direction, not because of biblical direction. And yet their existence and function are vitally important to the "business" side of the church. Their role ties in more to the relationship issues to be covered in later chapters, so we will postpone discussing their function until we reach those chapters. I have been a part of several Boards of Directors, and when they function within the right parameters, they are a true blessing to the church. When they try to function outside the right parameters, they can be a curse. But more on that subject later!

*Extra*biblical, but Not *Un*biblical, Roles

Every church has unique needs that require leaders and servants to meet them. Some congregations will need people to fill roles that other churches do not require, and many of these roles are not explicitly spelled out within the Bible. (The Bible did not prophesy the need for sound-team leaders or website managers!) Hence, the roles are considered *extra*-biblical (meaning that they are unmentioned in the Bible), but certainly not *un*biblical. On the basis of purely practical needs, we have developed other types of roles, some of which are unquestionably leadership type roles. Some of these roles include children's ministry leaders, worship leaders, shepherds (mature couples to help when you don't have elders yet, or to assist them when you do have elders), and other similar roles.

Since many smaller or younger congregations do not have elders or anyone qualified to be elders, appointing shepherding couples has found firm footing in some churches. In Phoenix, we have a Shepherding Training Program, and other churches are asking for help in starting such programs. (See Appendix Three, "Shepherding Training Subjects," for ideas and suggestions for developing such groups.)

In cases like these, we are merely recognizing needs in the church and identifying and appointing people with gifts and desires that make them suitable for filling such roles. Hence, we are using a type of leadership delegation, which has been done in both the Old Testament and New Testament. In Phoenix, our shepherding group meets once a month for breakfast, followed by a lesson from a member of our leadership team (alternating the type of leader—elder or evangelist) on one of the leadership topics from the list of shepherding training subjects. We provide each person an outline of the lesson and conclude with a discussion time.

Certainly we should strive to train and appoint qualified people to all biblically defined roles. We should also strive to train and appoint qualified people to other roles that are needed within our cultural and/or congregational setting. Moses did exactly that in Exodus 18, and we will often find ourselves innovating in similar ways to make sure that the needs of the people are met. And so, while our primary focus is on raising up people to serve in biblically designated roles, we must also have a secondary focus on raising up other people to serve in ways that are obviously needed. God grants us that freedom and responsibility, and he expects us to exercise it. He is the gift-giver; we are the gift-recognizers. Let's make sure we use all gifts available within any congregation, and enjoy the blessings of God as he uses the gifted to bless his family!

Part Three
Leadership Relationships

Chapter Eleven

Relationships:
Historical Origins of Challenges

A Matter of Perspective

It should be obvious that any book is written from a certain perspective, that of the author. I came into what I first called the "Discipling Movement" from a mainline church of Christ background. Actually, I was attracted to it by the very concept of discipling. One of the earliest definitions of discipling that caught my attention was that it was God's design to have "one another" relationships to help us deal with sin at the temptation level, rather than after it had damaged our lives. After attending my first conference of discipling churches in March of 1981, The Rocky Mountain Evangelism Seminar, I was hooked. I loved what I saw—the zeal, the evangelistic results and the courageous preaching. All of the criticism I heard and read about actually raised my curiosity enough that I decided to check into what was being said. The more negativity I heard, the more I was drawn in, both because of the results I was seeing and the lack of validity of most of what I was hearing.

Since those early days in my experience, I have come to understand the criticisms I heard early on, and yet I still saw the results and the good, which in my mind far outweighed the bad. I burned many bridges in joining this movement, and I have never second-guessed the decision that led to that painful process. I love our movement, complete with its mistakes and sins. As long as the church is comprised of humans and not angels, we are going to make mistakes and commit sins. I have never once thought about leaving it and never will. I'm in, and I'm in for life. But I'm not blind to our mistakes and sins, and with a combination of love and boldness, I want to give my perspectives about what led to those mistakes and sins. Criticism in the world is most often given because others are "down" on you; criticism in the church (one part of the spiritual discipling process) is given because others are "up" on you and want you to be your best. That principle applies in addressing sins in individuals and it also applies in addressing sins in our movement. Knowing what led to those sins will help us understand ourselves and our movement and will arm us to deal with future challenges righteously, having learned from history. I would think that my age, experience, service and sacrifice in the last thirty years would qualify me to share my perspectives about how we got where we are, and I know that my love for this movement should. With that in mind, let's have the courage to take an honest look at those challenges.

Challenges of Two Types

Relationship challenges of one type or another are always going to be a part of life for all of us—both inside and outside the church. Any husband and wife can attest to that fact, as can any parent and mature child. Even when sin causes the challenges, God will use them to help us grow—if we will let him. That is certainly his design and plan. In fact, much of our Christian growth comes through all kinds of challenges, and challenges in relationships are the most complicated and difficult kind that most of us will ever face for most our lifetime. They come in many forms, some expected and some unexpected. What I am saying in essence is that challenges in relationships are not a bad thing unless we handle them badly. Understanding how spiritual growth occurs puts terms like "challenges" in a whole new light (and a good one). We cannot afford to get into a reactionary mode when they come, as if they were an aberration. We must simply look for the hand of God in them and use the word of God to resolve and learn from them.

Relationship challenges may be categorized into two basic types: the incidental type that just happen due to the human element, and the systemic type. The systemic type is traceable to a system of behaviors that will continue producing tensions unless something is done to change the system. Systemic issues are issues of history, in which certain patterns have become well established and produce certain behaviors consistently. A good example of systemic problems in marriage can be illustrated by one husband's comment that his wife kept getting historical. His friend asked, "Don't you mean hysterical?" "No," the husband replied, "I mean historical—she keeps bringing up the past." The wife was keeping a record of wrongs and overreacting to present circumstances as a result of systemic problems in their marriage that had never been solved.

The systemic issues we have as a movement of churches are also a matter of history. Without understanding our own history reasonably well, we will keep bumping up against the same problems. Our backgrounds provide us with a "default button" to which we automatically resort in certain situations unless we understand how we got those buttons. Those background experiences form the DNA of who we are as individuals and as groups. Until and unless we gain an understanding of what formed that DNA and how it occurred, we will not change and stay changed in ways that prevent those systemic problems from recurring—thus producing ongoing relational difficulties. We all as individuals have to come to grips with our background experiences in order to deal in healthy ways with the present. Not only must we understand our own past experiences and their effects upon us, we also have to try to understand the experiences of other people in order to really understand them. Therefore, it should come as no surprise that the same insights are necessary for groups of people, if we want to understand the groups as a whole and how individual members of a particular group interrelate and interact with one another.

This chapter is mainly historical rather than solution-oriented. Once we gain a better understanding of our history in this chapter, the next chapter will suggest a number of practical solutions for the challenges mentioned here. And in this chapter I will not attempt a detailed account of our history, but rather a brief summary of the various stages, along with my analysis of the ways each of those stages have influenced our thinking, leadership style and church culture. So let's roll up our sleeves and jump into some pertinent history lessons.

Lessons from History — the Restoration Movement

Our movement's root system may be traced back to what we commonly call the mainline Church of Christ. That group was one branch of what was often called the Restoration Movement.[1] That root system is a part of our DNA, even if we are not aware of how it affects us. That background has profoundly influenced us in countless ways, especially in our approach to the interpretation of the Bible, along with our view of other groups who differ with us. Some of what we inherited is very good; some is not so good. I recommend Tom Jones's book *In Search of a City* (DPI, 2007) to help you understand our mainline roots and also how the next stage of our root system (the Campus Ministry Movement) developed from it. It will open your eyes to some captivating history.

My own doctrinal convictions were primarily developed within the mainline churches, and I am very grateful for much of what I learned from my biblical education in that setting. The concept of restoring New Testament Christianity and insisting on viewing the Bible as God's inspired word helped provide a foundation for my spiritual future. Most of what I wrote in my book *Prepared to Answer: Restoring Truth in an Age of Relativism* I learned from my education in the mainline church. I also gained a fair amount of legalistic tendencies from that same training, and I have had to deal with those tendencies in my thinking over the years. Thankfully, my early study of Romans and its principles has provided me great help in dealing with my deep-rooted legalism.

But the point is that without understanding how I developed spiritually in the mainline setting, I might not be able to make changes and would simply continue living according to my presuppositions. I hope that makes sense to you, because I know that some people are uncomfortable in talking about our past (for reasons that, frankly, I do not understand). We are products of our past, and we cannot understand ourselves without understanding our past to at least an appreciable degree—individually and collectively. The principle stated in Exodus 20:5 regarding God punishing the sins of the fathers to the third and fourth generation should have gained the serious attention of that generation; and that same principle of inheriting the consequences (not the guilt) of our spiritual fathers had better motivate us to want to understand what those sins were.

Lessons from History — the Campus Ministry Movement

More important to understanding the present is the next phase of our history, which I call the Campus Ministry Movement.[2] For many years, the members of mainline churches had sent their children to Church of Christ universities, with the hope that they would grow in a spiritual environment and meet a fellow Christian to marry. The concept of bringing the Word to worldly campus ministries was virtually nonexistent. But that changed—a little—in the 1960s. Although the mainline churches made some other forays into campus ministry, the particular effort that led to the ICOC began in the late 1960s.

In 1968, a mainline campus group called Campus Evangelism held a seminar in Dallas. There were about a thousand people in attendance, primarily college students from across the Bible Belt, Florida and California. A young man named Chuck Lucas was the main song leader for that seminar, and during the seminar, he was chosen to lead a pilot project to the University of Florida. The idea was revolutionary: Take the Word to a worldly university! Chuck started his work in Gainesville as the campus minister of the 14th Street Church of Christ and introduced many of the concepts and practices that we still use, including Bible Talks (called Soul Talks then), prayer partners, and a strong emphasis on total commitment, the authority of the Bible, and evangelism for every member. The church later changed its name to the Crossroads Church of Christ, and Chuck became the pulpit minister, and Sam Laing became campus minister.

Their goal was not only to have a great evangelistic impact on their campus; they also trained young men and women to start similar campus ministries on campuses all over America. They sent campus ministers to work in mainline churches that wanted to start campus ministries of their own. What began as an exciting idea soon led in most of these churches to some serious conflicts between the campus ministers (and their campus groups) and the older church leaders and older members. Conflicts ranged from differences in culture (imagine what happened when hippie college students were converted and entered a very traditional church setting!) to differences in standards on key issues like lordship, accountability, evangelism and devotion to the fellowship. The work at Crossroads had already been under a lot of criticism and had become controversial in the Churches of Christ. Over time, to some degree, Crossroads became reactionary against the status quo. Given the intense criticisms they were facing, their reactions were not unexpected, and in many ways, certainly not unwarranted.

Every person is a product of his or her environment, in good and bad ways. We either imitate (consciously or unconsciously) what we have been around, or we react against it. The same may be said of all movements, for they either bear the stamp of what spawned them, or they rebel against it. The concept of dialectical progression articulated by Georg Hegel, a nineteenth-century philosopher, seems more right than wrong when applied to movements historically. His view is often described in terms of this reactionary pattern: thesis – antithesis – synthesis, with the synthesis becoming the new thesis as the process continues. The stronger the reaction ("antithesis") against the status quo ("thesis"), the more the movement becomes defined by its differences with its source. The stage was set in the Campus Ministry Movement days to provide that antithesis. Although there may be great value in reacting against wrong things, the potential for overreacting to what we are in the process of rejecting is an ever-present temptation.

In this period during the 1970s and early 1980s, campus ministers who established campus ministries under the umbrella of existing Churches of Christ fought many battles as they tried to work with people who had traditional mindsets. Peaceful coexistence was virtually nonexistent—let alone cooperation or a sense of unity. This is not to say that campus ministers did not make many mistakes themselves that led to their own sins and set up the potential for future overreactions. Zeal without knowledge was not their main problem; it was zeal without experience in dealing with the circumstances they faced. In retrospect, I think the young campus ministers and older mainline leaders were almost equally at fault in the tensions and divisions that arose during those days. There was impatience, pride, self-righteousness and a rush to judgment on both sides. However, I place the greater responsibility on the older leaders, who reacted against the younger ones instead of patiently continuing to try to help them, understand them and work with them. Jesus had a couple of young leaders who wanted to burn down a city, but he kept working with them until they matured. Almost all young leaders are going to make mistakes of misapplied zeal, and older leaders are going to have to be like Jesus in order to help them mature. Young leaders are going to see weaknesses in older church members and may not understand why mature church members and leaders do things the way they do. But regardless of who deserves blame for what, the scenario was set for overreactions on the part of younger campus ministers.

One of their more obvious overreactions was their repeated emphasis on numerical growth. As the campus ministers saw it, the student ministries were growing quickly, while the older church members remained stagnant, with little (if any) growth. They viewed this as indisputable evidence of the older church members' lukewarmness. This attitude carried over into our churches for many years. I have heard many sermons preached among us, especially in the mid-1980s and early 1990s, in which speakers quoted growth statistics from the mainline Churches of Christ to show how poorly they were doing evangelistically. Those sermons go back to the past: Because these churches had persecuted the fledgling campus ministry movement, the reaction was something like, "We will show you!" The continued usage of these same statistics by some leaders through a couple of decades (again the 1980s, 1990s and even into the early 2000s) demonstrates the strength of the reaction. Certainly we ought to focus on converting people and growing numerically, but for biblical reasons instead of reactionary ones.

When Crossroads-trained campus ministers were beginning their ministries in mainline churches, the makeup of the existing congregations—the age, personalities, lifestyles and convictions of the older church members and leaders—yielded other reactions that were more subtle, and for that reason, potentially more harmful. The students developed a lack of trust for people in two basic categories, for somewhat understandable reasons. First, the average members of the churches were viewed as being lukewarm. Therefore, they could not be relied upon to help carry out the mission of evangelism in any serious way, and in fact the older members often resisted the efforts of students who were evangelizing in ways that were new and threatening to them. The problem is that some ministers who began their career as young leaders in such situations often retained a residual tendency to distrust members in our churches, however subtle the mistrust may have been. Suffice it to say that Romans 15:14 has been preached more than practiced by some of us. It reads: "I myself am convinced, my brothers, that you yourselves are full of goodness, complete in knowledge and competent to instruct one another." Are you convinced of that same truth when you think about the members in your church?

Second, the young students concluded that leaders of those traditional churches were not to be trusted, for they quite often represented the opposition as persecutors. In those churches, elders were unquestionably the leaders in control, and for this reason they were to be trusted the least. The carryover into our movement of a mistrust for elders cannot be denied. The highly influential role of elders in the New Testament church has not yet been duplicated in our movement, although significant progress has been made in recent years, and for that we are most thankful. Unfortunately, some of the progress was actually slowed down in some places after our firestorm, when elders were quickly appointed for wrong reasons—namely mistrust of evangelists by the members. Those elders did not get off to a great start in their relationships with evangelists. But those situations were more the exceptions than the rule. More and more elders are being appointed, and almost everyone is happy with that development.

Third, leadership style in our movement is another trait that has been influenced significantly by those campus ministry days. When a new church is planted, or when a leader is working in youth groups, including campus ministries, the leader should be the go-to person by design. A one-man leadership style is appropriate in those situations, but over time, leadership groups should be developed to help carry the load. Remaining in a one-man, top-down leadership mode is not a wise choice, but it became pretty much the pattern for our churches, since campus ministry was where most of our leaders had gained their training and leadership experience. They had also not learned how to treat disciples in an age-appropriate manner as they matured. How many mistakes we could have avoided had we learned this lesson years ago! Although we have made great strides in recent years, some churches may still need to learn it.

Tying together the previous three relics from our campus ministry days—focus on numerical growth; lack of trust; and leadership style—it's easy to see how these attitudes strongly influenced our definition of the role of the evangelist. To make sure that members (who were at least subtly mistrusted) would evangelize, many leaders felt that they must preach strongly and often on the need for evangelism or else the average person would not evangelize. Hence, the "push" mentality was built into our system from the beginning. Never mind that you cannot find this kind of motivation for evangelism in the New Testament—those basic assumptions (some of them likely unconscious assumptions) drove the preaching approach and biblical diet offered by the "forceful" leader. They were the foundation for his philosophy of preaching. Over shorter periods of time, this type of motivation for evangelism has produced some pretty impressive results. Over longer periods, the effectiveness in producing growth and spiritual health has waned in predictable ways. Our older, larger churches slowed in growth first, not simply because they were either older or larger, but because something had been amiss in our motivational approaches. Wrong motivation affects people much like taking drugs affects them—it takes a stronger and stronger "hit" to get the same results, until you reach a point when the same results can no longer be achieved, no matter how strong the "hit."

The motivation for evangelism found in the Bible is primarily relational in nature: love for God and love for one another. Outreach to nondisciples appears to have been based on a natural approach of sharing the good news (and to the disciples, it truly was good news!) with friends and family. Evangelism seems to have been as much a natural by-product of gratitude and joy as the result of specific, repeated emphasis in preaching and teaching. It seems that the principles of John 13:34–35 really worked, as people in the world were attracted by the love they saw among the disciples. Happy Christians are good advertisement! In the past (I refer here especially to the 1990s–early 2000s) many of our Christians were not too happy, precisely because of the preaching, teaching and treatment they received—an applied pressure to do what new Christians usually do naturally. An elder's wife made this comment a number of years back: "In our basic conversion studies with people, we stress that they are becoming a part of a loving family; shortly after baptism, they wake up feeling that they are in an army with very strong marching orders." I hope we have all learned to provide better motivation and a better balance in our preaching and teaching diet in recent years.

Before we move on to the next phase of our movement's development—the Boston Movement—I'd like to take a look at one more key reaction we had to the mainline church. During the campus ministry days, the mainline church was not very direct in confronting sins and fell short of "speaking the truth in love" (Ephesians 4:15). In reaction, some leaders among us evidently came to feel that almost any talk of a serious spiritual nature, private or public, had to be capped off with strong challenges to ensure that remorse and repentance were produced. This attitude carried over into the consistent use of strong confrontational approaches in both individual and congregational settings. The common "good point, bad point" approach used in discipleship groups found many other applications in private and public settings. The end result was that disciples were sometimes treated in ways that no thinking parent would treat his or her own children. We are all in need of much encouragement, and when encouragement is replaced or diluted significantly by challenges, spiritual insecurity is going to be produced. As much as challenge may be needed at times, Jesus' admonition in Revelation 3:19 ("Those whom I love I rebuke and discipline") is hardly intended to be the main ingredient in a diet of love. (Make sure you understand the context of Jesus' words in this text.) Thankfully, God's kindness is his favorite way of leading us to repentance (Romans 2:4), and we would do well to imitate him in our approach with others.

A part of our approach came out in what some have termed "agenda-driven" preaching: preaching to the perceived needs and finding scriptures that seem to apply. And most often, of course, those sermons were topical in nature. For example, if we believed the people needed to be more committed, our three lesson points might be: more committed in evangelism, more committed in giving financially, and more committed in attending all church activities. As each point was made, a verse would likely be read, quoted or referred to, but most of the sermon time would be focused on illustrations and correction. Even when we did set out to preach exegetical sermons (based on examining a particular passage, verse by verse), we still tended to use the text primarily as a springboard for accomplishing our own agenda of correcting and meeting specific needs. This tendency among preachers has been so common that we may not even realize we are doing it (and I count myself in that number). Sometimes such an approach is the right one, but a steady diet of it will lead to spiritual indigestion, malnutrition—or worse! However, I have been very encouraged by the strides we are making in changing this. I have noticed a greater emphasis in our preaching on more expository sermons rather than mainly topical lessons. (That is what I have been training leaders in a number of different settings and countries to do.)

It should also be noted that in past years, our emphasis on correction was not limited to those who taught and preached in public settings. It was also a tendency that many disciples had in studying with non-Christians and in discipling fellow Christians. We were trained to correct, and many of us became enamored with correction—minister and ordinary member alike. Though some people may still have that tendency, after 2003, most members and many leaders swung the pendulum much too far in the other direction, a problem we will address later on.[3]

Lessons from History—the Boston Movement

The work that began in Boston in 1979 was one of many that had connections to Gainesville and the training given there. While the Boston Church of Christ was one of few examples in which a campus ministry successfully functioned within a mainline church, it was not the only one. However, the Boston church and its lead evangelist, Kip McKean, did in fact lead the way in local church growth, coupled with a vision to win the world for Christ. It was an exciting time and an exciting place. Kip had gone to the Lexington Church of Christ, which had not grown numerically in quite some time, to put into practice what he had learned in his Crossroads training. The opportunity to establish campus ministries at schools like Harvard and MIT provided compelling motivation. But Kip's conviction was that they could not simply form a campus ministry within a mainline church; the whole church membership had to decide to come on board with the evangelistic and discipling concepts and practices—which those who stayed in the church did.

Although I didn't move to Boston until the end of 1987, people who were there in the beginning have reported that the rigid methodology of the later years was not dominant in the early years. The early 1980s were entrepreneurial years, when creativity was both appreciated and encouraged. However, with time, the system took shape and so did the systemic sins that accompanied it.

Several views and practices led to the development of the system. One was the increasing pressure brought about by the leadership, which was becoming more and more militaristic. Another was the exaltation of one gift (leadership) and one type of leader (evangelist). Being in the ministry was what nearly all young converts longed to achieve, and if they did not, they felt like second-class citizens. Even the phrases "being in the ministry" or "being in the full-time ministry" leave the impression that people not on staff are not in the ministry. If every disciple does not have the "ministry of reconciliation" (2 Corinthians 5:18), then we should quit preaching that passage. Furthermore, we are all full-time disciples if we are the living sacrifices Paul spoke about in Romans 12:1. I know what we mean by our terminology, but I also know that impressions are left by terminology, and I wonder if we are leaving an impression that is spiritually harmful.

Years ago in Boston, I was attending a function in someone's home, where I talked to a brother whom I didn't know well. He shared that he had been converted in the early days in Boston and that many of his friends had gone on staff and on mission teams, and that he had not been asked to do either. The way he described it hurt my heart. He obviously felt like a failure or something akin to it. And yet he had been a faithful disciple for many years, had married a disciple in the church and was raising his children to love God. Why should someone with that track record feel like a failure? Well, of course he shouldn't, and no one intentionally made him feel like that, but our way of doing things and describing things had left its mark on his heart.

Certainly when the church is growing rapidly, more and more leaders are needed, and some of them will be needed on staff. But how we motivate people and meet those needs is the real issue here. After a while, being a leader became such an emphasis that some people were basically called to "go into the ministry" even before they were baptized. Then add to the other systemic ills a growing emphasis on statistics and the competition that emphasis produced in each congregation and between congregations, and the mix was becoming somewhat toxic. Success began to be measured mainly by numbers of baptisms, and that led to more of an emphasis on having baptisms than making disciples. Through all of these things, the way our members viewed the church and its leaders was being affected significantly. To complicate matters, most leaders felt perhaps even greater pressure to produce—or else. We in turn developed attitudes toward the leaders over us (for pressuring us) and the people under our leadership (for failing to produce). Bad motivation affects us in ways far beyond the obvious. Please keep in mind that I am describing the general atmosphere and how the majority of leaders were affected and reacted. As always, there were notable exceptions.

Boston's main leader in those days wanted to make sure that he was given credit for starting "the movement," and he pronounced the year 1979 the magic year. At least by the mid-1980s, he started pointing to several changes he had made in the Boston church—he claimed they were different from the training he had received in Crossroads—as evidence that "the movement" had started in Boston. As I recall, he pointed to three differences: One, *all* members in Boston had to embrace the same expectations, regardless of age. Two, they had "discipling partners" instead of "prayer partners." (In retrospect, that over/under scheme with its strong military overtones was one of the most damaging parts of the system.) Three, they planted new churches of disciples rather than campus ministries within existing churches. Of those three things, only the third was really new. To say that the movement began in Boston in 1979 is an amazing example of revisionist history provided with a flair for arrogance.

Certainly it was a very important stage in our development as a movement (and we are still developing, and always will be), but it was not the beginning. In Appendix Four, I am including an article entitled "Appreciating Our History," which I suggest that you read. In Romans 11, Paul dealt with a growing arrogance in Gentile Christians in how they viewed their root system (Judaism). He reminded them that they were grafted in to the tree and owed their Judaic forefathers much. That article is an attempt to give credit where credit is due, especially to the Crossroads era. Make no mistake about it, I left the mainline group for very specific and serious reasons. I also treasure my sixteen years in Boston, mistakes and all. But if we are going to make lasting corrections, we are going to have to face what made us who we are, because relationships were affected in some very deep ways.

The success of the early Boston days, accompanied by the success in church plantings, led to a loss of the entrepreneurial stage and to the institution of more and more structure and the control that accompanied it. World Sector Leaders, Geographical Sector Leaders, World Sector Elders, World Sector Teachers, World Sector Administrators and other levels of leadership evolved, and evolved quickly. As the movement grew, it was natural that a more developed leadership structure be instituted. The real problem was not the organization itself; it was how it developed into a military model (discussed in chapter 4) that led to a hierarchal approach to organization. However, definite benefits came from being more organized, for organization and structure are needed and serve us well when applied properly. HOPE *worldwide* came into being during this period and has been a great blessing to the movement and to the world. Our organization enabled us to plant churches and support them in a systematic fashion. The good of that era was obvious; the bad was about to make itself much more obvious. The upheaval of 2003 was a long time in coming, but it was going to come through one means or another. Too much relationship damage had been done. I'm happy that I wasn't the one who lit the match, but the match was going to set off the firestorm at some point. The only question was, When?

Lessons from History—the Firestorm of 2003

Since this is the most painful time in our history as a movement, let me begin by saying that much progress on all fronts has been made since 2003. Few religious groups have the ability to deal with sin the way that we do—to look in the mirror, take the hits and repent. I am proud of us for this spiritual resilience. It is fairly unique. So, as we look back on our most recent historical challenges, which are always the most painful, let's not forget how far we have come in the present.

Those of us who love the church must view the events of 2003 as just being very, very sad. While I think a firestorm of some sort was inevitable, the way it happened created far too much collateral damage. I have already described and addressed all of that in the introduction and won't elaborate on it further here (though I am tempted). Suffice it to say that it was the worst time our movement has ever faced, and I pray we never face anything of that magnitude again. Let us hope we have learned the main lessons God wanted us to learn, and that those who haven't will learn them soon. I pray this book can be a part of that continued learning and changing. To use a phrase from Dickens, it was indeed "the worst of times," and as such, it left its impact on our relationships in all directions.

Almost all leaders felt the pain of being attacked and mistrusted, feeling like only our mistakes were seen (and often magnified) and the good things we had done for others forgotten. Of the hundreds of emails I received and conversations I had, the contents of some still bring a serious level of pain into my heart. But I also know that many of the people who made hurtful statements were victims of a mob mentality of sorts and needed to "come to their senses" (2 Timothy 2:26) due to the pain that they felt. What goes around comes around, and we reap what we sow. Leaders didn't trust others enough, and they lost their trust in us. Other such parallels can also be made. We leaders have to take a lot of responsibility for how people responded to us, and they have to take their own responsibility for the manner in which they responded.

We leaders were affected in many ways: Many didn't want to lead anymore (I speak here of leaders at all levels, from Bible Talk leaders to staff members), and many who did remain in leadership were sorely tempted to back off and quit challenging the members. In the aftermath of 2003, one of my close friends in a large church told me that of all the men on their church staff, only two were still functioning as evangelists. The others, in his estimation, had become clergymen. There was such a fear of criticism that some became like certain popular politicians—they had to take a poll to determine what their convictions were before preaching! Although I understand the temptations along these lines, we are preachers of the Word, and when times are most challenging, we will have to challenge as well. Having a lack of sensitivity toward those whom we lead is one sin; being afraid to preach strongly to them when it's needed is another sin. But without question, we as leaders felt hurt, disrespected, unloved and unappreciated. As the flames hit the Boston church, one of our evangelists said that their stock had dropped so low that the elders needed to step up and lead more. Although I generally agreed with his statement, and we elders did do more, it was only a matter of degree in our stock market value. The elder's stock position was in a *recession* but the evangelist's was in a *depression* (double entendre intended)!

On the other side of the river, members who felt unable to speak up in the past started speaking up. Some did it very well, and some did it very badly. Not a few developed a critical, worldly mindset and felt free to say almost anything they wanted to say and to repeat any bad news they had heard. Those who camped out on certain Internet forums soon lost touch with reality and became bitter roots in the fellowship. Most of them eventually left our fellowship, and many of those people eventually left any spiritual fellowship. As I said, it was a very, very sad time. Relationships were seriously affected between leader and member, member and member, and leader and leader. Satan was having his day. It reminded me of my mainline experiences, when the leaders would discuss what the members were having for Sunday lunch—namely, fried preacher, roasted deacon and stewed elder!

Lessons from History—Putting Out Fires and Rebuilding Walls

Our brief history as a movement, with its various phases, has contributed to both our challenges and our accomplishments in significant ways. I want to close this chapter by recounting some of the signs of progress in recent years. While I believe that we do have some default buttons that we need to be more aware of in order to dismantle them, it is obvious that we have already learned many lessons, which has enabled us to see more progress than we ever could have imagined back in 2003. For that, we must remain very grateful. But we must also be diligent in order to keep making progress and avoiding setbacks. It is to that end that I write this book.

On the whole, we are growing out of our funk and making serious progress—by the grace of God and to the glory of God. The International Leadership Conferences provide a good barometer by which to gauge our progress as a group of churches, and here I will briefly summarize my take on where we have been at each of the conferences since 2003. Our first post-2003 firestorm was actually held in Dallas in the fall of 2003, and this is the one I call the "Deer-in-the-Headlights" Conference. Leaders who attended were pretty much in a state of shock—understandably. But it was important to get together, and I appreciate the Dallas leadership for arranging the conference. Some things were said that could have best been left unsaid, but we were where we were. The next year, we met in

Chicago for the ILC, and people were generally in a better place, but most were still not doing great. Our world was still a bit upside down. Then came the ILC in Seattle, a conference that definitely showed our gradual improvement but had some awkward moments, as Kip McKean came and heavily recruited leaders for what was to become his new movement.

Two older friends of mine from the mainline church attended this conference. Both of these men were in their fifties and had a long church history. Over the years they have encountered a lot of difficulties within their own group. They made an interesting observation that tells me a lot about us: They said that although they could tell we had some serious issues going on behind the scenes, we were handling them in a far better way than they had seen similar situations handled within their fellowship of churches. That was a nice compliment and a testimony to our determination to take the high road in dealing with serious matters. It was after this conference that it became obvious that we would have to apply church discipline to our former leader. He had made it clear that in spite of repeated conversations with and pleas from a number of close brothers and sisters over several years, he was going to do his thing. He provided perhaps the ultimate example of a person who preached discipleship unabashedly and yet absolutely refused to embrace it in his own life. In my view, that chapter is the saddest one in the years since 2003.

Our next ILC was in Virginia Beach, and most of us had the zip in our step back, and faith in our future was obviously rebounding. We were not without our concerns, but the overall mood was pretty positive for most leaders. In 2007, the conference was in Long Beach, and the upward direction was evident at this meeting as well. The main glitch I remember was in seeing some tensions regarding the Plan for United Cooperation and the delegate approach for helping to keep our churches connected and cooperating. On that note, let me mention that I authored or coauthored three articles from 2006 to 2009 about the cooperation proposal, and I include them in Appendix Five, just to provide some insight into the development of this unity plan. Roger Lamb and the www.disciplestoday.org team have been more helpful than words can describe in helping us get this plan implemented and in helping our unity in many ways. At any rate, the Long Beach ILC was another testimony to our progress, and even the tensions about the unity plan led to some good resolutions in a number of cases. Like all challenges, if we face them openly, honestly and spiritually, good will always come, and it certainly has in this case. The unity we once had may have been somewhat forced, but we knew that unity was still vital to our future, and we have been willing to go through the pains of forging it—efforts that have been clearly blessed by God.

In 2008, our first ILC outside the US in many years was hosted by Shawn Wooten and the church in Kiev, Ukraine. For those of us from first-world countries, seeing the commitment and joy of people who live in very different conditions than we do struck our hearts in some wonderful ways. It was a mountaintop experience that those in attendance will never forget. I shed more tears of joy and conviction in Kiev than I have at any other conference in my life. It was special. I suspect that most leaders were feeling the same kind of convictions and soaring faith that I was, as we took a good dose of reality from a worldwide perspective. Next came the ILC held in Denver, a truly amazing event. Here is an excerpt from one of the articles I wrote on the church cooperation issue after that conference:

> As Roger Lamb observed near the end of this most recent ILC, there appeared to be a real "jump" to a new level of spirituality this year. We may not be where we should be individually and collectively, but it is obvious that the large majority of us really want to get there and are determined to act upon our convictions in a number of areas. I am most thankful for the Denver Church of Christ for their outstanding job as host church of this year's conference. Hundreds of Colorado volunteers did a marvelous job of making the time great, and God crowned their efforts with his blessings. Many leaders from all parts of the movement made their own contributions to what I believe will be looked back on as a watershed event.
>
> One part of the conference that was particularly encouraging to me was the continuing willingness of congregational leaders to keep considering the affirming of the Cooperation Plan. A number of additional churches have recently affirmed the plan, and the new Cooperation Plan Summary no doubt aided such decisions. The process of intentionally increasing the unity of our movement is working. Some leaders have been understandably unsettled about some of the mistakes of the past, when we were in a state of "forced unity," and have needed time to get their questions answered as we keep working toward a complete "forged unity."

Since then we have enjoyed two more leadership conferences, each of which demonstrated continuing progress. The spirit of these conferences has been clearly different than any conferences of the past. Gone is the feeling of worldly competition and a number of related worldly attitudes that too often colored our atmosphere in similar past meetings. It is a new day, signaling a new health and a desire to be our best for God and to help our brothers do the same. Between Dallas in 2003 and the American Leadership Conference in Boston in 2011, we have been up, down and all around, but we are finally in a place that we have never been before. Fires of testing bring pain, but they also bring refining. Through all the stages of our church history, we have been tested and we have been refined—all for one purpose in God's plan: to become what he wants us to become and to accomplish what he called us to accomplish in the first place—a world won for Christ. May we be the vessels through whom he can accomplish his grand purpose!

End Notes:

1. Gordon Ferguson, *Prepared to Answer* (Spring, Texas: Illumination Publishers), pages 113–135.
2. See Appendix Four: "Appreciating Our History," page 262.
3. Gordon Ferguson, *Prepared to Answer* (Spring, Texas: Illumination Publishers), pages 75–81.

Chapter Twelve

Relationships: Between Leaders and the Flock

Since this is a book about leadership, I am not going to focus on what the people under leadership need to do. I write here to leaders. Obviously, we have to help people get past their past as much as possible, especially if we played a part in the pain of their past. We begin by owning up to what we have done wrong, letting them talk through their issues if they still need to do that, then pointing them to the cross (1 Peter 2:18–25). Some could need professional help, and we can direct them to such a source. One mature Christian sister told me after 2003 that she could understand that people who had been hurt needed some time to work through it, but after a certain amount of time, if they remained stuck, then they had other issues. That was an astute observation. In many cases, people with deeper emotional issues had simply found something else besides themselves on which to blame their issues. Certainly, whatever we can do to help, we need to do. However, no matter what anyone has gone through, the solution is always the same: Imitate Jesus by surrendering to the Father and refusing to retaliate and become bitter. As the old song puts it, "The way of the cross leads home," and it's the only thing that leads us past the challenges of life in the world and in the kingdom of God.

The Crying Need for Righteous Motivation

What do we as leaders need to learn? Thinking back through the last chapter, we simply need to reverse some of our attitudes and practices and hold on to the good ones without wavering. Of course, the challenge is always learning to distinguish which belong in which category. We do need to take stock of how we typically motivate God's children. Several years ago, I wrote two articles about motivation. One was entitled "Motivation: Guilt or Grace," and the other was "Motivation Revisited: Correction or Inspiration." The principles in these articles are worth reading or reading again. They can be accessed on a number of websites, including mine (www.gftm.org).

One of the big needs in helping people view and respond to leadership biblically is to help them through their confusion (and make sure we are not confused ourselves). In 1 Corinthians 14:33, we are told that "God is not a God of confusion" (NASB). This means that confusion is spawned by Satan, who loves to confuse our thinking and bring disorder into our individual lives and into our churches. In the past few years, I have been amazed at how much confusion has entered into the thinking of many disciples. As a result, our convictions have become diluted and our lives often left without clear boundaries. It is vitally important to understand the underlying basis of this confusion. In order to help facilitate that understanding, I have often used the following illustration. As a movement, we can be described as a barbell having enormous weights at either end—one end represents the amazingly positive things that have been accomplished, and the other end represents the seriously negative things. However, when we think about the negative things, many (though not all) of these were actually right things done in wrong ways. Herein lies the root of our confusion. Motivation is the primary topic around which the confusion issue swirls.

If we fail to differentiate between correct biblical principles and wrong ways of implementing them, we will inevitably end up questioning the validity of those correct principles, and quit practicing them in any way—good or bad. Quite a few practices could be mentioned here: definitive preaching that both convicts and inspires; strong leadership; true biblical commitment to Christ and his cause; discipling (or whatever term you use) that helps us to carry out the "one another/each other" passages of the New Testament; evangelism; a study series designed to lead a person into a saved relationship with Jesus; financial contributions—of both the regularly weekly type and special contributions to support mission work; and a defined working unity between sister congregations in our movement of churches. Of course, the list could be lengthened, but you get the point. Have not many people lost their convictions about some of these basics of Scripture and basics of spiritual relationships?

Those of us who teach and preach have to accept responsibility for having emphasized the practices much more than the principles behind the practices. When the principles underlying our practices are not taught and retaught regularly, we usually end up believing that a way of putting a principle into practice is indeed *the* (only) way. Thus, the practice becomes the essential thing and not the principle that gives it validity. Our rather rigid "cookie-cutter" approaches in the past demonstrate this tendency all too well. However, the answer is not to eschew everything that resembles our former practices; the answer is to figure out the right and wrong of our past practices and to do right things in right ways. For example, our evangelism in the past was too often motivated by worldly means (numbers, goals, guilt, etc.) rather than by the heart of God for the lost. For his sake, let's not give up on the Great Commission—the world is still lost! Having some dating guidelines was not wrong; they were just applied wrongly in some cases and too often made into "laws." Discipling will always be the essence of spiritual relationships, but with an emphasis on mutually helping one another grow instead of an authority of "one over another." As one old seminary professor of mine used to say, we need simply to "sanctify and fumigate" the wrong applications—to throw out the bones but keep eating the fish!

The Twenty-Five Versus the Seventy-Five

Not surprisingly, our confusion in recent years has led to much of our organizational structure going by the wayside. I had an experience several years back that gave me an insight that I find applicable to the way we are trying to lead the church. The experience was going through the Dynamic Marriage Facilitator Training Program. (Dynamic Marriage is designed to help couples grow in their marriages, and the training program equips facilitators to lead the group discussions.) According to the instructor for this training, most marriages fall into one of three categories: twenty-five percent are healthy; fifty percent are stagnant; and twenty-five percent are on the verge of breaking up. The trainer said that the twenty-five percent of healthy marriages are in good shape because the partners in these unions are self-starters. They hear marriage lessons and put the suggestions into practice. They read the recommended books and talk to others and get help. If you extrapolate these statistics to people in general, and not just marriages, that would mean that about one-fourth of all people are self-starters and the remainder are not. From my experiences in life, I would agree that this is a fairly accurate figure.

By applying this principle to the church generally, we as leaders (self-starters) may be expecting virtually every member to become a self-starter spiritually. Leaders have often said that people need to take responsibility for themselves and their spiritual growth and not be dependent on leaders. That sounds noble and righteous, but is it actually in touch with reality? What we are really saying to people is "Be like me" (a self-starter). Yet people keep saying things like "I'm not pulled into relationships." "I don't have any friends." "I am isolated." We keep replying, "Well, have you initiated with anyone? Have you sought out help for yourself?" Are we expecting the impossible, or at least the improbable?

How do the Dynamic Marriage people deal with the fact that seventy-five percent of all people are not self-starters in their marriages? They provide very detailed structure, with specific expectations and accountability (all applied very positively). Otherwise, that large percentage of people will not get help in their marriages, and many will end in divorce. What did we as a movement provide for our church membership in past years? Detailed structure, with specific expectations and accountability. Was that wrong? No, it was necessary. What *was* wrong? The types of expectations, accountability and motivation used in many (but not all) cases. Strong directive leadership was not wrong; I think it was right—another example of a right thing too often applied in wrong ways.

Our people who are complaining about leaders not helping them with relationships and other components of the Christian life may sound like complainers who won't take responsibility for themselves. Could it be that they are simply crying out for help—

the kind of help that non-self-starters always have needed and will probably always need (at least at points in their lives until they reach real maturity)? The ideal is that all disciples should become self-starters, and hopefully with time and good direction to help them mature, many will. But if we don't lead people from where they currently are to where they need to be, they may not even stay in the church. It would be tragic to end up with only self-starter-type members, and long lists of immature or otherwise weaker disciples who have died on the vine. Food for thought, wouldn't you agree?

Lessons from the Past

Bottom line, what have I learned about Satan's plan to deceive and confuse? One, that over the years I was not nearly effective enough in helping to teach and reteach the principles behind the practices that I was calling people to. The actions themselves were too much the focus rather than the biblical basis for the actions. Two, in the more recent past (post-2003), I have allowed the importance of maintaining effective organizational structure to become diminished. I know of no organization, from the smallest family to the largest corporation, that can thrive without the right kind of motivation, expectations, and even accountability. Of course, all of these things can be done wrongly, but let's not forget that they can also be done correctly. May God help us to keep practices and structure in the proper relation to principles, and may he enable us to keep them all balanced with the proper biblical perspective. When that happens, Satan's efforts to confuse will be thwarted significantly, and we will all be filled with a faith that perseveres in spite of any and all challenges.

The Pressing Need to View Ourselves with Humility

In the last chapter, I explained how our early history during the Campus Ministry Movement era affected our view of ourselves, our members and other leaders. What do we need to do to make sure that these things are corrected and corrected entirely? I hope that a greater awareness of our root system will help. However, most of the answer lies in seeing ourselves and our roles in the right way. A good dose of humility will solve most of our relational problems in any type of relationship, at any level. Pride is not a joking matter.

God resists the proud (1 Peter 5:5), and so do godly people. If I had only one wish that could be granted for all of us who lead, the request would be quickly and easily made: *copious amounts of humility.* Pride has been at the root of most of our past problems, and humility is the cure. Therefore, to view ourselves rightly is to view ourselves humbly:

> For by the grace given me I say to every one of you: Do not think of yourself more highly than you ought, but rather think of yourself with sober judgment, in accordance with the measure of faith God has given you (Romans 12:3).

When Tom Jones and Mike Fontenot wrote their book on pride and humility, they adapted a popular phrase in our fellowship at the time for their title. It was fairly common for leaders to say in a somewhat lighthearted manner, "I'm just a prideful dog." Tom and Mike entitled their book *The Prideful Soul's Guide to Humility* (DPI, 2003). As they pointed out in the book, this subject is not a lighthearted one in the least. The Bible addresses pride in ways that should take our breath away just by reading. We would never say glibly, "I'm just a drunken dog" or "I'm just an adulterous dog." Why would we be so nonchalant about being prideful? Obviously, we have not put it in our list of serious sins. But we should and we must. Just look up all of the passages in the New Testament about pride and humility. Better yet, look all of them up in the whole Bible. We have to come to grips with the seriousness of this sin and then watch out for it like the plague that it is. In my life, Satan constantly tries to inject pride into my soul in new ways. Unless you have somehow become an angel, the same is true of you, and leaders experience this challenge in a measure beyond the ordinary person—simply because we are leaders.

Even the term "leader" has a way of influencing the way we view ourselves. That is why I dedicated one of the earliest chapters in the book to showing that we are first disciples of Jesus and second, servants of his people. Further, I repeatedly pointed out that leadership is a role and a function and not a position or a title. Do you think you understand what that means? A few illustrations will help. Suppose I am up in front of a group of ministry students in a ministry training session, which is often the case for me. I am not "Teacher Gordon," I am Gordon who teaches. As I teach, I teach with the authority of a teacher—humbly applied. But then when the day is over and I step out from behind the podium, what am I in relation to my students? Gordon the brother, the fellow disciple, the fellow sinner. I'm just one of the guys at that point, no more and no less. As we go out to eat or to fellowship, I'm just Joe Christian. Now since I am older and have the training and experiences I have, I get asked a lot of questions, which I try to answer. But in relationship to these students, I am one of them, not one above them.

How does that example apply to when I was serving in the role of a lead evangelist? The exact same way. When I was leading a staff meeting or a leadership team meeting or preaching a sermon, I was the person in charge of the particular function. But when it was over and I stepped out of that function, I was Gordon the brother. I did not, and do not, want to be viewed like a high-ranking officer in the military or the CEO of a company. When I am functioning in my role, I expect to be respected and followed while exercising that function. When I am not functioning in that role, I am just a fellow disciple and a servant. Then I am just hanging out with my friends, whose love I need and whose discipling I need. Isn't that simple? More important, isn't that *right*? If others exalt us in their minds in a way that isn't right, that is their problem (unless we have contributed to it in some way). If I exalt myself in my own mind, then that's my problem and it's a serious problem indeed. Some say that humble pie is hard to swallow and enjoy. If you are truly a humble person, swallowing that pie is not hard, and truthfully, you won't have to eat much of it anyway because you are already full of it.

The Urgent Need to Lead Confidently

Humility, properly understood, does not reduce confidence—it increases it. Why? If we are prideful, we are depending upon our own strength; if we are humble, we are depending upon God's strength. When I really feel that I am working in God's power, I am very confident in a way that leaves me relatively unaffected by what others may think of my leadership. In that mindset and heart-set, I am God's man doing his bidding. I can be humble and righteously confident at the same time, and that is the only way I can be confident spiritually. Leading out of arrogance may give the appearance of confidence, but it is a sham. Underneath it is an insecurity that comes out in sinful ways when opposition crops up. It's easy to be an angel when no one ruffles your feathers. It's only possible to demonstrate angelic qualities in the midst of feather-ruffling when you are God-confident rather than self-confident.

As the heading states, there is indeed an urgent need for confident leadership. Leadership is not about avoiding conflict and pleasing people. Even a casual reading of the Gospel accounts and their description of *the* Leader should make that clear. A few years back when I was still serving as an elder, the Southwest Elders' Retreat was being planned, and Bruce Williams left me a phone message asking me to speak and suggesting a title. He is a man given to succinct wording, and his message included pretty much a one-sentence explanation describing the title. It was, "Shepherd as a Father—Not a Grandfather!" I laughed when I listened to my voice mail, but I understood exactly what Bruce meant. In my physical family, I am both a father and a grandfather. Believe me, there is a marked difference in how you function in each of those roles! The message I delivered that year to my fellow elders and their wives was essentially this: "Be prepared to take the heat in the kitchen!"

Check Your Sentimentality at the Door

Some elders (and other leaders) have been tempted to show sentimentality and/or favoritism. Anyone who thinks they are not prone to do that in certain situations with certain people is not in touch with reality. That is why we must get others involved when we are dealing with close friends and relatives. I have seen some leaders who are very sentimental with the "old-timers" in the church, or with the children of old-timers, or with their own children, but they don't recognize it and will even deny it. They believe that they know these people so well that they are the best ones to advise them. That is foolishness. Theresa and I once gave a lesson about parenting teens. After the lesson concluded, we had a question and answer period. A former youth minister, whom I had known for many years, asked a very basic question about his teen, and I said jokingly, "You used to give advice about this all of the time in the past." Wisely he replied, "Yes, but when they are your own kids, you don't know anything!" Although he was joking back, he was on target in recognizing that when someone is very close to you emotionally, you are not the best one to supply the answers in difficult situations. I wish all parents were as wise, and that all leaders were as wise.

Beware the Vocal Minority

Some leaders can be guilty of listening too much to the vocal minority. Everyone should be able to express their views and concerns, but we have to be careful how much confidence we have in hearing one side of anyone's story (notice I said *anyone*). In the familiar Proverbs 18:17 passage, we read, "The first to present his case seems right, till another comes forward and questions him." At one point, I thought hearing both sides in two different settings would give you the whole picture needed. Not true. The passage speaks of a questioning process. Until I can get both sides in a conflict together to answer questions, I will not have the complete picture and therefore, not the accurate picture. People should be encouraged to work out their differences and to settle matters quickly (Matthew 5:25). In fact, we as leaders must insist that they do so, and refuse to allow those with ruptured relationships to coexist in our fellowship without resolving things, whatever that may take.

Further, those who continue to live with unresolved conflicts and who keep talking in ways that the Bible defines as slander and gossip must be warned. Back in 2005 as the Phoenix church was trying to emerge from the firestorm we were facing, the leadership of the church delivered some very pointed warnings. Here are a couple of excerpts from one such announcement:

> If you have a problem with another brother or sister, you must talk with them about it, not with others. Talking to others does not give them the opportunity to even hear the other side of the story, and it negatively influences their thinking toward the person being discussed. This approach, although common in the world, is unbiblical and unloving to the core. If you have problems with someone, talk to them and to no one else until Matthew 18 has been followed. We are urgently appealing to every member of this church to refuse to listen to another member talking negatively about a third member who is not present to give their side of the story. Proverbs 18:17 puts it this way: "The first to present his case seems right, till another comes forward and questions him." Please cease such talking and such listening, and obey what Jesus taught. If your brothers and sisters have problems with a fellow disciple, send them to that person to work it out and do not give ear to one side of the story. It is not righteous to do otherwise. Even if someone says that they have talked directly to the person with whom they have a problem, that doesn't give them the right to share those negative feelings with you later. In accordance with Matthew 18, if they couldn't resolve the problem in a meeting between the two of them, they should bring in the elders or other leaders to help resolve the issues of concern. . . .
>
> Our ministry staff has endured far too much scrutiny and criticism in the past couple of years, and your elders are saying today that enough is enough. If this

explanation and decision of the elders does not satisfy you, we remind you of the ending of that sermon noted earlier. Perhaps it is time for you to seek another church in which you will be happier. That is not our desire for you, but to have this continued negativity among us is not fair to the large majority of our members who desire a happier and more productive atmosphere in this church.

Announcements like this one (and we made several) were met with applause by the congregation. Most of the members are good-hearted disciples who just say or think, "Can't we just love one another?" I hope this example demonstrates the danger of listening too much or giving too much credence to the vocal minority who are critical and prone to negative attitudes about the church and about its leaders. We have to take the heat in the kitchen if we are true leaders.

The Sobering Need to Lead Boldly

Leading confidently is one thing, but leading boldly is one step beyond. The greatest degree of boldness is demanded of a leader in cases of church discipline. Applying church discipline in a public setting is not for the fainthearted. You can go to great lengths to explain the Bible's teachings about church discipline, but some people will still think you are being harsh. I have been involved in several situations in which staff brothers were being divisive. In every case, I delivered a sermon that I count among the strongest I have ever preached. Those messages were difficult to deliver, and I'm sure they were difficult for certain people to hear. But in order to stop the damage (and obey the Bible), the situation and people involved had to be addressed, and addressed strongly. Unless you have observed the harm that ensues when a leader becomes divisive and nothing is done about it, you will not have a fair estimation of why such bold denunciations are essential. If you have ever had the sober responsibility of carrying out such a mission, you understand how God's word can be sweet to the taste and sour to the stomach (Revelation 10:9). It is God's word and you love it, but preaching it in these situations with the boldness of a lion will make you sick to your stomach before it's over. But preach it we must. The flock must be protected.

Because this subject is so difficult to understand, embrace and practice, I have included an appendix that covers the subject of church discipline in great detail. I chose not to include it in this chapter both because of its length and because I didn't want to leave the impression that it should define in any way the relationships between leaders and those whom they lead. Yet because its practice will sometimes determine the overall health of the congregation, it should be studied out carefully and applied righteously.

Conclusion

Looking at mistakes we may have made as leaders is always unsettling and can be debilitating. Feeling unsettled is understandable and even needful, but being paralyzed by fear and regret is unacceptable. If we are leaders, we must *lead*. Years ago, I was asked to go with several other leaders to help a leadership group in a church outside the US. They were young and inexperienced and had made a number of significant mistakes in their leadership. They were already feeling bad, knowing that our presence meant that their failures were a matter of great concern. I spent several days with them and with the church, and my last talk to the leaders was simply about the need to lead. I explained that in a few days they had experienced a crash course in leadership and were now better prepared to lead. I also explained that all of us keep growing as leaders, but we cannot wait until a later time to lead. Their people needed them to lead, and those leaders needed to do so confidently. Whatever else might be said, they were definitely better leaders than they had been even a few days before. Plus they were humble learners, thus ensuring that God would in fact continue to bless them and to use them.

I am saying the same thing to the readers of this book. At whatever stage in leadership you find yourself, do your best, devote yourself to continuing to learn and grow, and pray about the rest. Jesus turned over his mission to save the world to some pretty young and inexperienced leaders, and their success in carrying out his mission was nothing short of phenomenal. If you are a disciple (a learner and follower of Jesus), a true servant of his people, and clothed with humility (Colossians 3:12), you will be just fine. I find myself concerned about two types of leaders: the more experienced ones who don't always take lessons on leadership seriously enough; and the younger ones who may take them too seriously. But I can only pray and trust that both types will be open to what I have written thus far—and to what you will read in the following chapters.

Chapter Thirteen

Relationships:
Between Elders, Evangelists and Teachers

An evangelist on our church staff in Phoenix recalls a statement made to him by his campus minister years ago when he first became an intern. He said, "The biggest challenge before us is not getting the gospel to the world; it is remaining unified as a movement." I think that statement was spot-on accurate, and all that we have been through as a movement substantiates it clearly. One of the most shocking statements in the Bible to me is found in Genesis 11:6. It was spoken at a time when the people were in rebellion against God, and yet they were perfectly united in that rebellion. "The Lord said, 'If as one people speaking the same language they have begun to do this, then nothing they plan to do will be impossible for them.'" Is that not shocking to you—that even at the height of rebellion, the power of absolute unity could absolutely not be blocked except by divine intervention? No wonder Jesus prayed what he did in John 17 and no wonder Satan never ceases in his attempts to destroy unity.

The three roles of elder, evangelist and teacher form the most essential grouping of leadership roles in spearheading our quest to change the world for Christ. While I have cringed at the mention of different types of leaders forming a balance of power, they do form a balance of perspectives. That balance is vital if we are to become, as churches and as a movement of churches, what God has in mind for us. I own a little plaque about marriage that is inscribed with these words: "The goal of marriage is not to think alike; it's to think together." In that light, people with different perspectives must have accurate expectations of others. We cannot get frustrated when others do not think exactly as we do or look at subjects and situations in the same way that we do.

We should embrace the perspectives of others as part of a vital process of making decisions that are not just acceptable, but the best. Paul put it well in Philippians 1:9-10: "And this is my prayer: that your love may abound more and more in knowledge and depth of insight, so that you may be able to discern what is best and may be pure and blameless until the day of Christ." If good, better and best are available choices, why wouldn't we always want what is best? One viewpoint will never yield what is best in all situations. Thus we see the need for a high level of trust and cooperation between the three key leadership roles in God's kingdom.

The Great Commission encapsulates the roles of elder, evangelist and teacher, and gives them direction. Although there is admittedly overlap in which part of the Great Commission the individual roles serve, the primary focus should be clear. The primary focus of the evangelist is on the initial disciple-making process—evangelism. He must set the example personally, call all disciples to be evangelistic, and then make sure they are trained to do it. Since the second part of the Great Commission is broader in scope and more long-range, it should be no surprise that both elders and teachers have that part as their primary focus. Perhaps we could make the distinction that teachers help disciples mature by encouraging their intellectual growth in their knowledge of the Bible, and elders help disciples mature by encouraging their emotional growth in applying that knowledge. Both teachers and elders, focused on the maturation process, help people grow more and more into the image of Christ.

Perhaps you are wondering what qualifies me to assert my opinions and assessments of how elders, evangelists and teachers should work together. In the spirit of Paul in Philippians 3, where he listed his qualifications for the sake of argument (though he did not derive his confidence from such things), I humbly offer a summary of my ministry experience, which will help you to understand the perspectives from which I write this chapter: I have been serving in the preaching, teaching and shepherding fields for more than forty years. For most of that time, I was on the paid staff of churches, although now I am supporting myself through a teaching ministry. But I have led churches and ministry staffs within churches with my evangelist's hat on; I have served as an elder for fifteen years in Boston and five in Phoenix; I taught in a ministry training school in my mainline days; and in our movement I have taught in leadership training programs in Boston, Europe, Phoenix, Asia and Kiev. All of these experiences have given me a firsthand view and personal experience of the needs and the potential threats to unity that arise in each of these three roles and among their relationships with one another.

From an emotional standpoint, I believe that I am even-handed in my evaluations of the needs and challenges in each role. (You will have to make your own judgment on that!) I have loved serving in each of these roles, and I have great friendships with many men in each of the three roles. Like the gifts in Romans 12, none of these roles is more important than the other. God doesn't make such distinctions, and neither should we. I honor and defend the value of all three roles, believing that they are all vital. On the few occasions when I have heard elders or teachers minimizing the role of evangelist, I may *feel* defensive, but I try to avoid *acting* defensive while speaking on behalf of the evangelist role. When I have heard evangelists or teachers minimizing the role of an elder, I have the same feelings and the same reactions as a defender of elders. When I have heard evangelists or elders minimizing the role of teacher, I likewise become the defender of that role. I say all of that to say this: When I speak about any of the three roles, and try to honestly evaluate how our movement has *in general* handled each role in the past, please don't get defensive. Know that I respect, value and (when needed), rise to the defense of each of these God-ordained roles. In the eloquent words of Delmar in the movie *O Brother, Where Art Thou?*, "I'm with you, fellas!"

Much of what I have written in other chapters has been aimed at helping us as individual leaders to become more self-aware and more in touch with what we have been in the past and what we need to be and become now. This chapter is aimed at helping us become more role-aware, and more in touch with how groups of leaders have worked collectively in the past and how they need to work in the future. To be candid, anyone who is defensive about his role and not receptive to critique and input has other problems—problems that have already been discussed at length in the book. And, of course, the taproot problem is nearly always going to be our pride in one form or another. Therefore, please hear me out and don't become defensive. Leaders should be the most humble people in our fellowship, not the least humble. We are learners, so let's be ready to learn some things as we read on.

The Evangelist Role

Although I do believe we need to vary our terminology for this role, the term *evangelist* does help us keep in mind the primary focus of the role. I was talking recently to a mature man of influence in the mainline church setting, and he made some interesting observations about where his group is now in their view of evangelism. According to him, when someone says something about the need to evangelize, a common reaction from a typical member goes like this: "That's just so '70s!" My friend was chagrined about this attitude, but he was being totally honest about where he believes his own fellowship is in this area. It makes me grateful for our fellowship's dedication to world evangelism—both as individuals and as a collective body—and it makes me grateful for all evangelists who have devoted their life to the mission of Jesus. I also understand, coming from our Campus Ministry Movement days, why we would want to call our guys in the pulpit by the term "evangelist."

Because I so appreciate evangelists, I want to make sure that other people view them in the positive light that I do. That brings me to the need to ask questions about the concerns that others have, or could have, toward evangelists. We have already addressed our past mistakes and the feelings they produced in the average church member. It was interesting to watch what happened in churches or regions of churches that lost their evangelists and couldn't replace them for extended periods of time. Some members seemed almost relieved to be without their staff leaders at first, but over time, the stock of leaders went up considerably. Those situations gave us a different application of the old saying, "Absence makes the heart grow fonder!"

In most of our churches, leaders are now appreciated, but in direct proportion to the degree that those leaders practice golden rule leadership. Really, it has always been that way. Leaders who led well were loved and appreciated, and leaders who led poorly were tolerated at best and resented at worst. The unpopularity of evangelists following the firestorm of 2003 was an aberration that lasted for different lengths of time in different churches. But as a movement, we are back in a much better and much more normal place now—thankfully.

Unity between leaders, regardless of role, is the bigger concern. How do leaders in other roles view evangelists? At the outset, we have to acknowledge that evangelists were more responsible for the leadership mistakes in our past than anyone else. For one thing, they outnumbered teachers or elders by a huge margin. Furthermore, in our movement, they were by design the leaders *over* all other leaders. In our old system, based as it was on the military model, many evangelists also led in ways that violated the principles of Matthew 20:20–28. Thus, we hurt others and we passed the same leadership approach down the line to lower-level leaders. All of that has already been established. The problem for we who served as elders at the time is that our input was sometimes not taken seriously. Had some evangelists been willing to listen to the few elders among us, much damage could have been avoided. As an elder, I came to view myself as a "seed planter" with evangelists who were higher up the leadership ladder. All I felt like I could do was express my concerns (some of them about very serious issues) and pray that what I said might eventually find some root in the minds of those to whom I expressed them. Sometimes that worked—usually after enough time had passed that the evangelist forgot where the idea had come from originally and thought it was his! (Yes, I'm being totally serious here.)

Teachers had similar experiences. The conflict here came because of the channel through which the teachers gave their input and expressed their concerns. Whereas elders were usually thinking about the emotional well-being of church members or staff members, the teachers had concerns that were more of a direct biblical nature. They studied subjects from a biblical perspective, and shared the lessons learned and the scriptures behind them. In my experience, evangelists had—and many still have—the tendency to respond to such input without opening the Bible to study out what the teacher has presented. Their answers are often simply pragmatic. The first question in their mind is usually, "How is this going to affect my job or my ministry group and our effectiveness?"

Although there are certainly exceptions to my observations, certain patterns generally hold true. Our tendencies are fairly predictable: Evangelists respond to an appeal to take a different direction by first thinking about how it is going to affect the mission; elders think first about how it is going to affect the security and emotional well-being of the flock; and teachers think first about what the Bible says about it. This is not to say that those in all three roles don't think at all from the other two vantage points, but their role does lead them into certain thinking patterns. Actually, none of that is bad as long as we work as a team, valuing the perspective of people who fill the other two roles. What matters is that we respect and seek the perspectives of people in other roles, inviting them to inform and complete our own viewpoint.

I recall one well-known evangelist, after he had moved from a church where he had served for a long time, saying that he had moved in order to get away from the elders and to be able to make decisions without any interference from them. That person was an extremist in many ways and is no longer with our movement, but the example shows the dangers of trusting in one perspective (especially your own) too much. Our present congregational evangelist in Phoenix, Gary Sciascia, had never served with an eldership before taking on his current role, and he has admitted that he has experienced a learning curve ever since. However, he understands the principles I have expressed and has done an admirable job of working with people in all three roles. Most of our evangelists have become team players with their fellow evangelists and with others in various leadership roles. My concern is not that we are now in a bad place. My concern is that we not allow ourselves to revert to earlier patterns, and also that we keep growing in our interrelationships. Growth in the right directions is the antidote to reverting to wrong directions. It's fine to say, "Thank God for the changes we have made," as long as we don't get complacent and quit striving to make improvements. That principle applies to all areas of Christianity, not just leadership.

The Elder Role

I first became an elder rather reluctantly. My experiences as a preacher in the mainline churches were characterized by tensions with certain elders. I had great relationships with some elders, but took lots of antacids in trying to survive with others. (And I don't pretend that the conflict I experienced with those elders was all their fault—I blame some of it on my own pride.) Elders in that fellowship were much like evangelists in ours in that they were viewed as being *over* all other leaders as well as the members. Once we get into the mode of thinking and arguing about who has authority over whom, we are already in dangerous territory. During my days preaching in the mainline church, we lived in that territory most of the time. Therefore, when I was approached about becoming an elder in Boston, I said, "No, I don't want to be an elder; I just want to be an evangelist." I said this in part because of my bad experiences in the past, but also because the evangelist role was *the* role among us, and to be really respected, you felt the need to excel as an evangelist. The interesting thing about that common feeling is that most of the average members in those days respected elders more than anyone. But we had not yet come to fully value all of the gifts and all of the *types* of leadership gifts. We have made much progress on that front in recent years.

I have had the privilege of working with some great elders, but elders have to be aware of what they do that brings concerns to other leaders. Perhaps at the top of the list is the fact that elders can be too calculated and slow in making decisions. A part of this reticence comes from being afraid to make mistakes. That fear may spring from a desire not to do anything that would negatively affect the flock they oversee. It may also trace back to a concern that they might end up looking bad. That motivation is called *pride*. We are all going to make mistakes, but after taking a reasonable time to consider decisions that need to be made, we must make them and move on. If the decision turns out to be a mistake, let's admit it, learn from it and keep moving on. I have been in some meetings with elders (sometimes as a member of the eldership) and left needing another antacid! We couldn't make decisions until we had examined every conceivable possibility and every possible result, which meant that we almost couldn't make decisions at all.

Another part of the difficulty in decision-making occurs when your premise of decision-making is that unanimity has to be reached, rather than broad consensus. There are some types of decisions that may demand unanimity, but not many. Most of what we deal with falls within the opinion realm, and a broad consensus is all that is required. When we first established an eldership in Phoenix, we had five elders and a slate chock-full of issues to address. If four out of the five were persuaded to take a certain direction, the other elder would say, "Fine. Although that is not my favorite option, if you other guys are so inclined, I can support it." We were able to move through packed agendas time after time. Given the condition of the church at the time, had we not been able to make that kind of progress, the church would have been left languishing in some very hurtful conditions.

Another factor that complicates decision-making is when every elder feels like he has to know everything about every situation before he can make a decision. This factor boils down to a lack of trust in the perspectives of others in the group who know the situation better. If everyone in any type of decision-making group has to know *everything* that *anyone* else knows, get ready to develop a hatred for meetings. In any group, some are closer to a given situation than others, and if you can't trust their perspective to a reasonable degree, either you or they need to leave the group. We have to trust the people who lead with us.

To use another illustration from Phoenix, when Gary became the congregational evangelist (taking over one of my roles), he immediately started leading staff meetings. At the time, I suggested to him that he and I should alternate in leading the meetings of the leadership team (comprised of elders and evangelists). We only did that for maybe two meetings. By then I was immersed in my teaching ministry and traveling a lot, and knew that Gary had a better feel for what was going on locally than I did (although I was still an elder at the time). It was logical to assume that he was the better choice to lead all of the leadership team meetings. If I couldn't trust his perspective, I couldn't trust him to lead the meetings—in which case I couldn't trust him to serve as the congregational evangelist in the first place. With my travel schedule, I had to trust the perspective of the people most closely involved in any situation. Even if I had been in town more often, I still would have given more weight to the opinions of the people closest to situations—even above my own opinions. Control freaks shouldn't be in decision-making groups. They will cause problems, and it doesn't matter what their individual role is—evangelist, elder or teacher. They bring delay and damage to the dynamics of the group, and therefore shouldn't remain in it.

Another challenge elders will likely face is in their relationships with younger leaders, especially leaders on the staff of the church. Younger leaders make mistakes, and older leaders will make their fair share as well. The young ones still need to feel supported and believed in by the elders. One of the most helpful contributions made by elders is in giving encouragement. Being commended by older people, especially those in leadership roles, is more meaningful than we could imagine. Conversely, criticism by older people carries quite a negative impact. Elders occupy a key place in approving and encouraging the staff. Each of us have certain relationships that are essential in helping us feel accepted and helping us to change through that acceptance. For example, our children can weather some pretty challenging storms in their relationships if we as parents remain "up" on them. A wife can endure many challenges as long as her husband is "up" on her. For staff people, their key approval comes from the lead evangelist and his wife, and if there are elders, the staff needs approval from the elders and their wives as well. If we are "up" on our staff, they will do their best. If there is doubt in their minds about how we view them, the insecurities will be large and growing. We are key people in helping them feel loved and supported, and this love and support provides the real foundation for their continued growth and change.

Another important point is in how elders view their role in relationship to the staff. Any tendency for elders to view themselves as employers with employees is unhealthy. Although that is a common practice in mainline churches, it is a deadly one indeed. Certainly elders do have a say in hiring and firing, but an employer-employee mentality prohibits the development of the kinds of relationships that are healthy and biblical. Jesus understood this principle perfectly, as may be seen in his statement in John 15:15: "I no longer call you servants, because a servant does not know his master's business. Instead, I have called you friends, for everything that I learned from my Father I have made known to you." Elders should likewise cultivate friendships with the evangelists and other staff members. When I as an elder have had to inform a staff person of their termination, the difficulty of that discussion for both of us was determined by our relationship. If I didn't shed tears in those situations, that was a bad sign.

The Teacher Role

I spent a number of years teaching in a ministry training school many years ago, a school from which I had graduated. Once I became a part of our movement, I never expected to use my teaching experience and training in the ways that I have. The early foundation of the ICOC had as one of its mantras the fact that we trained ministers like Jesus did—by walking with them rather than having them trained in classrooms. Somehow we seemed to miss the fact that Paul "took the disciples with him and had discussions daily in the lecture hall of Tyrannus" for two years, leading to the evangelization of Asia through this process of training leaders and sending them out to establish churches (Acts 19:9–10). While the on-the-job training approach will always be vital, it is not complete by itself, since Jesus is not the trainer. One weakness of this concept has been that the training was dissimilar in some ways to the on-the-job training that Jesus gave to the apostles. He taught them much Bible (see Luke 24:27,44–45), whereas we have tended to focus on what might be called "practical ministry," with no systematic teaching of the text of Scripture. Both approaches are needed—and both need continuing improvements. As far as I know, Douglas Jacoby was the first among us to start ministry training programs for staff members in the group of churches where he worked. The rest of us began similar programs by imitating what he was doing, and from there, all of us have continued to look for ways to keep improving the training and to expand the opportunities to more and more staff members and future staff members when possible.

We need more trained teachers among us, and quite a number of church staff members are getting advanced academic training. This will provide us with more resources for giving our ministry staffs more systematic biblical training. As much as the training is needed, we teachers have to be self-aware and role-aware of how what we are doing affects others. Teachers have created some tensions and certainly have the potential of doing that in the future. They generally approach issues in the church from a different perspective than do evangelists and elders, even when the evangelists and elders have academic biblical training themselves. We all tend to view the spiritual realm through the lens of our primary leadership role. After 2003, some teachers complained that they had felt somewhat sidelined or discounted in the past when they had brought up issues that questioned the status quo. When much of our movement structure was dismantled, or appeared to be dismantled, teachers felt more freedom to state their differing opinions than ever before, and we did. (Yes, I include myself.)

This gave the appearance that we were more out of harmony with the status quo than we actually were. Some of what teachers openly taught needed to be said, and other things taught were just opinion matters. In some cases, due to distasteful personal experiences and due to feeling muzzled in the past, teachers said things that created some negative ripple effects among other leaders (mainly evangelists). While that was understandable, especially considering the unsettled state of our movement at the time, it still strained relations between some evangelists and teachers. Mistakes on one side of the river don't justify mistakes on the other side. In spite of evangelists' mistakes over the years, whatever strains the teachers later created in their relationships with other leaders must also be addressed and resolved (if they haven't already been resolved).

During that unsettled period, I think teachers were emboldened by the widespread admission that we had not taught enough in-depth Bible to ground our people scripturally. This admission stated a real truth and exposed a real need, but many people soon adopted a naive view of the role of teaching. Their solution of choice for our problems was simplistic—namely, that all our problems could be solved with more in-depth teaching. People who adopted that mindset saw the teacher role as the "savior" of the movement. I attended one meeting of teachers and "wannabe" teachers that had me thinking, "These people have both feet firmly planted on the clouds." (Yes, I spoke up.) As much as I am doing to promote deeper teaching and study of the Bible, I believe it is only one part of the solutions we need—an important part, mind you, but not the only part. Ministers in the mainline Church of Christ have far more academic training than ours do, and that has not come close to solving all of their problems. The leadership improvement we need is multifaceted, and simplistic answers will not do.

Another concern some leaders have with teachers (or some teachers) is that their teaching is too academic in nature. I can understand that critique and would agree that teachers can sound as if they live in the intellectual world instead of the real world. We teachers must ask ourselves: What are we trying to accomplish in our training? I personally have a concern that teachers often overestimate our students' basic biblical knowledge level, and so we delve into areas that are beyond the scope of what our students really need. If this concern is valid, that means that we fail at two points: One, we fail to provide what they most need (or at least we limit it); and two, we confuse them by introducing topics that they are not yet equipped to handle.

My conviction about my role as a teacher (at whatever level) is that I should know the subject better than most of those whom I teach and should distill my teaching down to the essence of what the student most needs and is able to actually absorb and use. Then the student has to learn to follow that same principle as he passes down what he knows to the people who learn from him. There is a danger in wanting to expose students to topics that do not fit within the above framework. Perhaps that tendency is fostered by the fact that in the past, we were too limited in the number of subjects taught (and we were), and also because we felt that discussing certain other subjects was verboten (also true). But being reactionary is not the right response to past mistakes or stifling atmospheres.

And while all of our church members need more in-depth teaching, we need to put a lot of thought and effort into Bible training for our staff members. Our ministry people need more Bible knowledge, and they need it bad. The question of the hour is what type of training is needed.

The answer to that question is found in asking whether our primary emphasis is on training people to become evangelists or teachers. We must be clear in our own minds about that as we teach. If we are aiming our training toward raising up other teachers, the strong tendency will be to slant our teaching toward the academic side (not knowledge for knowledge's sake, of course)—rather than toward the practical applications that change lives and build churches. One of our nonstaff teachers made this observation: "It is my estimation that in any group of people in a church, there will be about five percent that have the teacher-type personality. They are drawn to the Bible and are curious about all the facts, the nuances and details of the structure, the history and the in-depth study of the Word." Other teachers might set the percentage at a higher number, but all teachers would surely agree that those with a teacher bent are a fairly small minority. I would estimate the figure at around ten percent, and while those whom we are training for ministry careers will have a higher interest than most in the more academically oriented study, the majority of them still want their training in Bible and Bible-related subjects to be focused on the practical applications that they will need in the ministry.

A word of advice to teachers who train ministers: Let us be careful not to let the minority of our students who are "teacher types" (those who are often openly enthusiastic about the "deeper" issues) overly influence our teaching focus. We must remain focused on helping train evangelists, not teachers.

When we are teaching a group of very mature disciples with good biblical and doctrinal grounding, discussions of deeper issues and controversial issues are fine—but such discussions should be reserved for those settings. As a teacher type myself, I enjoy such discussions, but I don't "go there" when I'm training younger, less experienced disciples.

When I encounter someone who desires to become a teacher, I encourage them to take more formal training at a conservative seminary, and I give them personal on-the-job training. Some brothers, however, are not equipped to handle some academic settings. Seminary is not for everyone—and not even for every smart disciple who loves academic learning. In my opinion, I would only recommend graduate school studies for people who have already developed a strong and practical biblical foundation within our movement, and who also have the emotional and spiritual maturity and stability to handle the intellectual and doctrinal challenges that they will certainly encounter. They have to be able to eat the fish and spit out the bones—with good discernment regarding which is which!

My associate in the Asia-Pacific Leadership Academy is Rolan Monje, a great young brother who has recently earned a doctorate in ministry. The personal and practical teacher training I do with him consists of the following: He takes my courses in the Academy; we have outside discussions and he does some extra assignments; he teaches some segments of courses he has already seen me teach; and afterwards we have debriefing sessions about his teaching. This approach is training him to be a teacher—but primarily with the goal of helping him become a trainer of ministers rather than a trainer of teachers. In other words, people with the teaching gift have to be taught individually, without sidetracking the main thrust of our ministry training sessions to meet the needs of that particular minority. Further, I think we have to be careful not to automatically assume that a large number of our ministry guys should seek advanced theological training, for some have already been adversely affected by doing so. I expect that some of our most experienced teachers are going to corroborate in developing an approach to training more teachers ourselves. I am very thankful for the increasing number of programs being established to train ministers, and we also need to develop a unified means of training more teachers.

My own thinking about these matters has been formed by attending two different schools for biblical education. One was called a school of preaching, and the other was a graduate school of religion (a seminary). In brief, the differences in the teaching approach in these schools had to do both with what was stressed and how it was stressed. Both taught in-depth Bible, but the school of preaching emphasized practical issues about life change and church-building, rather than the more intellectual, factual material. We still learned plenty of facts and memorized hundreds of Bible verses, but the emphasis was clearly different. Perhaps more important, these practical emphases were delivered with fervor and deep convictions. I was much more inspired and motivated to change the world by the school of preaching than by the seminary. Certainly, the Bible I learned in seminary was valuable, but all of us who teach must strive to provide inspiration, not just information, for those whom we teach. Although I personally love learning the more intellectual material, I try to keep in mind what most changes students' lives and convictions, and I teach accordingly. That, it seems to me, is what our training should provide, and if it does, we will avoid the charge of being too academic.

The other concern that I have heard expressed about teachers is the same concern Paul expressed in a different context, when he wrote: "We know that we all possess knowledge. Knowledge puffs up, but love builds up. The man who thinks he knows something does not yet know as he ought to know" (1 Corinthians 8:1–2). As we gain knowledge—and teachers thrive on that pursuit—pride in the form of arrogance is a very real threat. Perhaps that is why James wrote, "Not many of you should presume to be teachers, my brothers, because you know that we who teach will be judged more strictly" (James 3:1). In that context, James is talking about the destructive power of the tongue. We teachers do a lot of talking, and we must remember that "when words are many, sin is not absent" (Proverbs 10:19). God in the flesh once very humbly stated this truth about his teaching: "For I did not speak of my own accord, but the Father who sent me commanded me what to say and how to say it" (John 12:49). Both *what* we teach and *how* we teach it must be done with great humility. God's truth is a powerful thing—we must handle it with care and prayer. Let's not allow ourselves, whatever our role, to be adversely affected by the role itself, or by our accomplishments or our knowledge. And let's all help each other to remain humble, which means that we leaders must confront pride in each other without hesitation. We are our brothers' keepers.

A Marriage Made in Heaven

What should the relationship between elders, evangelists and teachers look like? A marriage made in heaven! Of course, like a marriage between a man and woman, marriages really aren't made in heaven—they come in kit form and must be put together on earth. But God wants the end result to look (and function) as though it was made in heaven. Surely he wants people who occupy the three key leadership roles to look and to function in that way. What will it take to develop and keep such a "marriage"? It takes great humility and appreciation for our fellow workers' different perspectives and contributions, and it takes all of us not worrying about who has the most authority. Authority is not our issue; humility and teamwork are our issues. The answer of what we most need is easy; the implementation is the challenge, but a challenge that we must, and will, meet.

Pendulum swings must be avoided at all costs, and this statement certainly applies when considering the marriage between roles. In my mainline church days, I was an evangelist in an elder-dominated environment, and in my early Boston days, I was an elder in an evangelist-dominated environment. (Teachers were all but absent in both equations.) Both environments are extremes, and both are unbiblical, impractical, unproductive and unhealthy. And both are reactionary in their developmental stages. No sooner do we throw out one extreme than we seek to adopt another—if we are focused on who has the authority. We must avoid such extremes, or we will reap the same consequences that we have already reaped in the past. We are a team of three types of Spirit-gifted leaders, and we must act like a team.

Dynamic Leadership

Being an avid football fan, I can't help but use a sports illustration. My favorite team is the New England Patriots—three-time World Champions! (Fans of other teams, I'm sure the generous spirit of Jesus will allow you to forgive my bias!) The three main roles of this team are reflected in its offense, defense, and special teams. They don't think in terms of "checks and balances" at all—although they have different roles, and when one part of the team is not on the field, they are cheering on the part that is. The respect they have for one another is obvious, and they are totally supportive of each other. They are willing to play on another part of the team if needed, no matter what their normal role. Their dominant mindset is well reflected in the old saying, "All for one and one for all!" Shouldn't people in the various leadership roles in the church have this same *team* mindset?

My first experience in a discipling church was in San Diego back in the mid-1980s. It was certainly the most biblical (and joyous) situation I had ever been part of up to that point. I came in to serve as the lead evangelist when I was in my early 40s, and soon thereafter was joined by co-evangelist Gregg Marutzky (then in his late 20s). George Havins and Ron Brumley were serving as elders at the time. The four of us formed a leadership team that worked together beautifully. We met weekly, usually with our wives, and led the church as a team. When I agreed to accept the evangelist role, the elders told me that they understood that I would be discipling them, since that was the accepted "ordering" of relationships at the time. Not accustomed to seeing such humility in elders, I was too shocked to say anything, but I knew what would happen in our relationship—we in fact discipled one another as equals. None of us thought in terms of who was "over" whom. We saw our roles as distinct, but overlapping in many ways. The evangelists focused on leading the charge evangelistically and the elders focused on meeting the needs of the flock. With both perspectives always co-joined, we planned as a team and made decisions as a team. It could be accurately called "a marriage made in heaven."

May God help us all to duplicate such relationships between all leaders of all types, and especially those serving in the roles of elder, teacher and evangelist. This is his goal for us in congregational settings and in the movement as a whole. We are God's team, united with him and with one another—filled with the Spirit and led by the Spirit. Amen, so may it be in ever-increasing measure!

Chapter Fourteen

Relationships: Team Leadership Principles

Definitions

Basic Concept

When the term "team leadership" is mentioned, different things come to mind for different people, depending on their own training and experiences. People who have more of a business background may think first of what leadership produces. They envision various people in a department doing their tasks well, resulting in progress that benefits everyone. Each member of the team does his or her job and does it well. The key word for them is likely something akin to *teamwork* or *cooperation*—cooperative efforts of employees for the good of a given department. For others, team leadership suggests a different picture: developing a good esprit de corps between workers, with a focus less on function and more on cultivating an overall positive group attitude. Of course, positive attitudes produce positive environments, and these in turn produce positive results. For yet other people, *decision-making* is the concept that registers first in their minds, and this produces either good vibes or bad ones, depending on their personal experience or observations of group decision-making.

I would guess that most church leaders, when thinking of team leadership, initially think about group decision-making—especially since the older leaders in our movement were trained with a one-man leadership perspective. This doesn't mean that these leaders expected to make totally unilateral decisions (although they often did so), but what they have been trained to expect is to make the large majority of final decisions. Once our movement began to change and these leaders started trying to institute what they thought was team leadership, they often found decision-making rather laborious at best and almost impossible at worst. And so for a while the idea of team leadership fell into disrepute—and some people still don't like it. No one would argue that the one-man decision-making approach is not quicker and far easier in the short run, but we all should argue that learning how to lead as teams is a worthwhile endeavor, for several reasons.

First, many minds are superior to any one mind in figuring out the best roads to take— unless, of course, that one mind is inspired directly by the Holy Spirit. (Think Jesus here, or one of the apostles or prophets.) Honestly, I think the fatally flawed viewpoint that our leaders were inspired by the Spirit was not absent in our past— at least in the minds of some rather narcissistic leaders. However, enough mistakes were made by those leaders to demonstrate that their own spirits were often leading them, when they thought it was God's Spirit! Proverbs 11:14 is but one of many passages in the Bible that direct us toward surrounding ourselves with many advisers rather than thinking that we always know best: "For lack of guidance a nation falls, but many advisers make victory sure."

Second, the atmosphere between leaders, and between leaders and nonleaders, is enhanced considerably when a group of mature, trusted leaders leads together as a team. Team leadership engenders trust in a number of directions, and does produce esprit de corps in unique ways. The more people feel valued, the more they give their heart to whatever a group attempts. Conversely, the more we feel that our views are devalued, the less responsibility we will embrace. Having our opinions valued is one of the best motivators of all when it comes to working effectively with others.

Third, relationships grow out of an atmosphere built on trust and teamwork. Team members can function reasonably well with just business-type relationships, but the more we feel like part of a close family, the more we will contribute to the cause. Of course, in the spiritual realm, the cause is *the* Cause! Jesus' words in John 15:15 cannot be improved upon to demonstrate this principle: "I no longer call you servants, because a servant does not know his master's business. Instead, I have called you friends, for everything that I learned from my Father I have made known to you." The Master understood that effective training of his closest disciples had to go far beyond information dissemination and methodology—relationship-building was at the heart of his leadership style. Clearly, a key component of building those relationships was in how he pulled others into his thinking and doing.

Important Distinctions

One important distinction to make within the realm of team leadership is that team leadership is one thing and forming a leadership team is yet another. Although the two ideas are closely related, there is some difference between them. The basic concept of *team leadership* assumes that a group of people with expertise in a given area is more likely to make better decisions about things in that area than any one person, no matter how much expertise an individual may have. Having a *leadership team* means that a small group of people is chosen whose maturity and experience has prepared them to function in the realm of overall leadership for an organization. This group functions as a top decision-making team, but this shouldn't mean that they necessarily make all of the decisions themselves in isolation. In some cases they oversee others who make decisions, while in other cases, they recognize their need to get input from those with the most expertise in a given area. Ideally, their decisions will consistently be influenced by input from a variety of different sources as they represent the members of their organization. Keeping in mind the difference between team leadership and having a leadership team is vital to building teamwork in a broader spectrum. Team leadership is more the philosophy, and having a set leadership team is more a practice. As long as a leadership team recognizes and accepts the concept of team leadership (they are willing to embrace broader inclusion as needed), it will block the isolation of one group (the leadership team) from the larger membership they represent.

Another important distinction to be made in speaking of team leadership is to understand the absolute necessity of knowing the difference between roles and relationships. For example, a church leader in a very responsible position (overseeing a whole country of churches) once asked me to assist with some difficulties he was having with some of the key leaders under his leadership. In my view, his request alone earned him very high marks in both wisdom and humility. Although he had developed a leadership team, it had become dysfunctional in some ways. I sat in the group (with the church leader present) and went around the circle of leaders, listening to each of them share about the dynamics that frustrated them. It quickly became apparent that the dysfunction had developed because the difference between roles and relationships had not been defined and understood.

These younger leaders had been converted and/or trained by the older leader, but they had matured, and now they felt that the older leader was not leading them in a manner that took their level of maturity into account. In other words, they didn't think that they were being led in an age-appropriate manner, and so they felt something amiss in their relationship with their trainer. From a role perspective, he was still over them in the Lord (1 Thessalonians 5:12) and knew more than they knew about ministry. However, from a relational perspective, they wanted to be treated as friends and confidants. They had grown up, but didn't feel the respect that growing up spiritually should have gained. Jesus understood this distinction and described it perfectly in John 15:5. Although he was still Master, he called his disciples his friends and made them feel like friends. If God in the flesh was moved to make this distinction, we had better understand and apply his example as well. The leader in the situation I described seemed to learn this lesson quickly, another credit to both his wisdom and humility. Understanding the distinction between roles and relationships is essential to effective team leadership. While we may not be peers in role, we must become peers in relationship.

Biblical Examples

Old Testament

The Old Testament is replete with examples of both the concept of team leadership and of leadership teams of many types. Since Israel was both a nation and a spiritual entity, leadership teams were found in the realms of military, political, and religious organizations. The religious type were evidenced most clearly by the

Levites and Aaronic priesthood. As Moses led the children out of Egypt, he was the unquestioned leader of the nation—but he was anything but a one-man show. Here are some interesting passages on the subject as the nation was being formed:

> Exodus 16:22; 34:31 – These passages both mention "leaders of the community" and constitute the first such mention in the Old Testament.
>
> Exodus 18:24–26 – This passage tells us that Moses, on the advice of his father-in-law, chose "capable men" and appointed them as leaders over groups of "thousands, hundreds, fifties and tens." These men served as judges, and lightened Moses' load by settling the simple cases themselves. Good leaders delegate, and in this case, a large organizational effort yielded leadership teams at several levels.
>
> Numbers 1:44 – This verse describes who those aforementioned "leaders of the community" were and how they were chosen, for they "were the men counted by Moses and Aaron and the twelve leaders of Israel, each one representing his family."
>
> Numbers 11:16 – In this instance, the Lord told Moses to choose seventy leaders, who are not all named, but the two mentioned in verse 26, Eldad and Medad, were not among the "community leaders" nor the twelve chosen to spy out the land in chapter 13.
>
> Numbers 13:2 – Interestingly, an examination of the names of the spies in verses 4–16 shows that these were all totally different men from the "leaders of the community," but as with those first chosen, the ratio was the same—one person per tribe.
>
> Numbers 16:1–2 – In this passage, the 250 Israelite men who rebelled in the situation involving Korah, Dathan, Abiram and On were also community leaders and thus members of an even larger council about whose initial formation we know nothing.
>
> Numbers 34:18–29 – In this passage, Moses chose one man per tribe to help divide the land territories once Canaan was conquered. Of previously mentioned leaders, only Caleb is in this list, since all of the older leaders besides him and Joshua had died before the land was conquered.
>
> Deuteronomy 16:18 – A general command was given to appoint needed leadership in the new land. The details were left up to those who were choosing the needed leadership: "Appoint judges and officials for each of your tribes in every town the Lord your God is giving you, and they shall judge the people fairly."
>
> Deuteronomy 29:9–10 – Note the four types of leaders who accompanied Moses near the end of his life and leadership role: leaders, chief men, elders and officials.
>
> Joshua 24:1 – Near the end of his life, Joshua had basically the same type of leaders

> in place. Elders and officials are the same groups mentioned in Deuteronomy 29, while the other two terms (judges and leaders) are slightly different in the Hebrew.
>
> 1 Chronicles 29:6 – We find similar types of leaders in David's time: leaders of families, officers of the tribes of Israel, the commanders of thousands and commanders of hundreds, and the officials in charge of the king's work.
>
> 2 Chronicles 1:2 – The description of leadership groups in Solomon's time was virtually the same: the commanders of thousands and commanders of hundreds, the judges, the leaders in Israel, and the heads of families.
>
> 2 Chronicles 19:4–11 – During the time of the divided kingdom, Jehoshaphat "appointed judges in the land, in each of the fortified cities of Judah… In Jerusalem also, Jehoshaphat appointed some of the Levites, priests and heads of Israelite families to administer the law of the LORD and to settle disputes."

In all of these passages, certain facts about leadership teams are obvious. One, many variations existed, involving numerous leadership groups, often comprised of significant numbers of leaders in some of the groups. Two, they were found in the realms mentioned earlier: military, religious and political. Three, although we are not told exactly how all of these groups were formed, the people often had a hand in helping choose their own leaders. Four, the nature of the teamwork aspect of the teams is not clearly specified, but taking into account human nature, we can infer that group dynamics were certainly at work, and some leadership training must have been provided by Moses or other leaders.

After looking at these passages, all that can be said about team leadership in those settings is that leadership teams were established as a way of delegating the top leader's authority and helping him lead the people. More important to our study is how the concept of team leadership was applied by that top leader. How did he work with other leaders under his authority, and how did he work with the average person whom he led?

David provides us with a good example of his leadership style in 1 Chronicles 13:1–4:

> David conferred with each of his officers, the commanders of thousands and commanders of hundreds. He then said to the whole assembly of Israel, "If it seems good to you and if it is the will of the Lord our God, let us send word far and wide to the rest of our brothers throughout the territories of Israel, and also to the priests and Levites

who are with them in their towns and pasturelands, to come and join us. Let us bring the ark of our God back to us, for we did not inquire of it during the reign of Saul." The whole assembly agreed to do this, because it seemed right to all the people.

He began by conferring with his leaders, but quickly brought the whole assembly of Israel into the discussion and decision. This exact principle is found in the New Testament, most clearly in the book of Acts. We will look at some of those passages in the next section. But we can conclude that David set an example in valuing and seeking the input of both his leaders and his people as a whole. Frankly, it is difficult to find biblical examples of singular leaders who made consistent unilateral decisions in either the OT or NT setting—except for leaders that we would agree were poor leaders.

New Testament

Acts is our go-to book for delving into the topic of team leadership. We begin with Acts 1:15–26 and the choosing of an apostle to take the place of Judas. Peter led the process, but the entire group of 120 seemed to be involved in whatever the specifics of the process were. In Acts 6:1–7, when the apostles needed help in seeing that the Grecian widows were treated fairly, they came up with a plan to choose seven brothers to help meet this need, then gave the spiritual qualifications by which to guide the choosing, but then had the church actually make the choices. The apostles then appointed the people chosen by the church. Just how the apostles guided the overall process we are not told, but their trust for the membership was obvious, and everyone benefited from the choices the church made.

Acts 15 illustrates the principles we saw in 1 Chronicles 13. Read the following verses carefully as you think about team leadership principles:

> Some men came down from Judea to Antioch and were teaching the brothers: "Unless you are circumcised, according to the custom taught by Moses, you cannot be saved." This brought Paul and Barnabas into sharp dispute and debate with them. So Paul and Barnabas were appointed, along with some other believers, to go up to Jerusalem to see the apostles and elders about this question. The church sent them on their way, and as they traveled through Phoenicia and Samaria, they told how the Gentiles had been converted. This news made all the brothers very glad. When they came to

Jerusalem, they were welcomed by the church and the apostles and elders, to whom they reported everything God had done through them (Acts 15:1-4).

This Jew/Gentile issue was likely the most dangerous issue the early church faced in its first decades and could have resulted in the whole movement being divided. Paul and Barnabas were the key leaders involved in the debate, but they and others were appointed by the Antioch church to go to Jerusalem to deal with the issue. They did not appoint themselves, although considering their roles and experience, it would not seem strange if they had. It is interesting and encouraging to note that after the church sent them on their way, they weren't so consumed with the lurking problem that they lost faith and quit rejoicing in all that God had already done through them. En route to Jerusalem, they took the time to report their good news to the brothers and sisters in Phoenicia and Samaria. Once in Jerusalem, the doctrinal issue surfaced quickly in front of the whole church. The next step was for Paul and Barnabas to meet with the apostles and elders from the Jerusalem church in a separate meeting. After this smaller group of the top leaders decided how to handle the situation, they came back to the church and not only reported their decisions, but included the church in helping decide who would deliver the decisions to individual congregations.

The church initially heard both the good news of mission work and the bad news of strong conflict occurring between certain leaders. Disciples are not going to be shielded from everything that's bad, if the issues are already known issues. However, we still have to keep Paul's admonition in Romans 16:19 in mind: "I want you to be wise about what is good, and innocent about what is evil." The issue in this case was dealt with behind closed doors, so to speak, by those most equipped by role, knowledge and experience to deal with it, but the membership was not treated as though they were fragile children. The way leaders lead is a matter of balance and common sense. An excerpt from my exposition of Acts 15 in *World Changers* can help us with that balance.

> The sequence here is very important. The leaders from Antioch were sent specifically to meet with the top leaders of the Jerusalem church, namely the apostles and elders. This they did, and it was in this setting that the issues were discussed and decisions reached. Then, the whole church was brought in and informed of the

discussions and the decisions, and their involvement was sought in deciding how to disseminate the decisions.

The church is a kingdom, not a democracy, which means that leaders are responsible for deciding the weightier issues. Sometimes the idea is advanced (often based on a misunderstanding of this passage) that everyone in the church should have an equal vote. Now that may sound very American, but it does not sound very biblical! Just imagine what would have happened at the Red Sea if Moses had left the decisions up to a democratic vote. The Israelites did have a vote of sorts in Numbers 13, as ten spies "outvoted" Joshua and Caleb. The result was disastrous, leading to forty years of wandering around in a desert while a couple of million funerals were held. Pilate asked for a vote from those assembled before Jesus, and they voted to murder God in the flesh. Majority rule in the world has never been righteous rule, because the majority are always on the wrong path (Matthew 7:13–14). Even among God's people, in the Old Testament or New Testament, God never instituted a one-vote-per-person process of decision-making. Leaders must do exactly that—lead. And the rest of us must follow that leadership. Judges 5:2 describes the happy occasion when leadership and "followership" work together correctly: "When the princes in Israel take the lead, when the people willingly offer themselves—praise the Lord!"

However, let me also hasten to add that the church must be involved in the decision-making process at appropriate levels. In this Acts 15 passage, they were brought in and informed in a way that they appreciated, and they were involved in deciding how and by whom the decisions would be spread. Back in Acts 6, another decision was made in a similar manner regarding how to meet the needs of neglected widows. The apostles decided just how the problem would be solved, and then they asked the congregation to select the men to carry out their plan.

Respect of followers for leaders and leaders for followers must be present in the hearts, expressed in our words and put into actions as we labor together. We are all a part of the one body described in 1 Corinthians 12, in which none are superior and none are inferior. Different roles we do have, but different value as children of God we do not have.

The most important point in these biblical examples is about how leaders view themselves, their role and the people they lead. Team leadership is a mindset that encapsulates these things, and results in the right kind of leadership teams. In any given environment, the way that the most influential leader relates to the other leaders most closely associated with him will trickle down to all levels. Having leadership teams is one thing; having leadership teams that function with the right concepts of team leadership is the most important issue. Having a leadership team doesn't guarantee a great spirit of team leadership, but a healthy spirit of team leadership guarantees that your leadership team will thrive. Chew on that idea for a while to make sure you grasp it.

We will bring our plane to a landing in a final chapter on team leadership *practices*, but suffice it to say at this point that any leader of any team must understand the concept of team leadership. Succinctly stated, if he leads his team well, he will often serve primarily as a facilitator of idea-sharing and a mediator of relationships and relationship dynamics within his group. He is not the boss, and yet he is the quarterback. To continue with the airplane analogy, he is the pilot who works with many other people and has the ultimate responsibility of landing the plane over and over again as he guides those under his charge. Therefore, his level of EQ (emotional intelligence) will either make him or break him as a leader. The experts in the EQ field say that one's EQ can be increased. I hope that my observations on the subject can help accomplish that increase in all of us who lead.

Principles That Cannot Be Ignored

An Understanding of Synergy

Synergy is defined by *Merriam-Webster's Collegiate Dictionary* as "a mutually advantageous conjunction or compatibility of distinct business participants or elements (as resources or efforts)." Said in another way, synergy means that the sum of output by a group is greater than the sum of the output generated by the individual parts added together. That's why I love a think-tank setting—lots of thoughts and ideas mix together, and God brings out of that mix what is best for us and the church. I am not sure just how synergy works, but it does. And, it is more than the obvious fact that multiple minds are more likely than single minds to figure out the best answers to problems.

My own theory is that groups produce some type of spiritual force field that we all can tap into when we are together in groups. If we are working as a group to pursue common goals in a defined agenda, all the better. But even in the absence of such a defined purpose, the force field still works when people of like mind are simply in one another's company. I have been in spiritual assemblies of all sorts and sizes when amazing ideas seemingly started coming out of nowhere! I know that spirits communicate with spirits, but spirits also prompt ideas in other spirits in some way that I cannot explain. We are living in a spiritual world that goes far beyond human explanation, and the Bible opens the curtain often enough on that subject to remove all doubts that it is true.

The brief stories involving Elisha's servant "seeing the unseen" in 2 Kings 6, and Daniel's encounter with an angel, often thought to be Gabriel, who was sent by Michael the archangel (Daniel 10) are enough to boggle the mind regarding the world that we cannot see with human eyes. A part of the spiritual world somehow influences our thinking simply because we are spiritual beings, seeking to "see" God and his spirit world. When we are in the presence of other beings who love God, our minds and hearts are influenced. When we are in a defined group of other beings who are trying not only to love God individually, but also to help figure out ways to help others love God more and serve him better, good things happen. God leads us beyond our own agendas to find his agenda and reach his conclusions. The concept of team leadership is based on that reality, and any leadership team that is truly seeking God's will above all else will be thus led by him.

Well, I had better change directions soon here, or I will weird out some of you even more! But my understanding of the Bible and my own personal experiences and observations have led me to the conclusions I just stated. If we are walking in the Spirit (Galatians 5:16–18), we should expect to be led in directions that maximize our effectiveness for God. As my friend Al Baird once prayed, "Lord, block the dumb." And in blocking the dumb, God leads us through the open doors into the light—the light of discovering his paths for us and the groups that we are blessed to lead.

Unified Relationships

All leaders are more than familiar with Jesus' prayer in John 17 about unity—*complete* unity, as Jesus described it. But do we have a unity that the world would approve or one that God would approve? We must have fine-tuned relationships *in* our leadership groups and *between* our leadership groups. To accomplish that noble goal, we must root out every vestige of an us-versus-them mentality at all levels and deal with all of the elephants in the living room regarding relationships. The us/them mentality can exist between leaders and nonleaders, leaders with other leaders, and between different leadership groups. We have already addressed this topic in several places and in several ways.

The elephant in the living room analogy means that we tolerate relationship issues between leaders that should not be tolerated. By nature, most of us are people-pleasers and conflict-avoiders. It is all too common for leaders to have what might be called "quiet reservations" toward other leaders, in and out of their own leadership group. The Leader of leaders, whom all disciples are to imitate, evidenced no vestige of conflict avoidance. He dealt with his friends and his enemies in exactly the same way—by directly addressing any issues or even unspoken reservations that kept people from being what God wanted them to be. My observations of disciples generally, leaders and nonleaders, would indicate that we have a long way to go in imitating Jesus in this realm. The principles in Matthew 5 and Matthew 18 leave us no choice if we are to obey him. All conflicts between disciples must be resolved biblically, and quiet reservations toward one another must be taken seriously. *Complete* unity is what Jesus prayed for, and he will settle for nothing short of that in the lives of those who wear his name.

The promotion of deep spiritual unity is much enhanced by the demonstration of mutual love and respect between all members of any leadership team. Sometimes we develop best-friend relationships with others simply because they make the first move in pursuing a relationship with us. This phenomenon occurs even when the other person is very different from us and someone with whom we would not likely have sought a close relationship of our own volition. But because of their efforts, a relationship develops that is for us very unexpected. As unusual as this process may seem, it is easy to explain with an important biblical principle. Listen to the "apostle of love" describe it: "We love because he first loved us" (1 John 4:19). Just as God's love for us causes us to reciprocate, another person's love for us produces the same result. What we all need to do in light of this principle is to make the first move to demonstrate love toward others, whether or not we are attracted to the person naturally. That is the Jesus thing to do, don't you think? It is a fundamental building block of true relational unity.

A Mutual Admiration Society

The essence of ministry is not to constantly correct. I have known too many leaders who functioned under that misguided premise. On the other hand, I have also seen too many leaders (past and present) who were prone to avoid giving corrections altogether—the opposite side of an altogether bad coin. If I could go back and raise my children over again, I would still correct them (how could you not?), but I would add copious amounts of praise. My own children seemed to have learned what not to do along these lines, and are much more adept at positive reinforcement than was their father. This provides another example from my life of being "too soon old and too late smart." However, you and I are not too late to praise God's children and our own fellow leaders in a way that provides them with eagles' wings to soar high for God.

We all remember criticisms and we all remember praise—especially what is done in front of others. My sixth-grade teacher, Mrs. Teacle, made it her aim to help me get out of myself and overcome my shyness. Other teachers' names I don't remember, but I well remember Mrs. Frances Teacle. She gave me reasons to believe in myself and to come out of my shell of shyness. I also remember one of my seventh-grade teachers, Mr. Renfro, who stopped me and my buddy Everett in the hall one day and made a statement that is still with me fifty-six years later. He simply said this: "You guys both have the capability to do tenth-grade work and you are not even doing seventh grade work." I suppose you could take that as a correction, but I took it another way entirely. That "backdoor" compliment planted a seed in me about my potential. To be honest, I didn't start living up to that potential for some years, but I did eventually discover that he was correct when I started training academically for the ministry, and I never forgot the encouragement I received from him.

Jesus didn't see a Cephas—he saw a Peter in the making. Jesus didn't see any of the Twelve for what they were; he saw them for what they could become, and all but Judas became the godly men he envisioned. (Judas also became what Jesus foresaw for him, sadly.) Thankfully, when Jesus sees us, he doesn't see us for what we are; he also sees us for what we can become. I am becoming misty-eyed as I write this, because like many of my brothers and sisters, I see my sins and weaknesses all too well and am tempted to give up on myself at times. But he doesn't, and I know that to be true intellectually even when I don't feel it emotionally. Only God knows how much encouragement we need, and he gives it to us primarily through other people whom he moves to demonstrate his love to us. We simply must learn to do that for one another, and leaders need it as much as anyone—at times we may even need it more. Leadership can be a heavy burden. All who lead understand Paul's statement in 2 Corinthians 11:28 all too well: "Besides everything else, I face daily the pressure of my concern for all the churches."

A part of being a mutual admiration society as leaders is to learn to appreciate differences in each other, not simply tolerate them. In the early days of our marriage, I sometimes discounted my lovely wife's perspective. I figured out what I thought needed to be done in a given situation and shared with her my fourteen good reasons for doing so. Sometimes she answered along these lines: "Well, I don't have an answer to those fourteen reasons, but something seems wrong about the decision." From my brilliant perspective at the time, if she couldn't answer my impeccable male logic, then my decision must be the right one! In time, after many mistakes, I learned that her female intuitiveness was in a different realm than my male logic, and I also learned how to put the brakes on a decision that she didn't feel good about. As I mentioned earlier, we received as a gift a little plaque made in the Amish area of Pennsylvania that read simply: "The goal of marriage is not to think alike—it's to think together." That principle goes far beyond the marriage relationship to encompass all relationships. We need each other's perspective because we don't know everything ourselves, although in our pride we too often think we do.

God grant us true respect for each other and for the differences in our backgrounds that make us unique. These differences influence each of our perspectives profoundly, and we can either be put off by differences in thinking, or we can see them as important to the process of the group and choose not to be too tied to our own opinions as a part of the mixture. Some leaders surround themselves with "yes men" and call that team leadership! Rest assured that it is not. A much more accurate term for that scenario would be "insecure leadership in action." A person's insecurity can be gauged accurately by his or her tendency to want control and avoid whatever and whomever interferes with that control. Are you a "control freak," or a true team builder who appreciates variety in thinking?

The nature of your team—its spirit and functionality—will provide the answer to this question. When you are secure in God's leadership, you will be a secure leader and you will produce security in those under your leadership.

Fun, Fun, Fun!

Some years ago, my wife was enjoying a day with one of her best friends in the kingdom. The sister's husband came in from a demanding day's work, and when he saw our wives laughing and enjoying life to the full, he vented some of the frustration of his day: "All you two do is have fun, fun, fun!" That has become an oft-quoted phrase among us in the intervening years. I think having fun, fun, fun should be a part of any leadership team. It is an essential part of building the kinds of relationships that make us function well in team leadership.

Several years back, when I was still a part of the leadership team in the Phoenix church, I pushed the idea of the elders and staff brothers doing more things just to have fun. One of the elders suggested that we have a bowling night, and while I was out of the country teaching, the event was planned for a late evening after the bowling leagues finished for the night. I arrived back home the night before the planned event after a long and tiring trip to Eurasia. No one expected me to show up late the following evening for the bowling outing, but I was one of the first ones to arrive. I had pushed the idea, so in my mind, I had no choice but to try and ignore my fatigue and jet lag and bowl with the boys! In each of my three games, I scored in the upper 180s, despite my exhaustion, and despite not having bowled in years. I couldn't bowl that well when I was young and bowling regularly! I think God rewarded me for encouraging something that was needed in our group.

Women shop; boys play! As a former ninety-year-old neighbor lady reminded me once, "Men are just boys grown tall." We have to play together as well as pray together and work together and share our hearts together. TOGETHER—that's the key word! Being a team means that we share life together with its ups and downs, its victories and defeats, its giving and taking. Memory-building is an essential part of family life, both in physical families and in spiritual families. Most of what remains in our memory is connected with emotions, both positive and negative ones. I have some heartaches associated with some of my leadership memories, and some big grins associated with others. You cannot be a leader without the heartaches, but you can strike a healthy balance with enough of the memories that bring a smile to your face.

Life goes by fast. Don't forget to have fun, and especially don't forget to have fun with those who share your leadership burdens. A real leadership team will cry together, make no mistake about that. A real leadership team will also laugh together—often. As I write this, I am finishing up my interim role as the congregational evangelist for the Houston church, and I expect to make one last trip to hand over the torch to the new leader. Replacing myself was the goal of my last role here, and at this point, I can say, "Mission accomplished." The thought of that accomplishment makes me happy and sad at the same time, and both emotions come from the experiences of team-building among the various types of leaders there and in the church as a whole. My greatest joy as I leave will be to see every leadership group functioning as a true spiritual team among themselves, and also with the other leadership groups and with the entire congregation. I love the way John stated the principle in 3 John 4: "I have no greater joy than to hear that my children are walking in the truth." The sad part will come from missing the people with whom I put these principles into practice, but this part still signals success. If the sadness were missing, it would mean we had failed to build team in the way that God expects.

Synergy, unity, encouragement and fun—these are the relational building blocks of team leadership that must be added to the conceptual principles. May God grant us the insight and the wisdom to lay all of these blocks well and to thus build buildings that make him proud!

Chapter Fifteen

Relationships: Team Leadership Practices

Introduction: The Need for Practicals

In the *Golden Rule Leadership* book, we focused more on the broad-brush principles of team building than on some of the more practical applications. Our thought was that one must buy into the philosophy before he will take the practical applications seriously. In many ways, this is a reasonable assumption, but some people are able to process the philosophy effectively only by visualizing the practicals from the beginning. This approach may also be helpful for those who are somewhat uneasy with a philosophical change in the first place. The purpose of this chapter is to provide some of these practical applications of team building. Special attention will be given to how teams can be developed at different stages and ages of churches or ministry groups. Being "age-appropriate" in building team is obviously needed, but figuring out just what that means is more an art form than a science. However, some pertinent ideas should help us move in the right directions without making significant mistakes as we go.

Building the Team

Building the Team in the Earliest Stages

It should be said that when planting a church or new ministry, we should expect the group to have essentially one-person leadership for a while. Most of the decisions for that new group will be made by that leader, in conjunction with whoever is providing direction from the sending church. The leader must begin in due time to build a leadership team from the ground up. However, building a leadership team is not his most pressing task in the very beginning. While it should not be on the back burner, neither should it be on the front burner. The initial evangelistic focus will in some ways slow down the development of a consensus leadership group. But he should start his work with the conviction that leading through a group is ultimately better than remaining a one-person leader for the church or ministry group.

The very nature of planting a new church demands a focus on converting younger people, and as younger people, they will not quickly be equipped to be a part of a leadership team. In the interest of building wisely over the long haul, the focus in church plantings should be on building the campus ministry first, singles second, young marrieds third, and older marrieds last. Several reasons lie behind this suggestion: One, the most viable future leaders of a church will most likely come from the campus ministry; two, you want to convert people first who are less encumbered with life issues and who can thus spend more time evangelizing in the early stages; three, those who are younger and have fewer life responsibilities will not have as many counseling needs as those who are further along in life stages, allowing leaders to continue concentrating on leading the evangelistic charge. Simply stated, the conversions of younger people in early plantings will ultimately provide a better foundation for the church, although developing team leadership will take more time.

This development should be planned out carefully. In the field of real estate, it is often stated that the three most important issues are location, location and location. In the field of leadership development, the three most important issues are thinking, thinking and thinking. Certainly leaders must provide good teaching and examples worthy of imitation, but their primary task in developing young leaders is teaching them to think and to think well. When building team leadership, your role as a trainer is to ask many questions in order to help those being trained to think through all important issues for their lives individually and for the church as a whole. Discipling cannot mean that we do the thinking for others; rather, it means that we train them to think—and think like Jesus.

Building the Team in the Intermediate Stages

In this stage of team leadership development, you begin including potential leaders in meetings and ministry discussions. You include those who are demonstrating two primary qualities: spirituality and leadership gifts. Without both qualities, they should not be included. At this point, the group you are developing is a discussion and input group, but not a decision-making group. As they mature as disciples and as young leaders, their input begins to carry more weight in decisions that are made, and at some point, the group begins to be more of a leadership team that actually makes decisions together.

Those who are chosen for this type of leadership training and participation may be drawn from the planting team or even chosen from the new converts. The leader's goal is to start training them to think critically and creatively, to help develop plans, and to gradually become a part of a decision-making process. Asking the right kinds of questions will lead them into this learning process. For example, in a meeting session, you could say, "Here is what I see as our needs and what I think could be done to meet them," and then ask, "How does that sound to you, and what are you seeing?" As leaders, we should avoid seeking feedback that only consists of positive remarks. Such feedback may stroke the leader's ego, but it doesn't develop younger disciples into wise leaders. Ask questions about what they think may help complete or balance your ideas and what the potential weaknesses may be in applying your sermons, teaching and directions. Participation is a valid part of getting people to buy in emotionally to your leadership, and this need is huge even in a campus setting where you are necessarily more directive. Your ultimate goal in developing a team is in helping them learn to think more deeply about ministry strategy and organization.

In a small church (which hopefully is small only because it is also young), one staff member or a ministry couple may constitute the whole staff. In larger churches, the staff may be quite a bit bigger and may interface more with other leadership groups. Ideally, in any size church, leadership should come from both staff and non-staff disciples in some form, to provide a broader perspective and complementing focuses. How decisions are made is always a factor that must be figured out and implemented consistently. The main issue is not one of who has the greatest authority, for that emphasis always brings in challenges and inflates our pride. The important issue is determining who is best qualified to make the more impactful decisions, and how those people reach those decisions. Regardless of who ends up in the role of making final decisions, input from people who have a variety of perspectives is paramount. Wise leaders seek as much perspective from as many different directions as possible. No matter the size of your ministry staff, no matter the size of your church, you will either seek these varied perspectives yourself, or you will receive them anyway—just in bad forms.

Building the Team in the More Mature Stages

Once a church grows and ages, you will have some members who are older spiritually and chronologically. You now have more choices in leadership development and in putting together leadership teams of various types. Developing younger leaders will be a continual need, as will utilizing your more experienced leaders. Including newer Christians who are more mature in life is also important in developing a leadership team. For example, I remember a fairly new convert in Boston being chosen to "meet the press" for an interview to be shown on national TV. Even though she was a young Christian, we chose her because she was very mature in life in general and in her career. Because of her age and life experiences, she did much better than most of our younger staff members could have done in handling difficult questions and explaining thorny issues. Certainly the spiritual inexperience of new Christians has to be taken into consideration, but even so, their level of common sense—earned through life—can often save younger staff members from making serious mistakes of judgment.

When Andy Fleming helped plant the Moscow church, he figured out pretty quickly that he needed a lot of input from the more mature converts in the new congregation (again, I mean people who were mature in chronological age, not in spiritual age). In time, he selected a consensus group of people who were not on the ministry staff to help the staff (who were mostly foreigners) understand the cultural issues. He asked them to help set the salary levels of the staff and to help make decisions about potentially sensitive issues, particularly issues that involved spending money. The value of including people with more life experiences who are not on the staff should not be overlooked. By this point in the development of a church, the church leader should have found both older and younger leaders to be peers and to help disciple him in natural peer relationships. Trusting that a discipler who lives in another city can meet all of your ministry and personal needs is a poor recipe for success. The best recipe in seeking help and input is (you guessed it) a both/and approach—help from two directions.

When we reach the stage of leading in an older, larger church, we should have developed a consensus group that represents several components of a more mature ministry: elders or shepherd types, evangelists, administrators, and perhaps people in other roles. By now, you have identified and trained some on staff to be a part of a consensus group, and you should have some nonstaff on the team as well. This group of mature individuals must be small enough to function as one group, a top leadership consensus team. They are the ultimate decision makers, or perhaps better stated, decision facilitators. It is essential that they continue to pull staff and nonstaff members into discussions and decisions in appropriate ways. Without doubt, nonstaff leaders must continually be identified, trained and empowered. A significant part of such empowering is to not only give them responsibility, but also sufficient authority to carry out that responsibility.

A mature leadership seeks to mature the church by broadening the input sought from the general membership who are not in this consensus group. It is obvious that not every disciple in a church can be a part of the top decision-making group, but it is also true that every disciple in a church should have some avenue for being involved in decisions that are made. In our movement in past years, it can be said generally that too few people made decisions, and that *far* too few people were included in giving any input into those decisions. However, figuring out how to improve our decision-making process can seem tedious and difficult. How are decisions to be made, and who makes which decisions? Those questions are highly significant ones for which answers must be determined if we are to move ahead effectively. The old system had this in its favor: Decisions could be made quickly. In the new paradigm we are in the process of forging, concepts like group decisions and consensus can slow down our progress unless we are clear on process.

Team Leadership Fundamentals

Expectations and Assumptions

Unmet expectations are one of the biggest challenges to any relationship or set of relationships. For that reason, participating in leadership groups while having basic unexamined assumptions can lead to problems. Many examples can be supplied to demonstrate this point. Suppose that someone is hired as a ministry staff person to lead a ministry group within a church that has an overall leadership team. If the new hire assumes that they will become a part of that team by virtue of becoming a part of the ministry staff, they could be in for a real surprise if the group doesn't function that way. Suppose that someone was appointed a deacon and he assumed that he would automatically be a part of a certain leadership group by being appointed. Once again, the stage is set for unmet expectations (and disappointment and hurt feelings) based on incorrect assumptions. Suppose that someone becomes a part of a leadership group and assumes that his group has the final say in making the most significant decisions for the church, but another leadership group assumes the same thing about their group. Troubles are right around the corner!

Such examples can be multiplied, and no list of such examples will ever exhaust the possibilities for producing relationship challenges between groups! As I have said, one of the cardinal rules of discipling is "Assume nothing," which is easy to say, but difficult to do. As life teaches us, sometimes we don't even know what our assumptions and expectations are until they go unmet! The only way to avoid relational tensions in this arena is to make sure that the parameters of any leadership group are well defined and understood by each person in the group—and by those in other groups that interact with them. My purpose is not to describe for you all of the potential challenges and their solutions, but to make you more aware of the need to anticipate challenges and to define parameters *clearly*.

The process involved in how we define our functions in a leadership group and how groups interrelate is key, particularly in how decisions of all types are to be made. Such issues of process directly affect attitudes and working relationships within and between groups. Let me say a word about decision-making in general. I'm sure some have had this feeling as they have read the many references made to decision-making by leaders: "Why do we always have to talk about who makes the decisions? Why can't we just all serve the flock and each other, and avoid focusing on decisions, as if that were the main element of leadership?" Who of us in leadership roles hasn't wished that we didn't have to spend time in meetings making decisions? However, we will never be able to serve in leadership groups without having to go through this often tedious and sometimes emotional process. Even in one's personal family, decision-making and the process it involves play a significant part in building and maintaining a healthy family. It is certainly apropos to be reminded that our primary task as leaders is not decision-making, but we cannot swing the pendulum to the point that we see decision-making as an unwelcome intruder into the leadership realm.

I recall a discussion among our leadership team in Phoenix regarding process that will illustrate why it can be such a sticky wicket. When our elders were appointed, they were immediately thrust into being the main decision makers during a challenging era (2004). In time, our leadership team became a blend of elders and evangelists, and at one point included me when I was serving only in the role of teacher. One of the elders discussed an issue with the other elders and they almost made a decision without bringing the matter to other members of the team. The situation was likely influenced mostly by two things: history and an assumption. The history part traced back to the time when the elders *were* the leadership team, and the assumption was that the matter being discussed was not a highly significant issue. And so the elders contacted me (as a former elder) and asked me to cast the deciding vote, since those serving as elders at the time had differing opinions about what should be done. But it became obvious that we needed to have a discussion on process. We decided that going forward, any matter having even potential significance would not be decided without having at least the elders and congregational evangelist in the loop, and normally the entire leadership team. Those are the kinds of process issues that can produce tensions—hence the need for discussion and definition about process.

The Decision-Making Process

To begin trying to clarify the decision-making process, we

should recognize the power of choice for all disciples. Freedom is a highly valued concept in the United States, to state it mildly, and freedom is mostly about having choices as citizens. In raising children, wise parents understand the power of choice. Giving even young children choices develops them in several ways. They learn to think better as they contemplate choices; they learn from the choices they make; and they feel valued and trusted by being allowed to make choices in the first place. The same principles apply to God's children. They need to be involved in appropriate ways in helping with the choices made for their ministry group and in being able to give input of some type into even broader decisions made for the church.

Obviously, no one can be or should be involved in every decision made, but what should the average member of the congregation expect regarding inclusion? Realistically, he should expect some decisions that affect his Bible Talk (or small group, or family group, or whatever his church calls the smallest organizational unit of fellowship) to be made by ministry staff. These decisions might include the need for everyone to be a member of a Bible Talk, and the expectation that Bible Talks will meet with a specified degree of regularity. On the other hand, Mr. Average Member should expect that other decisions will be left up to the Bible Talk itself, such as the time and location of meetings, outreach or fellowship activities, and the subject matter of the Bible Talk lessons. A wise Bible Talk leader will decide these types of things with his or her group rather than making all of these decisions independently. Thus, the members of the Bible Talk will function as a part of the decision-making process on some decisions, but will only give input to others.

In a mature group of any type, inclusion and input of the members must be funneled effectively to leaders making decisions. The higher the leadership level, the more creative we have to be in finding out what the feelings of the grassroots membership are about the direction of the church as a whole. Seeking input not only helps with decision-making at all levels, it provides a much-needed sense of inclusion for the people giving the input. Whether input is sought informally through casual conversations or sought more formally through meetings scheduled periodically to hear from different groups within the church, getting feedback is a vital part of building an effective decision-making process and a healthy church at the same time.

Mature churches will have different types of leadership teams, and each must develop an understanding of their decision-making parameters. When we first moved to Phoenix, it was obvious that such an understanding wasn't clear. The key leaders at the time went away for a three-day planning retreat, and the main focus was sorting out the answers to three questions:

- What type of decisions should be made at the different ministry levels?
- Who should make those decisions?
- By what process should those decisions be made?

At the end of the three days, we tested ourselves by mentioning examples of different issues to be decided, and we were able to quickly answer the three questions. Essentially, our retreat was a strategic planning session focused solely on the decision-making process. Once we had elders appointed, we held an abbreviated version of the planning session, adding the elders' role to the decision-making mix.

Without such definition and clarification, misunderstandings and tensions will inevitably result. If you don't know how to conduct such a planning session, bring in someone who does to help facilitate. It will be a worthwhile endeavor, trust me on that. Regardless of how many different types of leadership teams you may have, one of them is going to be the team that makes the final, most significant decisions regarding the direction of the church and the deeper problems that must be solved. This group especially must have a well-defined decision-making process. Understanding the term consensus is an essential part of the process. The term is defined in two ways: unanimity in which every member of the team agrees, or a broad majority agreement (but not unanimous). Some leadership teams put certain types of decisions into the total agreement category and certain other types of decisions into the broad majority agreement category.

It has been my experience that in smaller leadership teams, this dual strategy can work well as long as everyone understands which types of decisions belong in which category and no "self-willed" members are a part of the group. Everyone must be flexible and persuadable. In larger leadership teams, you will likely end up agreeing to only use the broad majority agreement approach in every type of decision made. Time constraints and the need to finalize decisions will most often lead you in this direction. If you insist upon total unanimity for every decision made, you will likely come to hate meetings and be tempted to harbor bad attitudes toward one another! Bottom line, those in decision-making groups must have a great combination of humility, a sense of fallibility and a willingness to be persuaded—along with a well-defined decision-making process.

Who Is on the Team?

When we are discussing a top leadership team, we had best begin by stating loudly and clearly: "Variations expected!" Leadership teams probably vary the most of any other type of group in the church. They may be comprised of only one group of leaders in a smaller church having no elders; in a larger church, you may find both an overall leadership team and supporting leadership teams within smaller ministry groups. (At this point in our history, many larger churches call their smaller ministry groups *regions*.)

In a church that has elders, the elders may be the main leadership team, or the elders, along with the congregational evangelist, may be the designated team. Or the team may be composed of some blend of leaders serving in a variety of roles: elders, evangelists, teachers, administrators, etc. There will never be an organizational formula for such teams, because it will all depend on the qualified personnel available. Further, the composition of any particular team will always be in a state of flux as individuals come on and off the team for different reasons. Building and maintaining functionality and unity between leaders with each other and with the flock is always going to be a work in progress.

One issue that should always be a consideration is just how women are going to fit into leadership teams at any level. To begin with, it should be noted that some congregations have women on the paid staff and some congregations do not. My strong preference is that they are on staff with their husbands (if married), for a number of reasons. Each of the congregations with whom I have worked in our movement of churches has had this practice—San Diego, Boston, Phoenix and Houston. The practice is admittedly within the realm of opinion, but my opinion is that this arrangement yields the best results—by far.

The decision to have women in meetings or not is also strictly a judgment call, but I am an unashamed pragmatist on the issue. I want to understand the women's perspectives as well as possible and I also want to save time. I have been in too many "men only" meetings in which decisions were made, only to go home and tell Theresa what we decided and hear something along these lines: "You decided what? Have you thought about this, and this and this?" After such conversations, I am most often (though not always) left with the feeling that we've made a decision without thinking through all of the issues. Therefore, I favor having the wives of the leaders present in the meetings to share their perspectives and input.

When I was in Boston, the last leadership team I was a part of had four couples in it. The men met separately at times, but the wives joined us for most of the meetings. I remember the women sharing their thoughts on how they wanted their role in the meetings to be viewed. In essence, they said that in light of the Bible's teachings about women not having authority over men, they were uncomfortable being considered as part of the final decision makers for the church, since both men and women were members of the church. They wanted it understood that while they might be decision *influencers* (and they were), they were not decision *makers* in areas in which both men and women were affected. The men in the group agreed with their wives on this point from a biblical perspective. Men should be viewed as the ultimate decision makers, but without question, women certainly influence those decisions—and they should, since at least half of most churches are women.

Leading a Team

Learning how to effectively facilitate discussions and move them along to making decisions is not that difficult. It takes focus on the leader's part and cooperation on the group's part. Even in a situation where the group is mainly an input group, make as many decisions as you can during the meetings. Sometimes you will have to thank the group for their input and tell them that you have to consider it further, but if it is your goal to make as many decisions as possible within the meetings themselves, you will be surprised how well even an input group can function. My goal is to always make as many decisions in any leadership group as possible, except in the cases where the stakes are higher than the group's experience equips them to deal with.

Husbands learn a lot about team leadership through their marriage, if they have a good relationship with their wife. When Theresa and I are discussing a subject that requires a decision, we usually end up agreeing. Sometimes when we start off with different viewpoints, I convince her of mine and sometimes she convinces me of hers. When we can't agree, as the leader I break the tie if the matter is a fairly insignificant one. If it is significant, we ask someone else to come in and help us reach a decision that is reasonably comfortable for both of us. A husband/wife team works well together if both understand and agree on process and if both have a humble spirit. The same may be said of any leadership team within the family of God.

In our leadership team in Phoenix (of which I am no longer a part), on several occasions we needed to seek outside perspective from experienced, trusted leaders. It always led to good results, not only because of the help we received but also because God blessed our humility in asking for help. When I first moved to Phoenix, the church had no elders. In the midst of their challenges at the time, they had appointed a temporary advisory group (the TAG). Even though this group was by definition an advisory group and not a decision-making group, we made many weighty decisions in those meetings. The group consisted of the ministry staff brothers and mature leaders within each of the ministry groups (regions). We had enough maturity, experience and humility to make many decisions that ended up blessing the church until an eldership could be established.

Every team must be led, although in a top leadership team, the leader is primarily a facilitator of the group. When the eldership was established in Phoenix, since I had the most experience by far, I led the elder meetings. Later, when evangelists were added to the group, I still led the meetings. Once Gary Sciascia was appointed to take my place as the congregational evangelist, he immediately began leading staff meetings. I've mentioned how I suggested to him that we alternate leading the meetings of the leadership team, and we did so once or twice. By then I was traveling so much in my teaching ministry that I wasn't nearly as in touch with local situations as Gary, so I suggested that he just lead all the meetings of the leadership team. He and I both handled the transitions in those roles seamlessly, as did the other members in both types of meetings. As long as the person leading the meetings knows how to do it well, it won't matter who leads, unless humility is lacking. Thankfully, in our situation, it wasn't.

But the leader must know how to lead meetings. Although I have no intention of providing all the details that could be provided, here are a few practical suggestions: First, build an agenda. Send out a request for agenda items to the people who will attend the meeting several days in advance. Give thought and prayer to the final agenda before the meeting, prioritize the agenda items, and go in prepared to move the agenda along at a reasonable pace. At the beginning of the meeting, share what your thoughts are regarding the order of priority items and an estimation of how much time should be spent on each item. Make sure the group agrees with both the priorities and the time allotted for discussion.

As the leader, you have to teach (and consistently remind) the group about how they should participate in the discussions. Help them to learn to say only what is necessary and to say it succinctly. If someone else has made your point, either say nothing or say, "I agree with the viewpoint expressed by brother so-and-so." ("Me-too's" are simply not needed and are time-consuming.) The exception to that is when each person is actually giving their vote about a very important decision and may need to explain why they as an individual feel the way they do about the decision being made.

The group should know at the beginning of the meeting which items are only informational and which are discussion items. Distributing as much printed information as possible at the meeting speeds things up as well. If any discussion item is taking more time than expected, and it appears that too little agreement can be reached, you may have to decide to discuss the issue more at a later meeting and finalize the decision then. When that becomes necessary (and it will occasionally), ask the group to really be praying and meditating about it in the interim—seeking God's will and not their own.

Bottom line, the discussions and decisions have to keep moving. The inability to make decisions and the postponement of decisions should be the exception, not the rule. Once in the meeting, you as the leader must lead the discussion, but in a manner that makes others comfortable expressing their opinions. You must keep the discussion moving and not let it get bogged down, for decisions have to be reached. After the meeting, notes should be provided via email, complete with action items, assignments and due dates carefully noted. These notes, or an abbreviated version of them, can be provided for other leaders who are not in this group, and you can ask other groups to provide you with similar notes from their meetings. This exchange is most applicable to the top leadership team and the ministry staff, for they are the two most influential leadership groups in most churches. These groups likely meet separately most of the time and have different decision-making parameters, so keeping everyone in both groups in the informational loop is very helpful. Although these two groups do meet separately the majority of the time in most churches, occasional combined meetings are strongly advised for relational purposes, as well as when issues with long-range implications for the church are being discussed and decided.

Team Leadership and Financial Issues

The Board of Directors

Most of the different leadership teams in larger churches are ecclesiastical in nature, meaning that their roles are focused on church activities and function. The exception to this is the Board of Directors, an entity formed in response to state and/or federal laws. Their purview is limited to the legal and financial arenas. In congregations without elders, some Boards have tried to function much as an eldership, making church decisions. Any such function is outside the authority and purpose of a Board, and has led in some instances to some rather unfortunate consequences. Now it may well be the case that some members of the Board are also members of church leadership teams, but as a Board, they should not be delving into the realm of church-function decisions.

When I first moved to Phoenix, their Board understood this principle and their subsequent limitations in the ecclesiastical realm. I was not a member of the Board initially, but they asked me to sit in on most of their meetings as a ministry advisor. One of the first challenges they brought to my attention was a financial crisis. In late 2004, the church was in firestorm mode and the contributions had dropped significantly. The Board informed me that the financial situation was such that five staff members were going to have to be terminated. They were very clear in stating that they should not register any opinions about who should be dismissed, but only the financial implications that made dismissals necessary. I appreciated their understanding of what their defined duties were and were not.

Like most Boards at the time, they did need clarification and training in other areas. We received a great deal of help by inviting Dave Malutinok in to conduct a workshop for the Board members. Dave had extensive experience with Boards, both in the business world and in the church. At the time, he was serving as the chief administrator in Boston, with the task of overseeing the administration of the churches in New England and continental Europe. Additionally, he had helped a number of congregations in New England initially establish their Boards. We provide training for most of our other leadership teams, and wisdom would dictate that training for our Boards would be quite important.

One immediate issue we faced when I moved to Phoenix was that no staff member was an official part of the Board. I became a member of the Board quickly, and we soon moved toward having a good mixture of staff and nonstaff membership. Some Boards have a percentage designation for these two types, perhaps one-third staff and two-thirds nonstaff. Some churches also have a designation for the number of elders to be serving on the Board at any point in time. Almost all Boards stagger their terms of service, meaning that new members come on and old members go off in such a way that they always have experienced members serving. Due to the nature of the Board's functions, having members with backgrounds in the fields of law, human resources and finance is a wise move. I have served on a number of church and church-related Boards through the years, and thankfully, all of my experiences have been positive.

Money Matters Matter

Of course, one of the main functions of a Board of Directors is to make sure that an organization has good policies in both financial and legal areas, and has a well-defined structure to ensure that the policies are being followed. Financial areas are especially sensitive to church members ever since 2003, when we faced many

Dynamic Leadership

unfounded accusations of the mishandling of money. This is not to say that there were not some genuine issues that needed correction, but the false allegations outnumbered the true ones by a wide margin. The Bible says a lot about money, because God knows that our purse strings and heartstrings are closely joined. Because they are a sensitive subject, all church leadership groups must deal with money matters sensitively and wisely.

Paul certainly had this attitude, as may be observed in the following passages:

> Now about the collection for God's people: Do what I told the Galatian churches to do. On the first day of every week, each one of you should set aside a sum of money in keeping with his income, saving it up, so that when I come no collections will have to be made. Then, when I arrive, I will give letters of introduction to the men you approve and send them with your gift to Jerusalem. If it seems advisable for me to go also, they will accompany me (I Corinthians 16:1–4).

> I thank God, who put into the heart of Titus the same concern I have for you. For Titus not only welcomed our appeal, but he is coming to you with much enthusiasm and on his own initiative. And we are sending along with him the brother who is praised by all the churches for his service to the gospel. What is more, he was chosen by the churches to accompany us as we carry the offering, which we administer in order to honor the Lord himself and to show our eagerness to help. We want to avoid any criticism of the way we administer this liberal gift. For we are taking pains to do what is right, not only in the eyes of the Lord but also in the eyes of men.
>
> In addition, we are sending with them our brother who has often proved to us in many ways that he is zealous, and now even more so because of his great confidence in you. As for Titus, he is my partner and fellow worker among you; as for our brothers, they are representatives of the churches and an honor to Christ. Therefore show these men the proof of your love and the reason for our pride in you, so that the churches can see it (2 Corinthians 8:16–24).

Several lessons jump off the page when reading these passages. One, giving to God will always be a part of our worship of him. Two, in one way or another, most of our giving is about meeting needs. Three, the handling of money given to God must be done in the best way possible in order to avoid just criticism. Four, those who do handle money must be both trustworthy and trusted.

All of our leadership teams, including the Board of Directors and individual leaders, must keep these lessons in mind. All of our church members must also keep them in mind. The leaders must be trustworthy and the church must be trusting. As someone who served on the paid ministry staff of churches for more than four decades, I have always tried hard to live as a frugal servant and as a generous giver financially. As a disciple, I felt I had the same responsibilities as everyone else in these areas and also that I had the same right to privacy in these areas as other disciples. In other words, my giving was between me and God primarily, although I often sought advice about how much I gave and was more than comfortable with the top leaders knowing exactly how much I gave. The same was true regarding how much I was paid. Those on the Board had ready access to my salary package, as did the elders and others from whom I sought financial advice. Other than that, I believe that a staff person's contributions and salary should be as private as any other disciple's financial matters in these areas. If not, why not?

During our upheaval years a decade ago, much was said about these matters, and some of it needed to be said. I do believe that leaders should have been more careful in money matters in some cases. I also believe that some members should have been more trusting and less critical of ministry salaries—and more careful in their own money matters. Most of these issues are now behind us, but human nature being what it is, all financial issues will never be behind us, nor should they be. Money matters do matter. Having said that, we have to be careful about how we view money from all vantage points and not let materialism and envy invade our hearts and lives. All of us are going to have to decide how we are going to look at money issues in the church and in our own lives.

For the most part, ministry salaries have been examined and re-examined and set by Boards of Directors according to proven salary models in the world that relate to ministry salaries. When all of these things were being determined afresh, the end result was that the overall church budgets were relatively unaffected on the whole, although the salary levels of some staff members went up and others went down. What did that tell us? That we were not that far off in the first place. I appreciate all of the work that went into setting or resetting salaries, based on solid data from not-for-profit business models, and I believe that due diligence was carried out in trying to decide things righteously and fairly.

As a ministry person for most of my life, I looked at my pay from several different angles. First, I wished I could have been totally self-supporting and not had to be paid at all. Second, since that was not the case, I deeply appreciated being supported to do what I loved to do. Not everyone is nearly that fortunate. Third, during the most challenging times, I thought to myself that what I was going through wouldn't have been worth it had I been paid ten times as much as I was being paid! Those pity parties normally didn't last long, by God's grace. Fourth, I believe in the principle expressed in 1 Timothy 5:18 when Paul said regarding ministry support that "the worker deserves his wages." With all of that in mind, I appreciate all of the support that I received for all these years financially; I appreciate the opportunities to give thousands and thousands of dollars to the Cause; and I appreciate the Scripture's assurance that I need not apologize or feel awkward about being paid.

All that I wrote in the preceding paragraph was said from the perspective of a ministry person. This next part is written from the perspective of a simple disciple. I take seriously what the Bible says about materialism and greed. In 1 Corinthians 5, Paul begins by addressing the grievous sin of immorality, concluding that church discipline is in order for a unrepentant offender. However, in the same chapter, he says that a number of other sins should prompt church discipline, or withdrawal of fellowship, including the sin of greed (vv. 9–11). The warning against the love of money are equally applicable to staff and non-staff members alike. Lest we become too critical of others about money, we had best look in the mirror of our own souls and in our own financial ledgers to see how we are using money in comparison to how the Bible says we should be using it.

From a team leadership responsibility level, we are going to have to set examples in the financial realm as individuals and make sure that God's will is being done in everything that pertains to money in the church. We have a responsibility to handle contributions and church expenditures carefully, and we also have a responsibility to help those whom we lead to be righteous with their money. We cannot speak of leadership and followership at any level without also addressing money issues. Indeed, money matters matter! Let us honor God in this area—as leadership teams and individual disciples!

Concluding Thoughts About Team Leadership

In the old leadership paradigm, positional authority reigned supreme, and with our strong one-man leadership model, decisions were most often dictated by one person. A slightly better model had decisions often made by the proverbial "Old Boys' Club" behind closed doors. Now we are trying to move more into the realm of influence authority, exercised through relationship and expertise. We are taking the time, and having the consideration for others, to discuss and persuade (but not force) those under our leadership—and we are desirous of hearing them out and working with them to forge decisions.

In this new paradigm, we have to first make decisions about the inclusion/decision processes themselves before moving on to the plethora of other decisions that wait in the wings. This initial step, believe it or not, is more tedious than most other decisions will be after the structure and procedure for overall decision-making is determined. It is not really that complicated, being more about common sense than anything else. Our problem is, simply stated, a training and experience problem. What may be simple to some by virtue of their background training, seems complex to others for whom it is new territory. Once we make the leap of faith necessary to figure out and act upon the paradigm shift before us, we will find the doors opening and the solutions forthcoming. May God move us through those doors quickly and efficiently!

Epilogue

From Good to Great!

What kind of a leader are you? Good? Great? Mediocre? Since I don't know who is reading this right now, I have no idea what the answer is for you. But I do know what you want it to be, right? You want to be a great leader for God. Just think about some of our common phrases in that regard: "I want to be my best for Christ!" "I want to do great things for God!" Those thoughts in our hearts, and others like them, drew us toward becoming leaders in the first place. We genuinely believed that as a leader we could impact eternity for God more than in any other way. My purpose in writing this book was to do all I could as an older leader to help you achieve the dreams that brought you into leadership in the first place, or to help you continue pursuing your dream of leading, even if you are not already serving in a particular leadership role.

I gave the epilogue its title for two reasons. First, I think the leadership in our movement right now is good leadership collectively. Some leaders are great; some are good; and some are likely mediocre. But we all have the seeds of greatness inside us by the Spirit of God. We just need to water them and let God make them grow. I am trying to let God use me to help with the watering process through writing this book. I believe he wants us to be great individually and collectively.

Second, I am captivated by the concept of continuing to improve in every area of my life, because I don't want to just be good at something if I can be great at it. That motivation explains why I was drawn to some concepts found in the business book whose title I borrowed for this epilogue. I must admit that I can scarcely think of this title without also remembering a specific way our churches at one time overused those words in keeping attendance statistics, combined with the word "awesome!" (I will refrain from going further with that thought—if you don't know what I'm talking about, good-great-awesome for you!)

The complete title for the book, written in 2001 by Jim Collins, is *Good to Great: Why Some Companies Make the Leap. . .and Others Don't* (HarperCollins). The author described the results of a comprehensive survey of American businesses that had moved from being mediocre or good to being great. The criteria used to determine greatness were so high that only eleven companies in the United States qualified. Although Collins's book has less direct application to our movement of churches than does *Primal Leadership*, a book I discussed in chapter 4, it is definitely worth reading. Its greatest value lies in what the researchers discovered about leadership style. They found distinct patterns of behavior in the people who led each company and in the people who followed them—patterns that relate directly to church leadership.

For me, the most remarkable finding in *Good to Great* was the description of the type of leader who helped companies jump into the great category. Without exception those leaders were humble, self-effacing types who took the blame for failures themselves and gave the credit for successes to people under their leadership. Make no mistake about it, they were ambitious leaders, but their ambition was almost exclusively for the success of the organization, not for themselves. The author confessed that the researchers had difficulty determining what label to use for these leaders, and were strongly tempted to call them "servant leaders." However, they rejected that choice because they thought the business world would discount the book if that terminology was used!

That should make quite a statement to church leadership. Is it not amazing that the leadership style judged most effective in business was exactly the same style that Jesus encouraged (and exemplified) two thousand years ago?

> Jesus called them together and said, "You know that the rulers of the Gentiles lord it over them, and their high officials exercise authority over them. Not so with you.

Instead, whoever wants to become great among you must be your servant, and whoever wants to be first must be your slave—just as the Son of Man did not come to be served, but to serve, and to give his life as a ransom for many" (Matthew 20:25–28).

How about you—do you want to be a *colonel* or a *servant?* And no matter what you say you *want* to be, what are you in the eyes of those whom you lead? Perhaps you could have some trusted, mature friends under your leadership read at least chapter 4 and then ask them. If your emotional reaction to that suggestion is hesitant, this suggests that you actually need to take that scary step and get such input. Admittedly, this thought is somewhat scary for any of us, but if it is overly scary for you, you could be stuck in your pride right now. The good news is: You don't have to stay there! Maybe you need to do some fasting and praying and studying on the topics of pride, humility and servant leadership. After all, servant leadership was exemplified by our Master to perfection, and we are called to lead like he did. If we are honest with ourselves, we all have a distance to go in imitating him. Let's all be committed to that growth for his sake and the sake of his beloved children. Then, and only then, will we be described as a great leader—by him.

We are all on a journey with him right now, and what happens to us on our journey of life is never the most important thing; how we respond to what happens to us is what ultimately matters most. As I look at my own history as a person, disciple and leader, I want to repent of all that has been wrong and be thankful for all that has been right. Then I want to formulate a plan for the present based on both of those elements, close the door on any negative impact of the past, and move on with today. While I am to some extent a product of my environment, I am not defined by it or bound by it. Learning from history is a needed thing, but being stuck in it is not an option for us as disciples, and certainly not as leaders. Let's close the doors behind us and walk (or run) through the doors before us with a God-given abandon that terrifies Satan!

Appendix One

Handle With Care!

An Article Written Soon After Golden Rule Leadership (2002)

After I write a book, I usually think of additional things I wish I had included. I either think of something I could have put within an existing chapter, or I think of another chapter that could have been added to improve the book. In the case of *Golden Rule Leadership*, I have some ideas that would fit within both categories, and Wyndham likely does as well. Had there been a second edition, we would no doubt have included those other thoughts. The one entire chapter I would add would be entitled *Handle with Care*, or alternately, *Proceed with Due Caution*. The purpose of the chapter would be to register a concern about being reactionary in reading and applying the principles in the book.

Several unhelpful reactions need to be avoided, reactions which can go to two opposite extremes. One reaction involves how the book and its authors are viewed. At one extreme would be to assume that the book is, or is intended to be, the best and final word on leadership. Any reaction along the following lines would be very unfortunate: "If Gordon and Wyndham, two very respected leaders in our movement, wrote it, it must be the gospel. Just give us the book and the Bible and we will have all that we could ever need on the subject of leadership." Rest assured that the authors would be as concerned by such a reaction as anyone. My original thought for a subtitle was "From the Perspective of Elders." I never imagined that the book would be exhaustive on the subject. Other writers have their own experiences and perspectives from which to draw, and we need books written from more than one perspective on such a broad subject.

At the other extreme would be the idea that a book on leadership by elders is not valid or important. Such a dismissive view could be expressed in terms like these: "What do elders really know about ministry leadership anyway? They don't even lead ministry groups and could not understand the pressures and challenges that we evangelist types face." For starters, Wyndham and I were appointed evangelists years ago and have led churches and ministry groups of various sizes. We have not forgotten all of those lessons we learned in the ministry-leading crucible. On the other hand, we will admit that we wear our elder hat most, and our perspective is definitely colored by that. However, it should be kept in mind that in both Old and New Testaments, listening to elders was/is highly commended, and examples of failing to do so yielded some dire consequences. Bottom line, we don't want to have the *only* word or the *final* word. We do believe strongly that we have an *essential* word which must be taken seriously.

Another potential reaction containing opposite extremes regards how we view our own grasp and practice of these principles of leadership. Some think they are further down the road of both the understanding and implementation of the principles than they are in fact. In the introduction to the book [GRL], I made the point clearly, accentuating it by putting it in the form of a warning. I even mentioned that those of us with the most experience may have the most trouble seeing ourselves. Is that surprising? The longer we have functioned with any given approach, the harder it is to see things without that approach coloring our viewpoint considerably. Thinking "outside the box" is easier said than done, including how we see ourselves and our leadership presuppositions. Proverbs 18:17 definitely must come into play here, and only one side cannot be viewed as the whole truth. None of us, including the authors, have the total picture of our own leadership style and ability.

The opposite extreme in how we view ourselves is to assume that we know little or nothing about leading and must put the book principles into practice immediately if not sooner! That view produces knee-jerk reactions which help nobody. As I taught some of these principles to the Boston church staff on various occasions, I usually ended the lesson with the admonition to avoid quick implementation of what they thought I was teaching. I advised them to think, pray, discuss and then develop a plan before proceeding with the implementation of the principles. Trying to change paradigms is never easy for any of us, and we must do it deliberately and carefully.

A third possible two-pronged reaction involves the word *criticism*. On the one hand, we can resist constructive criticism. Such resistance is prompted by either pride or fear or both. Leaders struggle with this issue on an individual basis. They can assume that being open about their shortcomings and sins will cause people to lose respect for them. Of course, the opposite is true. When we are courageous and humble enough to pull back the curtain of our heart and life and let others in, they are drawn to us in a remarkable way. God exalts the humble and so do people. Similarly, when we as a movement are able to constructively critique ourselves, it helps our people to trust us more, and it even limits what our destructive critics can do. It is hard to tear down those who are willing to openly discuss their own failures.

We do have a leadership system. The word *system*, according to the dictionary, can be simply "an organized or established procedure." Systems are necessary, but can be good or bad. Since even a good system can lose its effectiveness in a given situation, becoming protective of our system and being unwilling to critique it is a sign of creeping traditionalism. Humility and honesty must be co-joined into an ongoing "system" of evaluation. Let's fight the tendency to react emotionally against critiquing ourselves or even against allowing others to critique our leadership.

The other side of the criticism issue is also very wrong—to allow ourselves to sink to the level of becoming destructively critical. To think that our book would prompt some to go in that direction is a disquieting thought to its authors. For that reason, I want to deal with that possibility at some length. Co-authoring a book like *Golden Rule Leadership* has been a daunting task. Which of us thinks we have perfected Jesus' style of leading? Certainly not Wyndham or I. Our primary goal in writing this book was to give insight and input as peers with other leaders, all hopefully seeking to imitate Jesus, not as experts who have figured it all out. Our intention has been to prompt healthy discussion about leadership style at an important time in the movement. We have striven to be as humble as possible in addressing such an important topic, realizing fully that we are simply works in progress and not finished products.

All leaders are also followers in some settings. Therefore, when we read a book or an article on leadership, we can focus either on (1) how we are leading or (2) how we are being led. Perhaps it should go without mentioning that we should first think about how we lead others, but this is not our tendency, is it? We tend to immediately think about how we have been led, to contemplate whether our needs have been met or if we have been hurt, rather than contemplating how we may have met (or not met) the needs of those whom we lead.

Another part of the challenge in writing a leadership book is that some readers may respond in reactionary ways. For example, one such response might be anticipated as follows: "That's how I always thought leadership should be, but it isn't the way I have been led." This is a predictable response, but not the most spiritual. I am reminded of a sermon about the nature of advice that Randy McKean preached soon after he became the lead evangelist of the Boston church back in the early 1990s. At that time, some leaders in Boston considered their advice to be fairly binding, but Randy took exception to that view in his lesson, insisting instead that advice is simply advice unless a specific biblical statement or principle is clearly involved. Randy summarized his sermon by saying that three types of people would be challenged most in applying his lesson: those who had been *wrong* about the nature of advice; those who had been *right*; and those who had been *wronged*.

We find ourselves in a similar situation regarding the issue of leadership style. If you have led or have been led in less than a golden rule manner, your challenge is pretty much the same. Maybe you have been wrong in your exercise of leadership. You will have to be humble enough to admit this, repent and change what you can figure out needs changing. Or may be you have been right and have seen leaders leading in a nongolden rule manner. You will have to guard your heart against self-righteousness, another form of pride. Jesus uttered some very appropriate words for situations just like this: "If any one of you is without sin, let him be the first to throw a stone" (John 8:7). Or lastly, maybe you have been wronged by leaders. For starters, I must ask, "Who hasn't?"

In a recent author interview, Wyndham and I were asked why many leaders have not implemented better leadership dynamics sooner. My comments then fit well here. I wrote:

> My children could easily ask this question of me as a dad. It's a bit of a mystery that those most suited biologically to have children are the least experienced! As parents, we just have to learn as we go and do the best that we can figure out to do at the time. As spiritual parents, the challenge is the same. With our movement having grown fast, bringing fairly inexperienced disciples into leadership roles is a must. Remember that the apostle John started off as a Son of Thunder long before he grew into being the Apostle of Love. Sure, we have all made mistakes, some serious, as physical parents and spiritual parents. The two most important issues are our intentions and our progress. As a leader, I am not throwing stones, for even at my age (59), I still make mistakes and hurt people. But my intentions are good and my progress is real. Wyndham and I are simply trying to promote such progress by showing where changes are needed, while maintaining a grateful heart for all of the good we have experienced.

One of the greatest things about our movement is that we can look at ourselves and make changes as needed. Our leadership style has varied according to person, place and time. Many leaders have led by golden rule principles all along. Similarly, some ministries have been blessed consistently with such leadership. The passage of time has brought changes in leadership style as we have learned from our mistakes. Al Baird wrote an article some years back entitled "A New Look at Authority," in which he said that we had gone too far in how we applied authority to ordinary discipling relationships. As one of our most respected leaders, he was saying that we had overstepped certain biblical principles in this area and should correct ourselves, which, in large measure, we have attempted to do. Wyndham and I are trying to prompt a similar result on a somewhat broader basis of leadership style.

Much has been right about leadership in our churches, without question. Forceful, visionary leadership is sorely needed in all groups, religious and otherwise, and we are grateful that our movement has been characterized by the raising up of new leaders. *Golden Rule Leadership* is about developing a leadership style and structure that is biblically based and the most effective possible. In a nutshell, we believe that leadership style must change as congregations change in size and age, and this is the need we are addressing. Varying situations require different leadership styles, which must be selected or adapted to suit these different circumstances at any given time. Effective leadership depends upon many things: awareness of the nature of the task, the makeup of the group and its individual members, the environment in which the group is found, and particularly, the self-awareness of the leaders themselves. Younger and smaller churches will not have the option of working through strong leadership teams, but the leader(s) must strive to raise up other mature leaders who can share the load with them. I am thankful for our strong emphasis in the movement on leadership and "followership," for God has blessed us in planting churches all over the world. Now we must take it to the next level of growing larger and larger churches, which will demand some paradigm changes in leadership style and structure.

In the end, it is a matter of faith in God—truly believing that he is directing us, even through our weaknesses and mistakes. All we can ever do is to do the best we can with our present knowledge and experience, trusting that God will continue to help us learn and change when needed. Paul put it this way in Philippians 3:15–16:

> All of us who are mature should take such a view of things. And if on some point you think differently, that too God will make clear to you. Only let us live up to what we have already attained.

The one thing worse than having poor leadership is having no leadership at all. The one exception to that statement would be if the poor leadership was *terribly* harsh, and although I've seen a few leaders who would qualify as terribly harsh, I've not seen many. We are all works in progress, and if we were to wait until we had "arrived" before leading with confidence, none of us would ever lead! We can only do our best, pray about the rest, and trust that God will make up the difference as he continues to mold us.

As is often said, "Don't throw out the baby with the bathwater." Let's avoid having a critical spirit regarding past mistakes on anyone's part. Let's remain very grateful for all of the good things that have been accomplished. And let's trust that God is continuing to lead us all. Do we need more golden rule leadership? Absolutely. But that will only be possible when we all commit to being golden rule followers. Most of us are leaders in some sense, but all of us are followers. Rather than pointing fingers at others, let's look in the mirror and be the best disciples of Jesus possible. God will surely be pleased with such an approach.

Appendix Two

Matters of Conscience: A Deeper Look

I wrote this article back in 2007, when it was becoming in vogue to object to countless issues in the church, claiming that those things violated one's conscience. While we should certainly not violate our consciences, I believe appeals to conscience can be both misused and overused. And we must be careful *how* we make those appeals: At that time, once people objected to something based upon their own conscience, they essentially shut down any discussion on the matter and dismissed any further consideration. My goal in writing this article was to help us all have a more biblical understanding of what constitutes a valid objection based upon one's conscience. In some cases, people's objections related to the issues surrounding the Cooperation Proposal, and I believe that some people (certainly not all) were misusing the principle in discussing that proposal. However, people were pulling the "conscience card" rather quickly on any number of topics. I simply wanted to offer my study of the subject to a broader audience in hopes that biblical interpretation would be enhanced and deepened, helping us to avoid the misapplication of Scripture in the area of the conscience.

Common Misconceptions

The study of conscience biblically is a very interesting study, due partly to how misunderstood the subject actually is by many. For example, it is common to hear the old (mistaken) adage, "The conscience is a safe guide." It wasn't a very safe guide for Paul, who said before the Sanhedrin that he had "fulfilled [his] duty to God in all good conscience to this day" (Acts 23:1). That resulted in a slap in the mouth at the command of the high priest, but it had resulted in something far worse prior to this—he had helped kill Christians while believing that it was a service to God. He later stated in 1 Corinthians 4:4, "My conscience is clear, but that does not make me innocent. It is the Lord who judges me." The conscience is a safe guide only to the extent it is properly trained by the word of God.

Through the years, I have encountered several misunderstandings of just how the conscience was designed to function by God. Recently, I studied the Bible with a person who was deeply immersed in the teachings of Watchman Nee, teachings that I would call "neo-gnosticism." (See my recent article, "Watchman Nee's Teaching on Soul and Spirit: A Form of Neo-Gnosticism" at gftm.org) Essentially, his teaching is based on making a very sharp distinction between soul and spirit, and building an entire system on this distinction, which is very confusing to anyone not familiar with his system and its terminology. But as it relates to the subject of conscience, he says that the conscience is based on the intuition component of the spirit, which ushers in a type of gnosticism by claiming to have something of a direct pipeline to God's truths through hearing his voice in our inner self. Many religious people believe that God somehow speaks directly to their spirits, in a way that is better felt than told, and their consciences are often quite misled as a result.

Another misunderstanding, or in this case, blatant misuse, occurred with a ministry acquaintance of mine who often played the "conscience card" if his opinions weren't carrying the day. If his ideas were accepted, he was happy; if they weren't, he had a "conscience" problem with the directions chosen by the rest of the leadership group of which he was a part. This frequent appeal to conscience was nothing short of manipulation, and it likely isn't a surprise for you to hear that he didn't keep his job long.

An Historical (Almost Hysterical) Example

Another misunderstanding and misuse of conscience takes me back to my old days in the mainline Church of Christ. In that setting, a number of older leaders often mistook an immature or untrained conscience for a *sensitive* conscience, which supposedly demonstrated a high level of spirituality. As an anecdotal teacher, I can't help sharing an amusing incident in my life that illustrates this point all too well. Back in the late 1970s, I was preaching for a church deep in the heart of the Bible Belt. Once I took a week's vacation to go with my father and young son on a hunting trip, during which time I didn't shave. Although beards were none too popular for ministers to have in those days, I decided to let mine grow for a while. The negative reactions by church members to my sporting a beard were nothing short of amazing. I suppose the hippie years were in the too recent past for them to see beards and rebellion as anything other than inseparably connected.

I remember one older member asking to meet with me, and he started the meeting with the question of whether anyone had ever told me that I was hard to get to know. I was trying to validate his evident feelings in any way I could, but unsure of just where he was coming from with such a question. About half an hour later, I figured it out. In essence, he said that he thought he knew me and that I was a great guy—but then I grew the beard, which showed that he didn't know me at all! Wow, that was an enlightening conversation! But it did show how deeply some prejudices ran in that church at that period of history.

After a fairly short time, I shaved off the beard, but determined to address the issue of how I had supposedly "violated the consciences" of many members with my beard. It was obvious to me that the understanding of Paul's writing in 1 Corinthians 8–10, along with Romans 14, was woefully lacking. About six months later, I preached a sermon entitled "The Sin of Beards and Bowties." At the time, large butterfly bowties were still on sale in stores, but quite out of style anyway (except to one news announcer on a local TV channel). The night I preached the sermon, I wore one of the floppy things, and knew that a young ministry student with a beard would be sitting in his normal place in the second row in front of the pulpit. Thus, I had the props all set up for my sermon!

I began the sermon by talking about the importance of example and influence, and the sin of causing brothers to stumble (an oft-repeated claim in situations like mine). The "amens" started pretty early that night. I went on to show the biblical basis for not offending our brothers, by simply reading a number of verses in the chapters mentioned above. If you would like to read them, they are, in the order read, 1 Corinthians 8:1–2, 9, 12–13; 1 Corinthians 10:23–24, 32; Romans 14:13, 15, 19–21; 1 Corinthians 9:3–7, 11–15, 19–22; 1 Corinthians 10:31–33; and finishing with 1 Corinthians 11:1: "Follow my example, as I follow the example of Christ." I ended the readings with this statement, "If my bowtie bothers you, I ought to take it off; if Ralph's beard bothers you, he ought to cut it off!" The chorus of "amens" rose to a new level, as quite a number of people were evidently rejoicing to see that I had finally seen the light! My next statement was that since it had been a very short lesson up to that point (about seven or eight minutes, as I recall), surely there must be other things on the subject to notice and study out in the context of the passages read.

From there, since the last passage read was 1 Corinthians 11:1, I talked about the example of Christ in his earthly ministry. Certainly Jesus, like Paul, gave up many rights to influence people for good. Matthew 20:28 is a good passage on this point, as it states that "the Son of Man did not come to be served, but to serve, and to give his life as a ransom for many." Another good one is Matthew 12:20: "A bruised reed he will not break, and a smoldering wick he will not snuff out." However, some things Jesus did seem to point in another, somewhat contradictory, direction. For example, Jesus often healed on the Sabbath Day. Exodus 20 and Deuteronomy 5 were very explicit—work six days and do no work on the Sabbath day. In fact, the Jews cut their teeth on the teaching that they shouldn't do anything on the Sabbath that they didn't absolutely have to do. It is not a mystery why some might see Jesus' work on the Sabbath as at least questionable. Yet Jesus seemed to make a point of healing on the Sabbath. Sometimes Jesus disrupted those gathered in the temple or the synagogues for the purpose of worshiping God to the extent that bedlam ensued.

Don't you think the people had at least some reasons for their feelings? There were six other days in which Jesus could have healed, but he insisted on Sabbath-day healings! Even a more amazing situation was when the apostles picked grain on the Sabbath. Go back and read Exodus 16, which contains some very strong warnings about doing much of anything on the Sabbath. Also read Numbers 15:32–36, where it describes a man being stoned to death at the command of God simply for gathering wood on the Sabbath day! What would you have thought about the disciples gathering grain on the Sabbath day if you had grown up with these passages? They could have prepared food the day before—Israelites had been doing it for hundreds of years. Further, Jesus was criticized for the kinds of people he associated with, including prostitutes. (Likely, a minister in my '70s setting would have caused some serious buzz through such associations!) He was also accused of being a glutton and drunkard—but he didn't quit eating or drinking. The fact that his behavior and practices drove some up the wall didn't stop him from doing it. Why did he continue? We will answer that question a bit later in the article.

The Importance of Context

Studying passages in their context is a must, especially when sensitive subjects are involved or when addressing misunderstood texts. Look back at 1 Corinthians 8:4, 7–13, where the context gives a deeper insight to this subject of influence. First, notice in verse 9 that the wrong use of influence could cause someone to stumble. Verse 11 states that it could cause them to be destroyed. (Romans 14:15 uses similar terminology.) We must understand that there is a difference in causing someone to *grumble*, and in causing them to *stumble*. Second, 1 Corinthians 8:9–10 shows exactly how someone was caused to sin in this setting. Bottom line, they see your example and end up doing the same thing, but their conscience won't allow them to do it without seriously damaging them. So, to make the application to beards and bowties, it would mean contextually that my example or Ralph's example caused someone to wear a bowtie or grow a beard when their conscience wouldn't allow it without producing guilt!

Third, note that the weak person is the one that is caused to stumble, not the strong person. My experiences growing up often showed the supposedly spiritually mature brothers raising issues about nearly everything, and thus they backed others off a given choice so that they wouldn't be caused to "stumble." Frankly, those men were only grumblers and actually should have been the focus of church discipline, because in the words of Titus 3:10, they were divisive. Fourth, Romans 14 makes the other three points, but gives one additional point. It's about the attitudes the strong should have toward the weak, and also about the attitudes the weak should have toward the strong. Read verses 1–10 to grasp Paul's line of reasoning. Note that in verse 1, we are dealing with matters of opinion. The strong brother should not discount the conscience of the weak brother. The weak brother, on the other hand, should not judge the strong brother who has the stronger conscience and the freedom that goes with it. Either way, Romans 14 gives a clear call for tolerance towards each other. It should be quite obvious that my hearers in the long ago had looked at these passages in a surface way in the past, and had often given some incomplete or even wrong applications of them. To summarize, (1) Paul was talking about causing someone to fall away; (2) the way that they were made to sin was by following your example when their conscience wouldn't allow it; (3) the weak person is the one caused to stumble, not the strong one; and finally, (4) in matters of opinion, we must develop and exercise tolerance toward one another with different viewpoints.

But how do we harmonize what Paul taught here with the examples of Jesus already noted? Paul is dealing with young Christians, whereas Jesus was dealing with those who were supposedly mature. Paul was arguing for giving the immature time to grow, while Jesus was not willing to placate the ones who claimed to be mature—the keepers and defenders of the law of God! I have found that the young are typically not the ones upset about such things as beards and bowties—they haven't had time yet to become traditionalized. It is most often the supposedly mature who appeal to conscience being violated.

In my lesson of long ago, I went on to discuss possible objections, which although strongly felt, were emotionally based instead of biblically based. I decided as a result of that study that I would try to imitate both Paul and Jesus. In a nutshell, I wanted to be very careful with those who were newer Christians and thus immature in their faith, but not be manipulated by older Christians who were not willing to change their minds and alter their consciences. Real maturity is willingness to entertain the possibility of being wrong—of having a conscience that needs additional training. Digging in one's heels in the kinds of issues that Paul would call matters of opinion is not a very mature practice. Hardening of the arteries is probably an inevitable part of aging; hardening of the attitudes should never be.

Consciences Can and Should Be Retrained

All in all, I would never advocate someone violating their conscience, even in an opinion area. I believe that is what Paul was warning against in the passages referenced. However, I will always try to help someone retrain their conscience in opinion areas. The reason I make this distinction and feel strongly about it is intensely personal. I was raised in a church of about thirty people, all of whom believed sincerely that taking communion from multiple cups, having more than one tray of bread passed, and dividing the assembly into Sunday School classes were all sinful practices. We were technically called a "one-cup, no-Sunday School" type of Church of Christ. Once, we debated for six months whether we could change from using grape juice in communion to using wine, in order to have one couple join us on Sundays who were driving to another city to worship with a "wine, one-cup, no-Sunday School church." Although I was a preteen at the time, or maybe a young teen, I still remember vividly some of the heated conversations between my parents and other members of that little church. The memories are not good ones, but after a number of decades, sometimes they can seem at least a little humorous. During those conversations, the questions of violating consciences came up often.

When I married at the ripe old age of twenty-two, my (then) Baptist wife wanted us to attend church together. We at first agreed to switch off attending each other's type church, which we did for a few months. When it was time to attend the Church of Christ, I chose one of the more typical ones, with multiple cups and Sunday School, thinking that the little church of my childhood would be so different from what she was used to that it would seem too weird to her. After a few months, I just couldn't go to the Baptist church anymore, knowing how far off they were on the subject of salvation. In one service with a guest preacher, he had everyone close their eyes, and then asked those who wanted to accept Jesus to simply raise their hands. He kept telling us that one and then others were now being saved as they raised their hands. Although I honestly wasn't interested much in going to church anyway, I just couldn't stomach what I was observing in the Baptist church, and told Theresa that I wasn't going to go with her anymore.

That could have been the end of it, and I could have used my Sundays for fishing—which was more to my liking anyway! But she said that she would just go with me to the Church of Christ (which was not particularly good news to me). But we started visiting various mainline Churches of Christ at her insistence. It is a fact that the Baptist church teaching on salvation violated my conscience, based on passages about baptism and forgiveness of sins. And I believe that my conscience was correctly educated on that matter. It was not a matter of opinion.

However, like the folks being addressed in 1 Corinthians 8 and 10, I had conscience issues about other matters that were not as clear biblically—notably the use of multiple cups and Sunday School (which Paul could have called "disputable matters.") Fortunately for me, I became friends and fishing buddies with a preacher whom God used to change my life and my eternal destiny. I have written about him in the introductions of my books on *Surrender* and *Romans*. He introduced me to other scriptures about conscience and patiently helped me think through it all. He basically said that conscience shouldn't be violated, but it could be re-educated, noting that those addressed in passages like 1 Corinthians 8 and 10 and Romans 14 were younger Christians with weak consciences in areas related to their backgrounds. Those like Paul had stronger consciences, which meant in essence that they had better trained consciences. I'm sure one of the passages my friend used was 1 Corinthians 4:4, which we have already quoted.

While abiding within the boundaries of our conscience is important, the conscience is not always correct in its conclusions, however strongly the conclusions may be felt. With my friend's help, I was able to retrain my conscience and accept a number of teachings that once violated my conscience. Those same principles he taught me served me well when I first encountered the discipling movement and then later became a part of it. I did not violate my conscience (although at times it got "stretched" a bit!), but I did seek to ask the hard questions and try to deal with them biblically, and then prayed that God would help my conscience change in ways that it really needed to—moving from what would be classified as "weak" to "strong" (or at least "stronger" as the process continued).

Current Trends

In recent settings, I am hearing more about conscience than I have heard in a long, long time. Perhaps that is because some (most?) of us violated our consciences in our movement's past. But we have had far too many pendulum swings in the last several years, and this may well be among them. I would hope that matters of conscience would become more and more confined to biblically clear matters, not simply to what Paul calls disputable matters. People need retraining of their consciences far more than the strengthening of them in opinion areas. In the mainline church, we used to have an old saying: "In matters of faith, unity; in matters of opinion, liberty; and in all things, love." The problem I found with some folks was that their definition of faith issues was really broad. They didn't like to admit that very much of what they believed belonged in the opinion arena. The practical result was most often that they were able to hold others at bay who had different opinions. Otherwise, they reasoned, we would be asking them to violate their consciences.

I am not the judge of anyone's conscience. As Paul said, God is the one who judges. I am just pleading for consideration of possible weaknesses in how we are viewing conscience and conscience issues. My plea grows largely out of some of my own experiences in trying to work with others, and from my experiences in needing to retrain my own conscience—a painful but highly rewarding experience, for which I am most grateful. Had I not been open to that, I believe my life would have gone in quite different directions than it has, and I'm so thankful that my preacher friend (now deceased) was patient and loving enough to help me get past some things that were at first very difficult to deal with due to my background. And I do believe in looking back that my conscience was simply improperly trained in some areas, and hence according to Paul's definition, it was weak. As we mature, I think our opinion areas should become less important to us. Learning to properly identify the differences between opinion and faith areas is pretty essential for unity and harmonious relationships. And as we do that, the strength of our emotions in opinion areas should lessen considerably. One thing that has helped me since I have been in our movement is to realize that when good brothers who know the Bible well have sincere differences, this fact alone makes it highly likely that these differences fall into opinion areas. And in opinion areas, I want to remain tolerant and open to being persuaded to go in other directions than I might opt for personally, in order to work together most effectively. That is a worthy goal, and clearly a biblical one.

A Caution to Leaders

Back when Wyndham Shaw and I co-authored the book *Golden Rule Leadership*, I wrote the introduction. Near the end of the introduction, I included the following caution:

> **WARNING!**
>
> The greatest danger in reading this book is to assume that you really already understand the principles being discussed and are currently putting them into practice. This is especially true for our most experienced leaders. We do not see ourselves as we are; we do not see ourselves as others see us. Our strong tendency is to think more highly of ourselves as leaders than we ought to think (Romans 12:3).

Guess who got offended by my cautionary remarks? Not young Christians—they were saying "Amen." But a number of older leaders were definitely offended. What does that say to us? It says to me that as we age in leadership and years of service, we can be guilty of exactly what I penned in the quote above. In our former days as a movement, I was often cautioned about how I stated things, lest I offend the leaders. Now I am again being given exactly the same cautions. Something is wrong with that, and I think badly wrong. I can "lay it out" strongly to the average members, but I have to be careful not to offend the older leaders? Wow! Must history repeat itself again? Leaders ought to be able to hear challenges more humbly than anyone.

Certainly Paul argued in 1 Corinthians 8–10 that we must be willing to give up our "rights," and he used himself as a great example of such. But for whom was he anxious to give up his rights? The weak, immature ones in the fellowship who were struggling with their consciences over past pagan practices, and also for those not yet saved. Hence he was willing to become all things to influence the ones in those categories and to give up all things in order to do so. But he was not willing to compromise or change his approach in teaching to placate the ones who should have been more mature. His question in Galatians 4:16 was: "Have I now become your enemy by telling you the truth?" Rest assured that he was not directing that question to young Christians. Frankly, my biggest concern for us as a movement is our tendency in the direction of some of the unsavory elements of the churches of which I used to be a part. I suggest that you look up every New Testament passage using the term *conscience*. The only places that I could find where it was warning against violating the consciences of others were in 1 Corinthians 8–10. Romans 14 contains the same concept without using the word itself. In light of the context of who Paul's concern was about (immature Christians with weak consciences), and what the issues of controversy were (background pagan practices primarily), we need to be slow to play the "conscience card."

My best judgment about how to view and use money is not shared by all disciples, and that can bother me. My best judgment about the kinds of movies or television shows to watch or allow our children to watch is not shared by all, which also bothers me. My best judgment about alcohol consumption (especially where and with whom it is done) is not shared by all of my brothers. So once again I am bothered. But I don't intend to let those differences of opinion cause me to violate my own conscience by joining in to their practices, nor do I intend to become bothered enough to let it affect my love and fellowship with my brothers who have opinions and practices that vary from mine. What others do in opinion areas is ultimately their choice, and it is not about my conscience. In other areas more related to leadership decisions and directions, I am pretty flexible. If a real biblical issue is involved, we are going to have to hash that one out before proceeding, but if it is a judgment matter, I will for the sake of unity throw in my lot with majority opinion. Those are practical and workable paths to follow in our personal families and in God's family. Let's just keep conscience appeals out of places where they don't belong biblically. Generally, I like the old Restoration adage about faith and opinion, with this one change: "In matters of clear biblical doctrine, unity; in matters of judgment, freedom—but freedom exercised with a strong bent toward practical unity; and in all matters, love."

Appendix Three

Shepherding Training Subjects

The following is a list of topics that are helpful to cover when training shepherding couples to fill their role. Shepherding couples must be equipped to meet many needs within the fellowship, and these are some of the key areas that come up most often.

1. Pre-marriage counseling
2. Basics of marriage counseling
3. Family counseling
4. Parenting (different age children, include prenatal and postnatal challenges)
5. Meeting the challenges: second marriages, blended families, extended family, time and financial commitments
6. Marriage, divorce and remarriage
7. Crisis and grief counseling
8. Putting the past in the past—spiritually
9. Steps for real forgiveness
10. Confidentiality with sensitivity
11. The art of effective communication

12. Emotional IQ development
13. Conflict resolution skills
14. Special focus on helping singles in their roles and relationships
15. Biblical leadership roles defined biblically and practically (elders, deacons, evangelists, teachers, administrators—also leadership roles in the home)
16. Team building—within the roles, between the roles, and with the members
17. Equipping new Christians (discipling made practical)
18. Helping disciples mature through various ages and stages
19. Sound doctrine and church discipline
20. How to tell the difference between the weak, the uncommitted and the rebellious—and how to deal with each
21. Using hospitality to deepen relationships with and between members
22. Helping those with physical challenges
23. Helping those with addictions
24. Helping those with homosexual backgrounds or tendencies
25. Who Is My Brother? (based on book title—how we view those in other churches, and how dating relates to the subject)
26. Transitions of children to different stages (especially from high school into college)
27. Meeting challenges of financial commitments
28. Helping single moms/dads, widows and family
29. Mental health challenges
30. Shepherding without being legalistic

Appendix Four

Appreciating Our History

NOTE: This article was written back in 2002, prior to the startling changes in what we have called the ICOC. In some ways, therefore, it is somewhat dated. However, the biblical and practical lessons found in it are worth sharing in our present day. In some ways, they may be even more significant. See what you think!

As members of the International Churches of Christ, we are well aware of our emphasis on the brief development of our history as a movement. We remember all about the Gempels' living room on that fateful night in June of 1979. The details of those first church plantings in Chicago and New York City, followed by the first foreign planting in London, and then the first planting in a foreign language in Paris, are all a part of our memory treasures. We could go on and on, recalling the glories of such historic plantings as those in Johannesburg, Cairo and Moscow. We do glory in our history, because we are convinced that God was the one writing history by using our feeble but heroic human efforts to accomplish his divine purposes. Who could ever forget the Jubilee celebration at the completion of the six-year plan as those 170 flags were proudly borne high, each representing a nation in which a church was now established!

In our emphasis on our history, we are imitating our Jewish forefathers. Anyone even vaguely acquainted with the Bible is aware of their appreciation of God's hand in their lives as a movement. The sermons recorded in Acts are clear examples of this consistent historical emphasis. Stephen's audience in Acts 7 may have hated the latter part of his sermon, but they were all ears during the earlier part as he traced their history through renowned leaders such as Abraham, Jacob, Joseph, Moses and Solomon. The Jews loved recounting their past, for it demonstrated their tie with God above all other nations of the earth. Our love for the history of God's modern-day movement is but an extension of what his people have always reveled in. Indeed, God has done great things among us!

It is important to note that every part of sacred history has been glorious, but the glory of each has not been the same. Certainly in the Old Testament both high points and low points were all included, and to some extent, all appreciated. The low points taught lessons, which led to higher ground as God blessed repentance. 2 Corinthians 3:7–11 says that the old covenant was glorious, but not nearly as glorious as the new covenant of Jesus Christ. The fact that the latter was more glorious should not be used to dismiss the glory and appreciation of the former. Whenever God uses his people to accomplish his purposes, it is cause for rejoicing. The accomplishments of our children when they are in elementary school may not compare to their accomplishments in college, but they are precious memories to us nonetheless.

The Israelite movement of God was absolutely essential as a foundation for the new Israel, the church of God. Praise God for the faithful who awaited the coming of the Messiah and his greater kingdom. We thrill as we read of Zechariah and Elizabeth, the parents of John the Baptist; Mary and Joseph, who were graced with seeing God enter the world wrapped in the human flesh of a crying child; Simeon and Anna, whose presence graced the temple and whose prayers of thanksgiving were laced with prophecies about this child who would rule the nations. While it is quite true that most of Israel did not later accept the crucified Christ, they had been pursuing a law of righteousness which should have led them to him (Romans 9:31–32). A significant minority did follow the OT prophesies right into the church, beginning with the 3,000 on the Day of Pentecost, and continuing with daily conversions in those first days in Jerusalem (Acts 2:41–47).

We often see that early beginning in Jerusalem as one of the most glorious pieces in the history of the first-century church, but in some ways it had its limitations. For one thing, the church was filled with racial bigots for a number of years. It took God using a pretty nominal Jew, Peter, who could only be convinced that Gentiles were worthy of salvation through the rebuke of a series of visions. Even then, he later struggled with the application of those divinely revealed truths (Galatians 2:11–21). Toward the end of the New Testament revelation, the Jewish disciples in Jerusalem were amazingly still attached to their Judaic history (Acts 21). Until the destruction of the outward aspects of Judaism in 70 AD at the hands of the Roman army, the intermingling of the less glorious with the more glorious was still a reality. As the writer of Hebrews stated, the old glory that was "obsolete and aging" was soon to disappear (Hebrews 8:13), which it did at the destruction of Jerusalem and the temple.

What are we saying in all of this? Simply that in spite of the weaknesses in that early church, we still rejoice in all of its glorious history, for it all was the work of Almighty God, from start to finish. What needs to be said further is that we have a very similar lesson to learn regarding our modern-day movement. At best, we are failing to recognize and appreciate some of our own history, and at worst, we are guilty of the sins of ingratitude and arrogance. Let's begin this line of thought by looking at a very relevant but often overlooked passage in Romans 11:11–20.

> Again I ask: Did they stumble so as to fall beyond recovery? Not at all! Rather, because of their transgression, salvation has come to the Gentiles to make Israel envious. But if their transgression means riches for the world, and their loss means riches for the Gentiles, how much greater riches will their fullness bring!
>
> I am talking to you Gentiles. Inasmuch as I am the apostle to the Gentiles, I make much of my ministry in the hope that I may somehow arouse my own people to envy and save some of them. For if their rejection is the reconciliation of the world, what will their acceptance be but life from the dead? If the part of the dough offered as firstfruits is holy, then the whole batch is holy; if the root is holy, so are the branches.
>
> If some of the branches have been broken off, and you, though a wild olive shoot, have been grafted in among the others and now share in the nourishing sap from the olive root, do not boast over those branches. If you do, consider this: You do not support the root, but the root supports you. You will say then, "Branches were

broken off so that I could be grafted in." Granted. But they were broken off because of unbelief, and you stand by faith. Do not be arrogant, but be afraid.

By the time Paul wrote Romans, the church was becoming more and more Gentile in composition. The Gentiles were failing to see either themselves or the Jews in a realistic light, out of their own pride. Paul shows them that their inclusion in the kingdom was designed to provoke the Jews to jealousy in hopes of causing them to reconsider their own decisions about Jesus as Messiah. He further tells the Gentiles that they actually stood on the foundation of the Jewish religion, and that they stood on the basis of faith, not on their own merits. Instead of being arrogant and critical, they should have been appreciative of their Jewish heritage.

What is the application to us? Actually, there are several. Our movement has a history that goes far back before 1979 in Boston. We are built upon the foundation of what we now call the mainline Church of Christ, or by the more descriptive term, the Restoration Movement. The early days of this group were actually pretty glorious. Ministers from many different denominations banded together with the lofty intent of rejecting creeds in favor of following the Bible only. Surely we would all agree that this was, and remains, a noble goal. Many stories could be recounted from the 1800s that are impressive and thrilling. Thousands of people were baptized at the preaching of men who were sold-out for their cause, to the point that some of them actually gave their lives for it as martyrs. One of the best-known leaders, Alexander Campbell, developed the convictions that led to his leaving both the Presbyterian church and later the Baptist church, and through this process, he became the leading religious debater of his age, widely known and respected in and out of his movement.

Whatever else may be said about this period, it clearly had its glory and formed the foundation for what we enjoy today. Even in the mid-twentieth century, the Churches of Christ were said to be the fastest growing indigenous religious group in America. Although legalism eventually choked out the growth of many congregations, and thus led many of them to a position of being fairly nonevangelistic, lukewarm and doctrinally compromised, we grew up as a movement out of that root system. Virtually every doctrinal argument I used in my book *Prepared to Answer* I learned in that particular group. I appreciate all that I learned, although I did struggle with the persecution I received at the hands of some in that group. However, Paul had received more persecution from the Jews in his day than any of us in our day have received from our persecutors, and we have to keep that in mind. We must be diligent about keeping our hearts humble and appreciative.

Actually, the reason for writing this article is not primarily to help us be less critical and more grateful toward the mainline Church of Christ (although I hope it accomplishes that too). We have another part of our historical root system that is in many ways more important to us as a movement than the mainline background. Of course, I refer to the Campus Ministry segment of our history, which we often call the Crossroads movement. I think that this era was glorious in many, many ways, and yet the comments I sometimes hear regarding it vary from dismissive to derogatory. The claim that we have had a revisionist history regarding the Crossroads days is unquestionably true. The contribution of that era is larger than many among us admit, and the overall lack of gratitude toward it, combined with what seems to be purposeful avoidance of even discussing that period (by some), is very hurtful to those who came from that background. We simply must address this issue in an up-front manner and rectify our shortcomings regarding it.

Sadly, the end of that period was brought about by the sin of the Crossroads pulpit minister, which led to his dismissal by the elders. (Let me add the note that he and his family have done well in the years that followed, and I still consider them to be special friends to whom I owe much.) This unfortunate turn of events led to the demise of the influence of the Crossroads church, and subsequently, of those most closely associated with it. At the same time, the Boston church was growing in influence, and in a good way, Kip and the elders exerted a noble effort to unify the then-current movement by bringing key leaders into Boston for more training, hoping to unify the key leaders into one movement from their various sources. Certainly the movement tracing back to Boston days is the more glorious, but the Campus Ministry Movement blazed some trails without which none of us would be what we now are. Period. Anything bordering on disdain toward that era on the part of any of us who sit upon that foundation is nothing short of sinful, and

I strongly encourage repentance on the parts of those who need it.

I have plenty of sins of which to repent, but being critical of the Crossroads days is not one of them. I first visited the Crossroads church in 1981, and my life was radically changed as a result of that one-week visit and the later trips to speak at the Florida Evangelism Seminar. How that group was spawned out of the tradition-bound mainline Church of Christ of that day still amazes and thrills me. We may have taken things further in many ways (and we have, by God's grace), but their coming out of their labyrinth is, in my considered opinion, about as remarkable as what we have done since. My purpose is not to create some kind of prideful competitive comparison, but only to cause us to look back at all segments of our history in a way that is both realistic and spiritual.

I glory in the many positive qualities and achievements of the mainline Church of Christ, although my frustration with its shortcomings led to my leaving it, burning bridges in a way that necessarily left scars in my soul. I cannot defend everything I did in that process, by the way. I am grateful to be where I am, and during those many years since I came into our present movement, I have never wished to be back in that old root system. But I appreciate my history as I searched for that more excellent way. Similarly, I glory in the many positive contributions of the Campus Ministry Movement, for without it, we would certainly not be where we are today. Yes, they did some things wrong, but they did far more right than wrong, and my prediction is that we will actually reinstate some of their practices that we have typically deemed wrong in the past. I am grateful that we have all been delivered from that "church within a church" setting that was the case with many former campus ministry congregations, but I do not make light of all that we learned from it, especially the campus ministry part of it, which was not significantly different from what we do today—unless it be noted that their growth in campus baptisms often eclipsed our present growth on most campuses.

As to the specific contributions of the Campus Ministry Movement, many could be noted with but little thought, even by an "outsider" such as me. The insistence of total commitment as an essential component of repentance preceding baptism was a novel idea and sorely needed. Viewing the Bible as a standard for the attitudes and behavior of Christians, instead of simply being an idealistic standard, was likewise so needed. This mindset led to the kind of straightforward authoritative preaching that was all but absent from the pulpits of traditional churches. Discipleship in both its vertical aspect (commitment to Christ) and horizontal aspect (close, open spiritual relationships) was admirably stressed. The later focus on "discipleship partners" at all levels rather than the "prayer partner" arrangement of those days initially looked far better in theory than the practice has ended up, because of the tendency of over/under relationships to be mishandled. The emphasis on relational evangelism, with ample practical teaching about how to develop such relationships, stood out like a beacon for those not thus trained in other settings. Last, but certainly not least, an impressively large percentage of elders and evangelists in the most influential leadership roles in the movement today trace their roots back to Crossroads or to campus ministries led by those who were trained at Crossroads.

One mistake I often make in generalizing about the Campus Ministry Movement is failing to distinguish between the different commitment levels of churches who had campus ministries. The "church within a church" weakness often noted was generally true, in that the demands of discipleship were not equally applied to members of all ages. However, some churches were much more evenhanded in calling for and expecting such commitment from their memberships, with congregations like Crossroads and San Diego (Poway) being among this number. The amount of persecution each received is a pretty good testimony to that fact. The handling of said persecution by such churches paved the way for responding to later persecution after 1979, for many lessons were learned (positively and negatively). I do not believe that the commitment levels in congregations like these was where it should have been overall, but it should be noted that they were light years ahead of others within the more traditional Churches of Christ. I appreciate their determination and advances as they strove to emerge out of the denominational darkness from whence they came. They came further in many ways from their root system than we have since, for philosophically and practically, they had further to go. I would not want to return to where the better campus ministry churches were, to be sure, but I am both amazed and grateful for the progress that has enabled us to build upon their earlier foundation.

I pray that those who read these thoughts are both challenged and helped by them. I am concerned that our present slowdown of growth in the movement is directly related to the sins that are in our camp, one of which is described herein. God blesses righteousness and blocks unrighteousness; he exalts the humble and resists the proud; he rewards the spiritual and confuses the worldly. Let's be willing to examine our hearts individually and collectively as we seek to become more like the God who loves us. Let's absolutely and unequivocally appreciate our history, but let's not leave out any of it. The presence of the more glorious cannot be allowed to invalidate the less glorious, for both are glorious before God, and the greater would not be present without the lesser.

Appendix Five

FIRST COOPERATION PROPOSAL OBSERVATIONS REGARDING THE UNITY PROPOSAL
by Gordon Ferguson and Steve Staten
April 2006

INTRODUCTION

Dear Brothers and Sisters,

By now, most of you have received and read the Unity Proposal that has been written by nine of our brothers, with input from a number of others. The Proposal, and other related articles, can be read on the Disciples Today website (www.disciplestoday.com). Most of the content in the Proposal has to do with statements of shared beliefs that are quite relevant to our building greater cooperation as a movement of churches no longer held together by the organizational ties of the past. Another part of the Proposal concerns grouping churches according to geographical and relational settings for the purpose of aiding our helping of one another as congregations and also helping to care for the mission works that depend on older and more mature churches. Just as individual disciples don't do their best in isolation, neither do congregations of disciples. We need each other in many ways, and the Proposal addresses some practical ways to help one another.

The questions that most of us will want answered before embracing this Proposal have to do with the content of the shared beliefs and the recommendations for the alignment of churches for discipling and supporting missions. Two items follow this introduction which hopefully will be helpful in answering those questions. First, find a letter written by me (Gordon) that I wrote to a number of personal friends who asked for my perspective. Recent experiences of the Phoenix church leadership provide the basis of some relevant comparisons within this letter. Second, find part of a letter by Steve Staten, a brother with much education in the field of church history, addressing concerns that some have about the Proposal being some sort of a creed. This letter was addressed to me, but I am including excerpts from it (with his approval) along with my own letter. Steve's comments are very important because any written document used as a means of promoting cooperation will be seen by some, at least initially, as some sort of creed. Those of us with historical roots in the Restoration movement are most likely to experience that first reaction. Steve's observations are very helpful in understanding some distinctions in definitions about the Unity Proposal—what it is and what it is not.

I certainly understand that each congregation has to determine their own evaluation of the Proposal, but wanted you to know something of the perspectives of two teachers within our movement of churches, and the reasoning that has been a part of our own viewpoint of the Proposal. Thank you very much.

—Gordon Ferguson

Gordon's Letter

Dear _____,

I know that there are some different perspectives among the leaders of the various churches, and certainly some who will differ from my own thinking. But that is expected with different personalities with different backgrounds and experiences. Having said that, I wish to add some of my perspective, although I am not at all agitated by differences that many brothers have with me on a number of issues. That's one good thing about being 63—I am not overly concerned about what people think of me or my perspectives at this stage of life! With that said, I would like to register a few thoughts.

I see the current unity proposal as something temporary, designed to help us bring more order out of the fairly chaotic situation in which we have found ourselves for the past three years, not a creedal statement designed for the ages (as is the case with most denominational creeds—which begin simply and end up longer and more complex with the passage of time). There are times historically, especially in the midst of upheavals, when some clarification and order must be given to restore some semblance of common sense in practical areas—in all sorts of organizations. I do think that churches who have good relationships with other churches and are healthy overall will have to be careful not to judge everyone by themselves. Frankly, such churches or congregations who have gotten healthy are definitely the exception rather than the rule. I would remind healthy churches of that fact, just as I remind our leaders in Phoenix that most churches have not progressed to the point that we have as a congregation, and we cannot let our unity locally keep us from seeing the need globally that most other churches have—a pretty dire need at that, in my judgment.

In view of this sort of thinking, perhaps an example from our congregation's recent history could serve as a good illustration. Theresa and I moved to Phoenix in mid-December of 2003 and found the church to be in quite a bit of turmoil. We began meeting with small groups of people and with individuals or couples to get as much perspective as we could about what people saw to be the big issues. We received an earful, as might be expected, with certain reoccurring comments, concerns and questions. One concern was that the Phoenix church didn't have elders, even though the church had been in existence for at least a couple of decades. In my opinion, some people wanted elders for good reasons, and some wanted elders mostly because they had lost their trust of the ministry staff. So, one of our first tasks was to start an elders' training class and begin moving toward the selection and appointment of elders. I and four others were appointed as elders in September of 2004.

A question that many people asked was about our identity as a congregation. They knew what the church had been in the past and were confused about where we were at the present, and they definitely wanted to know what we were going to be like in the future. To answer that question, I preached a lesson early on entitled, "What Do We Now Believe?" Further, we gathered all of our leadership groups together to discuss what we ended up calling "Core Convictions of the Phoenix Valley Church of Christ." Both of these articles are on our web site (www.phoenixvalleychurch.org), should you want to read them. Once all of our leaders agreed to the content of the Core Convictions article, we asked everyone to attend either a Friday night devo or a Saturday morning devo. In that setting, we presented the article, handed it out in written form and then posted it on our website.

A couple of months later, we elders were appointed, after months of elder training and teaching the congregation about the eldership—their qualifications, the selection and appointment process. Our elders felt very deeply the newly accepted responsibility as shepherds of the flock. Hebrews 13:17 especially got our attention: "Obey your leaders and submit to their authority. They keep watch over you as men who must give an account. Obey them so that their work will be a joy, not a burden, for that would be of no advantage to you." The part that made impact on us was the statement that we must give account for the flock under our care. The church was in such a state that we weren't even sure who were members and who wanted to be members. In our minds, something had to be done to clarify the identity of the flock.

To help with that, we developed a membership pledge (a "shepherding sheet" as it came to be called). Other churches have called similar documents "membership covenant," and this very idea sends some of my good friends into orbit! We asked each person to commit to what we saw as the most fundamental basics of living as a disciple. At the end of the simple one-page document, we offered three possible responses:

1. I am ready to commit at this time.
2. I am not ready to commit at this time. Please contact me to help me resolve issues that I have.
3. I am not willing to commit to being a member of this church.

I doubt that many checked the third possibility—they most likely just left. A number of people did check the second possibility, and we got with them individually or as couples and were able to resolve most of their concerns. Thankfully, most people simply checked the first possibility. At any rate, as elders we felt that unless people were committed to be a participating part of the church, we really couldn't be accountable for them. We saw this approach to be a temporary one, meant to clarify in a time lacking clarity (to put it mildly). Looking back to that time, I would say that it was helpful, although certainly not a cure-all. My mention of the Core Convictions and pledge documents is only meant to illustrate that we needed some means of clarifying and unifying our church during a time of serious upheaval and confusion, and never did we intend for these documents to become creeds in any way. Frankly, they have served their purpose (helpfully so) and have all but faded into the sunset already.

I see the current unity proposal to have the same purpose our documents had here—to unify and clarify after a time of very confusing and disunifying events. Wyndham and I wrote a book only a few years back that ended up as such a document—one with a temporary purpose to address issues that were in vogue at the time. Let me assure you that *Golden Rule Leadership* is not required reading for anyone now (only a few years after its writing) because it served its purpose (I pray) and is quite outdated. The current unity proposal will in all likelihood follow the same path as the needs and atmosphere of our movement changes and progresses. Our movement was at some extremes prior to the upheaval of the past three years, but predictably, we swung the pendulum from one extreme to the other. We went from being overly organized to being fairly unorganized. Certain people reacted to almost any type of organization or any attempt at some type of uniformity. Interestingly, from a source outside our movement, I came across an insight that I wrote up into an article entitled: "Self Starters and the Rest of Mankind." This article may also be found on the Phoenix Valley Church website. I know of no organization that can function without a pretty good organizational structure, beginning with one's individual family. Please note that I am not defending our military-style organization of the past, complete with its (often) unwritten creeds. But I know that we have members in many different stages of maturity and we cannot make the mistake of expecting the less mature to think and act like the most mature have learned to do. Organizational structure and expectations in one's own family have to meet the needs of that particular family at a particular stage in that family.

Anyway, take this letter for what it is worth to you. I believe that our leadership in Phoenix will sign on with the unity proposal. I also believe that quite a number of other leaderships will not sign on—at least in the short run for sure. I am not too concerned about who does and who doesn't, to be frank. God in time will help us work it out and work together. About the only real concern I have is what our biblical and practical reasoning processes are that cause us to sign or not sign. And I have heard some reasoning by those on both sides of the issue that seem questionable to me. Paradoxically, in the reaction of some against what they see as demands for uniformity, they themselves are demanding their type of uniformity—though I'm quite sure that they wouldn't see it as that. Interesting times! One old Restoration slogan I did like is this: "In matters of biblical truth, unity; in matters of opinion, liberty; and in all things charity (love)." Our problem, as always, is distinguishing what is truth and what is opinion—we all get the two confused at times, given our own limitations and sinful nature. Thanks for listening.

Steve Staten Letter Excerpt

It is easy to overreact to formal creeds with silent creeds, and to group Confessions and Statements of Beliefs together with creeds. These are not the same when seen in their historical settings. Statements like our current Unity Proposal can help keep our integrity higher and foster an openness in areas when our past movement may have been ambiguous on some beliefs. Those who worked on the Proposal clearly admit it would be constructed differently at a different time and thus should be evaluated from the vantage point of passing time. It was developed by mere pilgrims to identify those who shared our highest common ideals, build trust, pool strengths and NOT intended to draw lines or alienate any of God's children whether or not they ever sign on. As you read the following definitions, it should become obvious that our Unity Proposal is neither a creed nor a confession of faith, but rather a statement of faith or agreement—of commonly held beliefs:

Creeds—a reed or measuring stick of all timeless truths used to establish orthodox faith from heretical forms. The Roman Creed, Apostles Creeds, Nicene Creed fall into this category. These were used to identify which books, letters and congregations held to the historical apostolic faith. They still serve as a witness, especially in how we received our canon. Creeds do not address lifestyle standards, just core doctrine. They are practically never revised.

Confession—a description of beliefs held by a body of Christians of a historical grouping. These come about as the result of a crisis, split or awakening, such as the Reformation. These begin to address lifestyle or moral standards. These are practically never revised until another split occurs. The Westminster Confession is a good example of this kind of a statement.

Statement of Faith—Some statements of belief also include covenant agreements (see below). This is the case with The Plan for Unified Cooperation. These statements are usually lists comprised of interpretations of Scripture to let members and outsiders know their core doctrinal positions.

Covenants/Agreement—Identity agreements for affiliation or participation are regularly revised because internal challenges and outside influences may force an organization to state clearly where they stand on something (for example, alcohol, dating, homosexuality). Institutions are usually flexible to having their majority constituents influencing these agreements because it sometimes reflects philosophy and course heading. The Plan for Unified Cooperation has a section under The Church Community which is more or less a covenant of long-cherished practices and lifestyle convictions, some of more or less importance than others. The motivation behind such agreements, such as in Acts 15, is to engender a healthy and respectful environment for cooperation.

COOPERATION PROPOSAL #2
THE COOPERATION PROPOSAL REVISITED
by Gordon Ferguson
October 2007

About a year and a half ago, Steve Staten and I coauthored an article entitled "Observations Regarding the Unity Proposal." It was a combination of a letter I had written to answer questions about the proposal (now called the United Plan for Cooperation) and Steve's very relevant comments about various types of written documents in religion. Over 350 churches have affirmed the Cooperation Plan. Many others are prayerfully considering it. In the months since that article was published, many of us have continued to answer questions and clarify issues as some among our movement of churches have continued to express reservations and raise questions about affirming the proposal. (Note that I use the term *affirm* rather than *sign*, which is more accurate.) In rereading that earlier document, I feel much the same now as I did then, but I do have additional observations I would like to share, given the nature of the reservations expressed and questions asked since then.

A Brief History

But before proceeding, let me go back to the beginning of the upheaval in our movement several years ago. As soon as it began, I had immediate concerns for its impact especially on smaller churches and less mature disciples. The foremost of these concerns at the time was about how mission churches that were dependent on outside support were going to fare. Unfortunately, some of my worst fears were realized. One example that is near and dear to my heart is what happened to the churches in the Philippines (which my home church in Phoenix helps support).

Before the firestorm hit our movement, Manila had been one of the fastest-growing churches among us. They had about 4,300 members and had planted fourteen other churches in the Provinces of the Philippines. They had over one hundred people on staff in Manila and another twenty-eight in the Provincial churches (men and women). They had an annual budget of $420,000 a year. One year later, due to rapid loss of financial support, they had only eight brothers on staff in Manila (no women) and eight on staff in the Provinces (one of which was a woman). They were devastated by the rapid loss of staff and financial support—which dropped to $150,000 for that year. Thankfully, their support has gradually improved, more are being put on staff, and they are growing once again. They have planted four new churches and plan to plant another four in 2008. Churches in developing nations have suffered more than most of us can imagine unless we have been there to see the situation with our own eyes.

They need more financial support, to be sure, but that alone will not solve their problems. Sometimes we assume that the main thing lost was finances, which is not true. Last year, the Philippine leaders asked that some of us come over to teach and encourage them—by taking money for travel out of our special contributions designated for them. This meant that they would rather have emotional and spiritual support through personal visits from supporting churches than more staff, which the money would have enabled them to hire. Some of us went to encourage both leaders and disciples, and the results of that were more than we could have imagined. Suffice it to say that scores of churches in the developing nations suffered similar fates in loss of support of all kinds. They felt isolated and abandoned. The Cooperation Proposal encouraged them tremendously by restoring their hope of a united brotherhood, who would once again wrap their arms around them.

My next biggest concern was that our congregations would swing from the end of the pendulum in our interrelationships (of dependency on "Big Brother") to the other end (of independence and isolation). This concern has also become reality in many cases, although good progress has been made, thanks in part to the Cooperation Proposal itself. The proposal has caused us to examine more closely what we once took for granted. We have been moving from a forced type of unity to a forged unity, and the forging has not always been easy nor the results ideal. But thankfully, we are in process and are making progress.

The Unity Proposal was designed to address these two concerns of meeting needs on the mission front and promoting congregational relationships. Additionally, it was also an attempt to help clarify the beliefs and practices that we shared in our past history. Probably this part of the proposal was the most controversial initially. A number of people were concerned that putting these things in writing would produce some sort of creed that would take on a life of its own. I don't think this has proved to be the case, but I understand the concerns. (You might want to see Steve's relevant comments in this regard in the aforementioned April 2006 article, in the previous appendix.)

The Present

At the present time, the concerns I continue to hear are about the second part of the proposal regarding congregational relationships, but perhaps most concerns are still about the third part of the proposal regarding commonly held beliefs. The concerns about the congregational relationships and grouping of churches in geographical settings are largely that one congregation will exert an authority over another against their will. No one will argue that this was not a problem in the past, but the question is whether we will revert to the old ways in time. All I can share on this point is what I have experienced. The churches in the Southwest part of America were grouped together in the proposal with former "Big Brother," the Los Angeles Church. In Phoenix, given the history of sending people and money to the West Coast, we were apprehensive—to put it mildly. I expressed this apprehension to Bruce Williams, congregational evangelist in LA, and to Al Baird, one of the elders there. Bruce, Al and John Mannel (another elder) made a trip to Phoenix to meet with our elders and staff brothers. Concerns and hurts were expressed and questions were asked by us, all of which were met with sensitivity, gentleness and apologies. The humility of these three men dispersed our fears in one fell swoop. We suggested that they also take trips to at least two other SW churches that had an eldership, a suggestion they were happy to follow.

Since that time, we have enjoyed a very harmonious relationship. I'm not concerned in the least that we are somehow going to revert to practices of the former days. I believe the brothers in the larger churches have truly changed, and I know the rest of us have changed as well. I am not going to have another church dictate what we in Phoenix are going to do, but I very much want their input and help, have asked for it, and have graciously been given it. Relationships among congregations need to be viewed with a good dose of common sense. Church plantings need to be very submissive to the church that planted them until they reach a reasonable level of maturity. Then they and the more mature church should have a relationship much like we older folks have with our grown children. We want to have a close relationship, and because of that relationship and our added maturity, we still want to give input—but the decisions they reach are their own decisions. Period. Surely that should describe relationships between more mature churches and less mature churches. Where the maturity level is similar, brotherhood should mean that we provide mutual help to one another. Just as disciples need other disciples in their lives, church leaders need other church leaders in their lives. Independence and isolation are a curse. Interdependency and cooperation are a blessing— for individuals and for churches.

Some brothers have expressed the concern that organizations tend in the direction of more and more centralization and control. This is likely true overall—unless the organization is aware of that trend and intent on functioning in a way that avoids it. Truthfully, organizations can start well and degenerate, while others can start poorly and make positive changes. Again, all I can share is what I have experienced. One year ago at the International Leadership Conference, we delegates from the affirming churches selected a group of nine well-respected brothers to continue attempts to help us become more unified and effective in our collective efforts. This year, the group of nine, by their own recommendation, was replaced by ten committees, with a chairman chosen for each committee. (That's called *decentralization*, I believe.) The chairmen were asked to form their own committees, and no stipulations were given for those choices. Committee members could be chosen from churches who had affirmed the Cooperation Proposal or from those who had not. Before the committee idea was approved, those from the group of nine kept restating that they were in no way a governing board, but only a serving group to facilitate what the larger group wanted to do. When someone says repeatedly that they don't desire or intend to act as from any authoritative position, I believe them— especially when their entire demeanor and speech is clothed with humility, as theirs was.

What about the concerns of the other category in the Unity

Proposal—the statement of shared beliefs and practices? My religious background was in the mainline Church of Christ. We prided ourselves in not having written creeds. Our oft-stated battle cry was "No creed but Christ; no book but the Bible." But that group took division to a whole new level. Did they avoid creeds simply because they didn't write them down? Hardly. They divided into many different flavors and had quite well-defined unwritten creeds—but creeds nonetheless. Some of my friends who have not affirmed the Cooperation Proposal are worried that we will devolve into something akin to the Catholic Church. I am much more worried that we will devolve into the independent, highly autonomous churches from which we originally evolved. Even with my mainline church background, I don't understand the fear of written statements of shared beliefs. In our techno age, everything stated verbally can quickly be put into print. When our leadership in Phoenix delivers messages regarding sensitive areas (finances, church discipline, etc.), we often print them and hand them out and then put them on our website. I would far rather people know exactly what we said than embellish and distort it into gossip and slander. In actual fact, this part of the proposal has received a lessening emphasis, as the other two parts about cooperation in mission efforts and intra-congregational relationships have received the most attention. Said another way, the Unity Proposal has evolved into the Cooperation Proposal for good reasons.

Why did those who collaborated to write the original Unity Proposal believe that the beliefs and practices section needed to be included? One, Kip McKean was saying and writing that we had lost all of our convictions in these areas, and he was having a very negative impact on younger disciples and churches. With our mature leadership in Phoenix, it wasn't a problem for us—we dealt quickly and decisively with Kip's Phoenix satellite church in our city. But the large majority of our churches outside the US (which outnumber those in the US) do not have the same maturity of leadership and thus were being influenced negatively. They needed the more mature leaders and churches to state what was true and untrue regarding Kip's allegations. They needed clarification and assurance. Two, these same less mature churches were full of disciples whose world was shaken by the upheaval we experienced. They were asking (often with tears) if we were still a movement and if we still had convictions about these issues addressed in the proposal. These disciples in these churches (and they do constitute a majority) were relieved at the offering of the proposal. Most of them affirmed the proposal quickly, because it addressed directly all three areas of concern that they had. Further, they were (and are) puzzled when this was not done by a number of our more mature leaders and congregations.

The Future

Now for the toughest question: Why have thirty percent of our churches not affirmed the proposal? For reasons noted already, to be sure. Others are focused on very basic needs in their own churches, and some are difficult to contact. A few will probably not cooperate in the near future. But I believe that something more subtle is involved as well. I would call it unintentional myopia. We tend to see the situation of others from our own perspective, in spite of the fact that our situation may be quite different from theirs. Some time back, I wrote an article entitled "Self-Starters and the Rest of Mankind." The gist of it was that self-starters don't need as much structure and motivation as others do. Better stated, non-self-starters (who comprise the majority of humans) need more structure and outside motivation than do self-starter types. But it is the self-starters who tend to judge the needs of others by their own needs. As one insightful person pointed out to me recently, it is the self-starters who are basically insisting that every Christian be a self-starter. In an unintentional way, they are essentially saying, "You should be like me." Well, maybe they will be in time, but we must meet them where they are presently and keep helping them to grow in this direction. Anything less suggests a lack of humility and genuine care for others, whether or not we intend it or realize it.

Applying this to the Cooperation Proposal, the more mature may well insist that they agree with everything (or nearly everything) in the proposal, but don't feel the need to have their name on a list of affirmers. They don't see the need for any defined structure in a movement of sister churches. I understand that line of reasoning on a personal basis. I'm sixty-five years old now, and I know what I believe and what I am committed to. I don't need to sign or affirm anything, for myself—but I think others need for me to have my name on that list. They need the reassurance of knowing that someone with my history in this movement wants to cooperate in every way possible to keep our churches working together as closely as possible. To me, it's a simple matter—why not publicly assure them in a way that all know where I stand, whether they live in my state or in the southern tip of Africa or of South America? And by the way, if I had written the Proposal, I would have worded a few things differently, and I'm sure most of us would say the same. However, my focus is on the general tenor of things relating to the purpose of promoting healthy unity and cooperation, rather than on a few details that I might have said differently. If we have to agree on every last detail to have unity and cooperation, we will be frustrated and unhappy in every relationship known to man, including marriage!

I know that some will inevitably feel that articles like this one are an attempt to force them to put their name on the list of affirming churches. Let me assure you that such is not my intention. Forcing anyone to do anything is counterproductive and unbiblical. However, I am unashamedly trying to persuade you to reconsider your position if you have not affirmed the proposal by giving your heart to cooperation with brothers and sisters around the world and having the name of your congregation added. My love and acceptance of you as members of God's family is not in question. But I do believe we need to think seriously about the impact of our example on less mature disciples and churches. What I may think I need is not the key issue here—it is what others need of me. Please think and pray about these things. Call or write me if you want to discuss it further. And please forgive me if my intentions were not expressed in the best way, in spite of my goal to do so! May God help us all to work hard in continuing to forge the unity for which Christ prayed and died!

COOPERATION PROPOSAL #3: MOVEMENT COOPERATION: PROGRESS AND IMPORTANT CONSIDERATIONS
by Gordon Ferguson
September 2009

I recently returned from the International Leadership Conference held in Denver, filled with gratitude for the amazing progress our movement of churches has experienced in recent years. Each year since our movement was disciplined significantly by God in 2003, these conferences have shown gradual but significant improvement in our churches as we have responded righteously to God's discipline.

As Roger Lamb observed near the end of this most recent ILC, there appeared to be a real "jump" to a new level of spirituality this year. We may not be where we should be individually and collectively, but it is obvious that the large majority of us really want to get there and are determined to act upon our convictions in a number of areas. I am most thankful for the Denver Church of Christ for their outstanding job as host church of this year's conference. Hundreds of Colorado volunteers did a marvelous job of making the time great, and God crowned their efforts with his blessings. Many leaders from all parts of the movement made their own contributions to what I believe will be looked back on as a watershed event.

One part of the conference that was particularly encouraging to me was the continuing willingness of congregational leaders to keep considering the affirming of the Cooperation Plan. A number of additional churches have recently affirmed the Plan, and the new Cooperation Plan Summary no doubt aided such decisions. The process of intentionally increasing the unity of our movement is working. Some leaders have been understandably unsettled about some of the mistakes of the past, when we were in a state of "forced unity," and have needed time to get their questions answered as we keep working toward a complete "forged unity." As one who has written articles regarding the overall issue and as one who continues to be asked some of those questions of concern, I believe I better understand those who have a reluctance that I have not had personally, and I also believe I better understand the bigger picture. In the interest of helping answer questions, prayerfully in a golden rule fashion, hoping not to portray any sense of condescension (which I do not feel), I offer a few considerations that have been helpful to others recently.

CHURCH UNITY AND COOPERATION

The first consideration comes in the form of a question: "Do we still want to be a movement of churches?" I believe the answer to that question for most of us is a resounding "yes." Coming from years spent in a mainline church setting, remaining a united movement is a precious thought to me. I remember at age five experiencing a split in our little church that brought great pain to my parents and other friends and relatives. Unfortunately, such experiences were not infrequent in the churches of my youth, and those experiences, combined with my convictions about Jesus' words in John 13–17, fill my heart with a huge desire to see unity prevail among those of us in the International Churches of Christ. From the time I joined this movement in its earlier stages, even the imperfect unity we had was encouraging to me. Now as we pursue a true John 17 type of unity, I am moved to prayers of thanksgiving in tears. God help us keep working toward that perfect unity for which he prayed!

The second consideration is that if we want to function as a movement of united churches, decisions will have to be made that affect us all. Otherwise, we will be only autonomous congregations rather than a movement. Thus, another question must be asked: "How can we as a movement make decisions?" Some logical reasoning has to help us answer this one. I can only see three possibilities in addressing this question.

One, we could go back to having a few people at the "top" make major decisions for the rest of us. I doubt many of us would cast a positive vote for that one. I certainly wouldn't.

Two, we could figure out some grouping of all churches which were formerly a part of our movement, and select delegates from that grouping, no matter where they stand currently on any issue of doctrine or practice. Knowing where some churches do stand on key issues, their inclusion would lead to a state of disunity instead of unity. I would not want to be in a delegates meeting comprised of such a combination. It would remind me too much of some Men's Business Meetings in the mainline church that still give me knots in my stomach when I think back about them.

Three, we can do what we are already doing by agreeing upon basic doctrines and directions, grouping ourselves by geographical considerations, and choosing trusted brothers in those groups to represent us in delegate meetings. These delegates would make some lesser decisions as a group and then take back to their churches potential decisions of a more serious nature for further discussion. In the latter case, the decisions will be finalized at a later time after local leadership groups have added their input. I see no other valid option, but what I have seen in how things are functioning through our present (and ever-evolving) approach qualifies for "golden rule leadership" as I understand it. In delegate meetings, I have not seen anyone driven by worldly ambition for position or recognition, but rather only willing volunteers who want to see our movement unified and moving forward to affect eternity as much as possible for our Savior. Whatever lingering small doubts I may have had in the earliest stages of our present approach have been totally dispelled by what I have seen and experienced since then. I long to help others who still have lingering doubts to be able to get those removed and to enjoy a type of unity I have only dreamed of in the past.

Hopefully that line of reasoning can help others, for it has already helped some. For us to be a movement, some implications must be considered and decisions made regarding them. Embracing some type of structure is obviously necessary. A couple of years back, I wrote an article entitled "Self-Starters and the Rest of Mankind," in which I used the Dynamic Marriage program as an illustration. (Most of us familiar with that program are very positive about it.) The illustration addresses what they do to deal with the fact that the large majority of married people are not self-starters and need more help than they can provide for themselves. In this program, the help comes in the form of structure, expectations and accountability—all done excellently. The fact that these three things may have been done wrongly in our past movement history does not invalidate them. Right things can be implemented in wrong ways or right ways. Wrong approaches to parenting and marriage should not make us reject either institution. In fact, in the smallest organization possible (two people in a marriage relationship), structure, expectations and accountability are essential for a positive functional relationship.

Financial Cooperation

One discussion in the most recent delegates meeting involved how we can financially support HOPE *worldwide* and the *Disciples Today media* (now chosen by the delegates as the official media for the

International Churches of Christ). Decisions are in dire need of being made by us as a movement. I have heard some say that we should all just give freewill offerings for such needs and that will more than take care of them. That has been our approach in the past six years, with the result that both organizations mentioned above are in genuine danger of ceasing to exist unless we unite to support them. The process of accessing needs like these and then asking churches to give at a certain rate according to the size of their membership is the only approach that will work. Some seem to think that this approach somehow removes the joy of giving and makes it an assigned duty. I can speak for only one on that point, and that is for myself. I am all for being made aware of needs and meeting them, and I gain joy from doing so.

Maybe an illustration will help us on this point. When grown children have aged parents who can no longer care for themselves, the children have to figure out the needs and then determine how to meet them in a fair and equitable manner. The responsibility of thus providing does not diminish the satisfaction of having done the right thing by seeing that the parents' needs are met by those who love them. Meeting specifically designated needs is not mutually exclusive of giving joyfully. At the beginning of this year, being off staff of a church, our income was impossible to predict. (We are now supporting ourselves with Social Security and my teaching ministry.) But in faith, we set a substantial weekly contribution figure, which we have consistently given, and have been blessed by God as a result. Additionally, we have given to help individuals who needed help in a variety of ways. Recently, our congregation completed our Special Contribution for the year. The leadership (of which I am still a part) set a budget for that contribution and shared with the church that the amount would be approximately 11 times our weekly contribution. I was happy to know the specifics of the need, in order to plan our giving and do our fair share. We ended up giving more than the requested amount, and as always, gave with joy, knowing the needs of the mission at home and abroad.

Some may fear that asking for specific amounts per member to support HOPE and Disciples Today could lead to abuses in the future. I'm sure most of us have wondered about that and hopefully have asked questions and had them answered. The bottom line of this issue has several parts. One, none of us wants to abuse the approach, since that would ultimately destroy what we are trying to accomplish. Two, no one can force any church to do anything that they don't want to do. Three, those having affirmed the Cooperation Proposal can remove themselves from that affirmation list at any time. I for one want to know what the urgent needs are among us as a movement and do all I can to help meet them. Meeting specific and specified needs and giving joyfully have never been mutually exclusive for me, and at my age, I don't anticipate that this feeling will ever change!

Congregational Relationships

Another aspect of structure needed for us to be a truly unified and growing movement is how we interrelate with our sister congregations. In this realm, many joint endeavors come to mind, such as regional conferences, retreats, camps, and the like. Also, just as individuals need discipling (by whatever term you prefer), churches need the same. Otherwise, in our isolation, we fail to see ourselves clearly. Outside influence is a wonderful thing to help keep us aware of our strengths and weaknesses and keep growing. Again, I understand that some worry that "Big Brother" will start making our decisions for us. At the beginning of the formulation of the Cooperation Proposal, I had that concern, since we were in the same geographical grouping with the Los Angeles church (definitely "Big Brother" in the past!). Three brothers from the leadership group of the LA church—Bruce Williams, Al Baird and John Mannel—came to Phoenix to meet with our elders and staff brothers to address our concerns. Their humility and expressed desire to be givers and not takers alleviated our apprehensions, and time has shown them to be true to their word. They have provided us much valuable help and input, for which we are most grateful.

But you may be wondering how discipling works between churches in a righteous way. Back in 2003, while still in Boston, I used my grown children as an illustration of how I thought churches should relate to each other. With my grown children, I wanted to keep a really close relationship; I wanted them to value my age and experience and seek advice from us; but, in the realm of making final decisions, that was their task. I would hope that my adult children would have the same kind of relationships with each other. Is this not how churches with their own leadership groups should function? Input is sought and valued, but final decisions are up to local leaderships. Of course, in church plantings and situations where less mature churches are being supported financially by more mature churches, the mature churches will be involved more in decision-making. Similarly, if I loan my grown children money, I would expect to be involved with them in making decisions about how that particular money is going to be used. Churches providing financially in such situations may well want to be involved more in joint decision-making. Note that I am not talking about this process being applied to mature First World churches sending mission support to mature Third World churches. However, in those situations, budgets and annual financial reports are certainly in order.

Let me share one more illustration to help show how the discipling relationship works between churches. In Phoenix, we once had an unfortunate experience with a staff person and asked for input from the LA brothers, which was gratefully received. After following their initial advice, another issue came up in the situation that had to be dealt with. After our local leadership group decided how to deal with it and did so, Bruce Williams called to say that some leaders in LA had a concern about how we handled one aspect of the situation. After talking it through in some detail, Bruce asked if our leadership team (comprised of both elders and evangelists) would reconsider that one aspect of our decision—to which I replied, "Sure." I explained the request to our leadership and we met to reconsider our decision with their concerns in mind. After much discussion, we decided to stick to our original decision in the matter. I called Bruce to inform him of that, and he thanked me for our willingness to at least reconsider the decision. That was the end of the matter. He never brought the subject up again, as far as I can remember, and there was not the slightest hint of any strain or awkwardness in our relationship with him or with LA leaders after that time. Quite the contrary, because our working relationship has been excellent before and after that particular issue.

Although the LA leadership is much larger and more mature than ours, the input and advice has gone both ways, as it should. I think it provides a fine example of what relationships between congregations looks like in the present. I disciple our congregational evangelist, Gary Sciascia, but he also has a discipling phone time with Bruce regularly, which Gary and the rest of the Phoenix leadership appreciate greatly. Most of our elders have ongoing relationships with LA elders as a part of our desire to avoid any hint of isolation and the damage that it causes. I think our relationship with LA preaches a good sermon about spiritual maturity, mutual trust and respect, unity and cooperation, and what it means to be united in a movement of churches sharing a common history and a common mission to change the world.

CONCLUSION

In conclusion, let me thank you for reading far more material than I intended to write in this article! However, I do believe that what I wrote about it is all interrelated to the overall subject. I have found others to be helped by it, and my only desire is to be helpful and a promoter of the type of unity that Jesus prayed for. I feel better about the unity of our movement at this point than I ever have. As churches, we have a ways to go in getting the majority of our members back on the cutting edge of evangelism and discipleship, but we are making definite progress. And I am convinced that our growing unity as a movement is the most important tool our God has used in helping us make significant and numerous changes for the better. I believe he shares my joy at the changes that are occurring daily. The future is as bright as the promises of God, or as Tom Brown put it in a great lesson at the recent New England Conference, "The best is yet to come!"

Appendix Six

The subject of church discipline is one that deserves a place in a book on church leadership. The following material was originally published in my booklet, *Love One Another*, later included in an appendix of *Romans: The Heart Set Free*, and has been adapted for use here.

Introduction

In this lesson we will consider the topic of church discipline, or as it is often called, "withdrawal of fellowship." This topic is obviously not a pleasant one, but it is a necessary one and a biblical one. In Protestant churches, the concept of church discipline has often been called the "forgotten commandment." In most churches, including ours, the concept could accurately be called the "misunderstood commandment." Therefore, our task will be to clear up both ignorance about the subject and misconceptions surrounding it. I hope that raising and answering several key questions will clear up the misunderstandings of this sobering biblical doctrine.

What Is Church Discipline?

In a broad sense, church discipline includes all efforts to train Christians in the way of the Lord, just as the discipline of children includes all training. In the more specific sense that we are considering, it means the purposeful exclusion of a church member from the fellowship of other Christians because of unrepentant sin after biblical procedures have been followed. To those who have not studied what the Bible has to say on this subject, this definition may sound unloving, judgmental or harsh. However, God calls for us to carry out church discipline in certain situations, and if we refuse to do so, he will hold us accountable for our disobedience.

In Proverbs 13:24, we are told that the one who withholds punishment from his child actually hates the child. The same would be true in the case of spiritual children. Although a type of judging is forbidden by God (Matthew 7:1–2), the judging that would relate to church discipline is clearly commanded by God (1 Corinthians 5:12–13).

As to the charge of harshness, consider some of God's disciplinary actions in the Bible. In the Old Testament, we have the accounts of the flood; Sodom and Gomorrah; Achan (Joshua 7); Korah, Dathan and Abiram (Numbers 16); and many others, all situations in which God was very direct and strong in his response to sin. In the New Testament, God's customary approach is to wait until the Judgment Day before dealing directly and forcefully with sin, but the case of Ananias and Sapphira in Acts 5 should convince us that the nature of God and his hatred of sin have not changed in our day. After looking at such accounts, it becomes obvious that many of us do not see clearly both the "kindness" and the "sternness" of God (Romans 11:22).

Key Biblical Texts

Let's summarize a few of the key texts about church discipline.

Matthew 18:15–17

If a brother (or sister) sins against you, go to the person privately for the purpose of bringing about reconciliation between the two of you. (Note that the phrase "against you" is not necessarily in the original Greek manuscript.) If the person does not repent, take others with you in attempting to resolve the situation. If this approach fails, share the situation with the church. Ultimately, lack of repentance demands that withdrawal of fellowship be practiced.

Romans 16:17–19

In this passage we are taught to watch out for and avoid people who cause divisions by their false teachings. Note that Paul does not state that the divisive and false teachers are necessarily within the fellowship of the church, nor does he command that they are to be excluded from the fellowship. Neither does he mention any action we should take in reaching out to them or warning them. He apparently left this issue somewhat undefined in order to allow the directions in the passage to be applied as needed—to *anyone* causing divisions and putting obstacles in the way of Christians. The passage will fit a member of the church who becomes destructive to the faith of others, a former member who is destructive, or even a total outsider. The focus is not specifically on the identity of the sinful person, but rather on the damage he causes, which cannot be neglected.

1 Corinthians 5:1–13

The sin here is sexual in nature, as a man was sleeping with his father's wife—evidently his stepmother. The church failed to deal responsibly with the sin—they were prideful about the matter (proud of their understanding of grace?). Paul's response was unmistakable in verses 11–13:

> But now I am writing you that you must not associate with anyone who calls himself a brother but is sexually immoral or greedy, an idolater or a slanderer, a drunkard or a swindler. With such a man do not even eat.
> What business is it of mine to judge those outside the church? Are you not to judge those inside? God will judge those outside. "Expel the wicked man from among you."

2 Thessalonians 3:6,14–15

In this context Paul addressed a situation in which some people in the church were idle and not even looking for work. The first response to the problem was to refuse to feed such a person—*no work, no food!* (v. 10) The second response was to take special note of this idle person who refused to obey Paul's instructions and to stop associating with him until and unless he repented. We will examine other related passages later on in the lesson, but these provide us with clear directions about the need for, and nature of, this type of church discipline.

Titus 3:9–11

This passage is a very important on this subject for two reasons. One, it adds another text on the topic of divisiveness, thus complementing what Paul said in Romans 16:17–19. Two, it does not suggest the same procedure that Matthew 18 does—namely, getting the church involved in the process. Matthew 18 addresses an unresolved issue between two disciples, not every possible case of church discipline, and certainly not this one due to its nature. The charge, "Warn a divisive person once, and then warn him a second time. After that, have nothing to do with him," was given to Titus the evangelist. We can conclude from what Paul said in Titus 1:9–16 that once elders were appointed, they would help share in this task of silencing the rebellious. We cannot expect the average disciple in our churches to know how to deal with divisiveness, since it is often subtle and difficult to recognize. The use of "objective negativity" is not easy for less mature Christians to recognize. Objective negativity occurs when someone starts off sounding both spiritual and concerned about another person or situation, but in a very subtle way plants seeds of doubt and mistrust in those who listen. I have included an appendix examining this subtle but highly dangerous sin in much more detail. Biblically, King David's son Absalom (see Appendix Seven on page 298) was the master of using this approach. Note what is said of him in 2 Samuel 15:2–6:

> He would get up early and stand by the side of the road leading to the city gate. Whenever anyone came with a complaint to be placed before the king for a decision, Absalom would call out to him, "What town are you from?" He would answer, "Your servant is from one of the tribes of Israel." Then Absalom would say to him, "Look, your claims are valid and proper, but there is no representative of the king to hear you." And Absalom would add, "If only I were appointed judge in the land! Then everyone who has a complaint or case could come to me and I would see that he gets justice."
>
> Also, whenever anyone approached him to bow down before him, Absalom would reach out his hand, take hold of him and kiss him. Absalom behaved in this way toward all the Israelites who came to the king asking for justice, and so he stole the hearts of the men of Israel.

Which Sins Necessitate Withdrawal?

Some sins are mentioned specifically in connection with the withdrawal of fellowship. As we have already seen, both idleness and immorality are grounds for withdrawal, unless repentance occurs. In 1 Corinthians 5:11, in addition to sexual immorality, other sins are listed, including greed, idolatry, slander, drunkenness and swindling. (In passing, it is interesting to ask how Christians would recognize the sin of greed in another person's life. Materialistic attitudes would be a part of the answer, but the level of financial contribution would be involved as well.) In Titus 3:10, a divisive person is to be warned once, then a second time, and if repentance is not produced, then the church is to have nothing to do with him. Romans 16:17–19 is similar, but would be applied to anyone destroying the church, whether a disciple, a former disciple or a nondisciple.

Some sins are not specifically identified with withdrawal, yet are included by necessity because of their impact on a person's relationship with God. Withdrawal of fellowship is actually a recognition that a person has already lost fellowship with God due to unrepentant sin. Therefore, the church cannot be in fellowship with someone who is out of fellowship with God. Many sins would qualify for this category, because most of the sin lists end with admonitions like this: "those who live like this will not inherit the kingdom of God" (1 Corinthians 6:9–10, Galatians 5:19–21). Obviously, not all sins are easily observed, and some may never be seen by other disciples. But in this case, God will ultimately handle those situations, as 1 Timothy 5:24 states: "The sins of some men are obvious, reaching the place of judgment ahead of them; the sins of others trail behind them." In the sin passages and the discipline passages, it is abundantly clear that known, unrepentant sin cannot be tolerated by the church.

What Is the Procedure for Withdrawal?

When considering administering church discipline, we must first pray for the person (1 John 5:16). Second, we need to go to them and try to turn them back (Matthew 18:15–17, James 5:19–20). We must make sure that we go in a spiritual manner (Galatians 6:1–2). We must also be gentle, careful about our own lives (not self-righteous) and willing to help carry whatever burdens the ones in sin are carrying. Third, we need to take others—leaders—with us as the needs dictate. Fourth, if the person is not moved to repentance at this point, we must warn them (1 Thessalonians 5:14, Titus 3:10). Fifth, after they have been warned and have refused to heed the warning, we must inform the church to stay away from those in sin. After they are formally withdrawn from, no social fellowship is allowed (Matthew 18:17; 1 Corinthians 5:11; 2 Thessalonians 3:14; Titus 3:10). What is our attitude toward them then? What can we do to help them at this point? We must not regard them as enemies, but we need to continue to pray for them, and when we do see them, we must warn them as fallen brothers (2 Thessalonians 3:15).

As stated earlier, the church at large is involved in some issues of church discipline, as in Matthew 18 and 1 Corinthians 5, but not necessarily in others, as in Romans 16 and Titus 3. Divisiveness is one sin that is best dealt with directly by mature church leaders, for reasons noted.

What Are the Purposes for Withdrawal?

The reason for the withdrawal of fellowship is first for the purpose of obeying God. He commands it. Refusing to obey his teachings on the subject may appear broad-minded and nonjudgmental, but it is unspiritual and rebellious. Our society is so existential that taking almost any stand for biblical righteousness is labeled as bigotry. Our concern must not be what the world will think of us if we practice church discipline; it must be what God will think of us if we do not!

A second purpose for withdrawal is to keep the church pure in two ways. First, withdrawal keeps the church pure by protecting it from guilt as an accomplice (2 John 9–11). Second, it protects the church from sinful influence (1 Corinthians 5:6). In this passage, sin is compared to yeast, which works through an entire batch of dough. Once unrepentant sin enters the body through one person, Satan gains easier access to other members of the body. There is a spiritual principle involved that is subtle to the casual observer, but devastating in its results over a period of time. When sin is not purged, it leads to a toleration of sin. Toleration leads to an acceptance of sin, and finally, the acceptance leads to the practice of sin!

A third purpose of withdrawal is to serve as a warning to the church (1 Timothy 5:19–20). It is also to show the world that disciples are totally committed to living for God and his mission on the earth. In 1 Corinthians 5:1, Paul was highly upset about their lack of example before the world—they were doing worse things than the world was! In Acts 5:1–11, God practiced some church discipline directly when he killed Ananias and Sapphira: "Great fear seized the whole church and *all who heard about these events*" (v. 11, emphasis added). The church was highly regarded by the non-Christians, though they were afraid to join the church for a while (v. 13). Nevertheless, the church continued to grow "more and more" (v. 14).

Finally, the purpose for withdrawal is to restore the fallen Christian if at all possible. Notice the hopeful wording regarding restoration in the following passages: Matthew 18:15; 1 Corinthians 5:5 (see 1 Timothy 1:20 for similar wording); 2 Thessalonians 3:14–15; James 5:19–20. However, this highly desirable result does not happen the majority of the time in real-life situations. When this serious act of discipline fails to move the person to repentance, the Bible has not failed; the church has not failed; God has not failed! Only the person has failed, by failing to respond to the love of God expressed through the church. (Revelation 3:19 comes to mind: "Those whom I love I rebuke and discipline.")

Withdrawal of fellowship is a last resort, much like an emergency operation. The odds are not good for survival, but sometimes it saves a life and therefore must be tried. However, even when repentance and restoration do not occur, all of the other purposes of such discipline are still accomplished and the victory is still the Lord's!

Appendix Seven

Objective Negativity

We Live in a Negative World!

The subject of negativity is a broad one, and although we are going to focus on a certain highly dangerous type of negativity, some general observations will prove helpful. In case you haven't recognized it, we live in a negative world. Bad news sells and good news doesn't. At least that seems to be the message of our modern media organizations. Further, many of us grew up in negative families. I know I did. My parents would not have been characterized as positive thinkers and talkers by any stretch of the imagination.

Then, besides the effects the environment has on our perspectives and subsequent conversation directions, we have our own inner struggles with which to deal. We all develop some forms of insecurities as we grow up, and a common way to compensate for our bruised egos and warped self-images is to tear others down in an attempt to feel less inadequate about ourselves. This brand of negative speaking about others is far more common than the so-called "common cold" (and it makes us a lot sicker!). Those who are consistently critical of others are first of all critical of themselves. They may act otherwise, but rest assured that it is only an "act."

When I was in high school eons ago, we spoke of certain classmates having a "superiority complex." There is no such thing. That prideful and smug presentation of oneself was a charade, a cloak used to cover what we called an "inferiority complex." That last term is relatively accurate, although outmoded in this era. Now we just say that a person who feels bad about themselves is insecure or has a poor self-image. If we are familiar with Schema Therapy, we would perhaps say that they have a defective schema. In other words they feel defective as persons.

Get Your "Buts" in the Right Place!

Anyone not really comfortable in their own skin has the problem thus described, and one dead giveaway is that they are defensive and handle almost any form of correction (however well-intentioned and well presented) poorly. They already feel bad about themselves and don't seem to realize that input from others can help them change—the end result being that they feel better about themselves. Another evidence of this malady is seen in how they view and talk about others. They do tear others down in order to feel better about themselves, but it never works. Sin cannot make you feel better inside your heart of hearts.

Those in the church who have not yet conquered this problem have certain patterns to their negative speech. One pattern is just to talk negatively about others behind their backs, thus committing what the Bible defines as gossip and slander. Another pattern is saying both good and bad things about others, but doing it in a certain order, thus creating a certain emphasis. Compare these two sentences in how they affect your feelings about someone we will call Betty for purposes of illustration:

> "Betty is a great wife and mother, but she doesn't seem to get very involved in serving others."
>
> "I don't always know what Betty may be doing to serve people generally, but I do know that she is absolutely a great wife and mother."

The point of the illustration is to show that whatever we say after the little conjunction "but" is what our hearers go away with–it is what they tend to remember. In the first example, we are left with the thought that Betty doesn't serve those who aren't in her family very well, and in the second example we are left with the warm feeling that this woman really loves her husband and children and shows it by her actions. Note a couple of things in the first example. The speaker is making an assumption (shown by the word seems) and leaves us with what appears to be a conclusion. If you want to have troubled relationships on all levels, assume what you don't really know to be factual and state it as a conclusion!

Don't Be Fooled by One of Satan's Favorite Tools!

Both of these speech patterns described are negative and hurtful to relationships, but they are not nearly as dangerous as the one this appendix is mainly addressing—objective negativity. The most dangerous form I have ever found of unhealthy talk is also understandably the most subtle. This form is one of Satan's favorite tools for destroying relationships on both an individual and group basis. I have seen several of his human agents use this tool in an almost unbelievably effective way (in being destructive). But rather than simply describing how they used it, we have the perfect biblical example in a child of a king (and a very good king at that). Turn to 2 Samuel 15:1–6 as we read about Absalom.

> In the course of time, Absalom provided himself with a chariot and horses and with fifty men to run ahead of him. He would get up early and stand by the side of the road leading to the city gate. Whenever anyone came with a complaint to be placed before the king for a decision, Absalom would call out to him, 'What town are you from?' He would answer, 'Your servant is from one of the tribes of Israel.' Then Absalom would say to him, 'Look, your claims are valid and proper, but there is no representative of the king to hear you.' And Absalom would add, 'If only I were appointed judge in the land! Then everyone who has a complaint or case could come to me and I would see that he gets justice.'
> Also, whenever anyone approached him to bow down before him, Absalom would reach out his hand, take hold of him and kiss him. Absalom behaved in this way toward all the Israelites who came to the king asking for justice, and so he stole the hearts of the men of Israel.

Absalom's work described here very nearly led to the killing of his father and to his usurping of David's throne. He stole the hearts of the men of Israel, Scripture says. He didn't merely win their hearts by serving them; he stole their hearts by tainting their thinking toward the king whom they had loved and followed for years. How sad! How powerful is Satan's tool of objective negativity! Negativity we understand to some degree, but how does the term *objective* fit in to its use? Now that is a hugely important question, make no mistake about it.

We have all come away from certain conversations saying something to this effect: "Wow, that guy is really something; he's about the most negative person I have ever heard in my life!" Someone skilled in the use of objective negativity never evokes that reaction, but what they do to a person's heart is something akin to what a hidden cancer does to a person's body. It is an undetected destroyer, doing its deadly work mostly in secret until drastic results emerge. The presentation of such soul-damaging information is cloaked by the sense of objectivity created, and the more spiritual it sounds, the better the cloak. With that in mind, we shouldn't be surprised that those looked upon as spiritually mature, or better yet, as spiritual leaders, are the most effective in using this approach.

In actuality, those skilled in this deceptive work are basically "seed planters." They plant tiny seeds that grow quietly inside hearts until a plant or a tree is produced. Isn't that exactly what Absalom did? He kept planting seeds as he validated the concerns of people and showed them affection, and those seeds were aimed at undermining trust in his father and building trust in himself. He was one sharp dude, one smart cookie. He knew exactly what he was doing for the four years he did it. Gossips tend to be impatient and have to say it now; the Absaloms of the world are patient and content just to plant and water, waiting for the tree of doubt, discontent and rebellion to grow.

My intent is not to make anyone mistrust spiritually mature people or spiritual leaders—far from it. I think most would say that I would fall into both of those categories. But like Paul, I want to help you not fall prey to those whose skills are found in this form of negativity that we are discussing. In 2 Corinthians 2:11, Paul said that he didn't want his readers to be unaware of Satan's schemes. Thus his teaching was aimed at exposing Satan's schemes (and he has many). Paul could not have described a person skilled in the deadly scheme of objective negativity any better than in this passage from the same book. "For such men are false apostles, deceitful workmen, masquerading as apostles of Christ. And no wonder, for Satan himself masquerades as an angel of light. It is not surprising, then, if his servants masquerade as servants of righteousness. Their end will be what their actions deserve" (2 Corinthians 11:13–15). Well, what do such people sound like in everyday life? Here are some samples from a very long list of possibilities:

> "I really love our elders, but some people have shared a few things with me that sometimes make me wonder..." But you do have to appreciate their sacrifice of time and energy.
>
> "I think we have a great staff, but I did hear one or two things in confidence that have made me a little nervous. I guess we will just have to trust the Lord that he will work out whatever needs to be worked out."
>
> "I appreciate the fact that our leaders are following a carefully planned process of looking for additional staff members, but I really hope that they will keep _____ in mind and not just make decisions out of personal preferences. I am glad, though, that they seem to be focused on finding someone soon."

"I am certain that our small group leader has a real heart to serve, but I do wonder if he has the time to be serving in that role right now with all that he has on his plate. But don't you just love their two little girls—they are the cutest things!"

"The couple we have leading our small group really loves people, and that is such a valuable and appreciated quality. I have heard some disciples question whether they had the gift set to be able to do it. But getting people to lead is no easy matter, so I suppose that we should just appreciate their willingness to serve in this way."

"Betty is one of my best friends and I feel like I can tell her anything, but I am praying that she can keep a confidence. We all need a safe place to share our struggles."

"I really love this church and have a lot invested in it for these nine years that I have been a member. I hope our direction for the future is clearer to others than it is to me. I guess I just need to pray more."

My examples mention leaders quite a bit, as I'm sure you have noticed. There is a reason for that. Satan knows that he can destroy churches if he can erode trust in leaders. I'm not defending bad leaders, and the fact that Wyndham Shaw and I wrote a little book a decade ago entitled *Golden Rule Leadership* should demonstrate that point clearly. Although what we wrote is now "old hat" and widely accepted in our movement today, it was strongly resisted by a number of leaders in high places when it was first published. Having said that, Satan has always, and will always, do his best to destroy trust in all leadership—not simply that which you and I might agree is poor leadership. Destroy the mom or dad in any family, and you'll see the family severely damaged.

Maybe you are thinking that those who practice the fine art of objective negativity sound almost the same as those who have their "buts" in the wrong place. Well, they are similar in some ways, but different in key areas. Both use the word "but" as a key part of their processes. However, the Absalomic approach sounds much more spiritual. It not only begins with positive statements; it also ends with them. The effect is much more subtle. You hear a person like this, especially if you trust them and/or look up to them, and you leave the conversation feeling mostly good. You can recount the positive, spiritual-sounding things they said. On the other hand, the more spiritually in tune you are, the more likely you leave feeling unsettled, perhaps ever so slightly. Seeds have been carefully planted, and if you do not come to realize that something is amiss, those seeds may well grow. I have seen people thus influenced who eventually left the church that I never imagined would possibly leave.

What is the Solution—the Antidote?

The solution to dealing with this malady is to pay attention to your own heart. If something seems slightly out of kilter after a conversation, tending to pull you in a negative direction, go back to the person with whom you talked and start asking questions.

"When you said that some have questioned the leadership gift of _____, who are those some?"

"You expressed some doubt about your good friend Betty being able to keep a confidence. Have you told her that?"

"That statement you made about the direction of the church—what exactly are you questioning here? I think you and I need to go talk to some of the leaders of the church together, because I want to make sure that your doubts are dealt with and not spread to others—including me."

Bottom line, we need to be very careful about what we listen to that has a negative bent to it about anyone or any group that is not present for the discussion. The Lord knows that we must learn to talk to others about sensitive issues and concerns—but we need to do it with them, face to face and not behind their backs. People sometimes ask me if I am feeling something toward them that isn't positive, and the answer is pretty simple: "If I am, you will be among the first to know it, because we will be talking in an up-close and personal way." If someone seems to perhaps have funny feelings toward me, I ask them about it. If they do, I want to encourage them to come to me, but I am quite willing to go to them as well. Matthew 5 and Matthew 18 say that we should meet each other going and coming if relationships are not in a good place.

Disciples are learners. That's a basic meaning of the term itself. Let's learn to recognize sinful speech, whether it is coming out of our own mouth or the mouth of another. And by all means, let's learn to get beyond our conflict-avoidance tendencies and resolve relationships that are strained or that we think may be unsettled in some way. If we have good marriages, we have done it hundreds of times because we don't want to be under the same roof with another person with whom we are not at peace. For the Lord's sake, let's refuse to live under his same big sky with our brothers and sisters without cultivating and maintaining that same peace. It is the will of our Father, who loves us all as his dear children. Amen and Amen!

Dynamic Leadership

Illumination Publishers International

For the best in Christian writing and audio instruction, go to the Illumination Publishers website. We're committed to producing in-depth teaching that will inform, inspire and encourage Christians to a deeper and more committed walk with God. You can email us at our website below.

www.ipibooks.com